ROTH FAMILY FOUNDATION

Music in America Imprint

Michael P. Roth
and Sukey Garcetti
have endowed this
imprint to honor the
memory of their parents,
Julia and Harry Roth,
whose deep love of music
they wish to share
with others.

The publisher gratefully acknowledges the generous support of the Music in America Endowment Fund of the University of California Press Foundation, which was established by a major gift from Sukey and Gil Garcetti, Michael P. Roth, and the Roth Family Foundation.

Moral Fire

ALSO BY JOSEPH HOROWITZ

Conversations with Arrau (1982)

Understanding Toscanini: How He Became an American Culture-God and Helped Create a New Audience for Old Music (1987)

The Ivory Trade: Music and the Business of Music at the Van Cliburn International Piano Competition (1990)

Wagner Nights: An American History (1994)

The Post-Classical Predicament: Essays on Music and Society (1995)

Dvořák in America: In Search of the New World (for young readers, 2003)

Classical Music in America: A History (2005)

Artists in Exile: How Refugees from Twentieth Century War and Revolution Transformed the American Performing Arts (2008)

Moral Fire

Musical Portraits from America's Fin de Siècle

Joseph Horowitz

UNIVERSITY OF CALIFORNIA PRESS
Berkeley · Los Angeles · London

University of California Press, one of the most distinguished university presses in the United States, enriches lives around the world by advancing scholarship in the humanities, social sciences, and natural sciences. Its activities are supported by the UC Press Foundation and by philanthropic contributions from individuals and institutions. For more information, visit www.ucpress.edu.

University of California Press
Berkeley and Los Angeles, California

University of California Press, Ltd.
London, England

Library of Congress Cataloging-in-Publication Data

Horowitz, Joseph, 1948–.
Moral fire : musical portraits from America's fin de siècle / Joseph Horowitz.
p. cm.
Includes index.
ISBN 978-0-520-26744-2 (cloth : alk. paper)
1. Music—United States—19th century—History and criticism. 2. Music—United States—20th century—History and criticism. 3. Music patronage—United States—History—19th century. 4. Music patronage—United States—History—20th century. 5. Musical criticism—United States—History—19th century. 6. Musical criticism—United States—History—20th century. 7. Higginson, Henry Lee, 1834–1919. 8. Krehbiel, Henry Edward, 1854–1923. 9. Holloway, Laura C. (Laura Carter), 1848–1930. 10. Ives, Charles, 1874–1954. I. Title.
ML200.4.H67 2012
780.973'09034—dc23 2011045448

Manufactured in the United States of America

20 19 18 17 16 15 14 13 12
10 9 8 7 6 5 4 3 2 1

In keeping with a commitment to support environmentally responsible and sustainable printing practices, UC Press has printed this book on Rolland Enviro100, a 100 percent postconsumer fiber paper that is FSC certified, deinked, processed chlorine-free, and manufactured with renewable biogas energy. It is acid-free and EcoLogo certified.

For Agnes, Bernie, and Maggie

Contents

Illustrations

Introduction

Fully twenty years ago, I decided that the most dynamic decade for classical music in the United States was the 1890s—a finding that contradicted conventional wisdom both about American music and about the "Gilded Age." The latter term, roughly designating the period between the Civil War and 1900, originates with Mark Twain's first novel, co-written with Charles Dudley Warner in 1873: *The Gilded Age: A Tale of To-Day.* Its genesis was a conversation in which the two writers expressed discontent with the state of American fiction. They also shared their discontent with the state of American democracy. The result is a long and tangled tale of Washington politics. Hypocrisy and bribery, poverty and violence are major themes. Readers of the book easily recognized Senator Abner Dilworthy as Kansas's Senator Samuel Pomeroy, a watchdog for temperance and the Sunday School, who was caught offering cash for a nominating vote—and yet was cleared by a committee of Senate colleagues. The Crédit Mobilier scandal of 1872, in which a fraudulent company was found to have siphoned federal railroad money, was equally a fresh national memory. To many, the harsh iconography of *The Gilded Age* seemed just. And the label, with its pejorative associations, stuck.

I am far from being the only present-day writer for whom Mark Twain's notion of a Gilded Age mischaracterizes a time and place he himself embodied. To be sure, historians need to periodize and label; to be sure, all such distinctions and designations generalize and mislead. That said, not only is "Gilded Age" atypically pejorative, as far as historical labels go; it also happens to be a belated polemical construct. Unlike "Elizabethan" or "Victorian," "Progressive Era" or "New Deal," "Gilded Age" was not employed during the decades it identifies. True, it originates with Twain and Warner. But not until the 1930s did works of history commonly apply this term.*

Its general usage, that is, originates not with *The Gilded Age: A Tale of To-Day,* but with the "Young Americans" movement after World War I. This quest for a "usable past" devoured the parental generation in favor of venerable antebellum ancestors and a vital present. Chapter 3 of Van Wyck Brooks's *The Ordeal of Mark Twain* (1920), titled "The Gilded Age," marks the first influential deployment of "Gilded Age" as a tool of periodization, evoking an era in which the pursuit of wealth was a "sacred duty," and in which a "vast unconscious conspiracy" crippled "the creative life"; Twain is depicted crushed between commercial and genteel forces. Following his mentor Brooks, Lewis Mumford, in *Sticks and Stones* (1924) and *The Golden Day* (1926), engaged in "a bit of preliminary house-cleaning and rubbish removal" by way of discarding "the barbarism of the Gilded Age."[1] In the 1930s, such significant historians as Charles and Mary Beard, and Vernon Parrington, as well as such influential popularizers as Matthew Josephson, embedded the rubric and imagery of Gilded Age America.

In retrospect, this genealogy tells more about interwar intellectual life than about the period in question. Brooks and Mumford, especially, were writers of irresistible panache. Their exhilarating polemics successfully instigated new thinking: they cast a shadow on the past in order to brighten the present. But their books remain polemics whose pertinence and plausibility have long faded. Just as the Young Americans needed to rediscover Hawthorne, Emerson, and Thoreau, others would subsequently make startling discoveries amid the ostensible rubbish of turn-of-the-century America.

My own such discoveries include the momentous contributions of Henry Higginson, Henry Krehbiel, and Laura Langford. Charles Ives

*A historian who searched could find only two uses of "Gilded Age" from 1873 to 1919 "that referred to the present generally and were not direct references to the book [*The Gilded Age: A Tale of To-Day*] or the play [the book as adapted for the stage]." See Alan Lessoff, "Van Wyck Brooks, Lewis Mumford, and The Gilded Age: Provenance of a Usable Past," a talk delivered March 2, 2005, at the University of Illinois at Chicago.

was of course discovered by others, but not long enough ago. Seeking candidates from the Oedipal generation of Brooks and Mumford, Serge Koussevitzky's Boston Symphony Orchestra searched in vain for a Great American Symphony during the interwar decades. Ives's Second Symphony, an American masterpiece from 1900–1902, only came to light in 1951. By then, Brooks and Mumford, their purposes served, had both recanted. As early as 1931, Mumford was singling out such figures as Albert Pinkham Ryder, Thomas Eakins, and Louis Sullivan en route to a revisionist perspective. Brooks—in *New England: Indian Summer, 1865–1915* (1940) and *The Confident Years, 1885–1915* (1952)—undertook his own sympathetic reassessment of reviled Victorian decades. As Mumford later approvingly observed, both he and Brooks had "purged" the "negative" and "querulous" tone of their earlier writings. But Mark Twain's notion of a barbaric Gilded Age remained.

Indulge in a moment's reflection. We think of the caliber of the founding fathers: intrepid. We think of the pre-bellum culture bearers the Young Americans extolled: bracing. We think of the interwar modernists: clever, subtle, fresh. Think now of post-bellum arts and letters: of Frederic Church and Albert Bierstadt, James Russell Lowell and William Dean Howells: Victorian, reverent, naïve; fettered, whether by habit, belief, or attire. But the earnestness of this period, its seriousness about life and its responsibilities, may also be read as a strength—the "moral fire" of my title.

Will "Gilded Age" ever be popularly displaced by a better nomenclature? Alternatives have been floated. In the pages that follow, I nominate "fin de siècle" for the culturally eventful closing decades of the nineteenth century—and ponder the ways that Europe's fin de siècle did or did not resemble America's.

• • •

When *Moral Fire* was in its final stages of creation, a distinguished publisher advised me that my book would prove a hopeless marketing challenge because it "fell between the cracks," the cracks being American Studies and Music. I had to smile ruefully: between the cracks is where I live.

As a cultural historian specializing in classical music in the United States, I have long explored subject matter ignored by nearly all other cultural historians. When not writing books, I produce concerts. While I would never claim that the beleaguered men and women who administer orchestras and present concerts don't read, American concert life, generally, is securely divorced from American intellectual life. Separated by a crack, classical music occupies a more isolated niche in the world of contemporary culture than do film, dance, or theater.

How I wound up between the cracks began with a job and a book. The job was reviewing concerts for the *New York Times* from 1976 to 1980—an activity that persuaded me that most classical music events were redundant or otherwise superfluous. The book, *Understanding Toscanini: How He Became an American Culture-God and Helped Create a New Audience for Old Music* (1987), was my first attempt to comprehend the classical music cul-de-sac.

One thing led to another. I no longer review concerts, except on rare occasions for the *Times Literary Supplement*. My eight books mainly deal with the distinctive institutional life of American classical music. Two of them, *Wagner Nights* (1994) and *Classical Music in America* (2005), incorporate admiring cameos of Henry Higginson, Henry Krehbiel, Laura Langford, and Charles Ives—portraits greatly expanded in the present volume.

As my *Toscanini* jeremiad also led to an unexpected opportunity to run an orchestra—the Brooklyn Philharmonic at the Brooklyn Academy of Music—I today spend about as much time creating musical events as I do pondering their past and future. In Washington, DC, I am the artistic director of PostClassical Ensemble. I frequently curate festivals for orchestras and presenters throughout the United States. My approach, invariably, is thematic and cross-disciplinary: an attempt to infuse fortifying humanities content into the classical-music agenda. Naturally, I seize every opportunity to translate into public programs the topics I write about. "Dvořák and America," "American Roots," "The Russian-American Jazz Connection," "American Transcendentalists," "The Gershwin Moment," Copland and the Cold War," "Hollywood Composers," "The Idea of the West," and "Artists in Exile" have all generated concerts including film, theater, dance, and pertinent scholarship.

My efforts to bind History and Music have also included a pair of "Dvořák and America" projects sponsored by the National Endowment for the Humanities. The first spawned a young readers book and an interactive DVD (by Robert Winter and Peter Bogdanoff) for Social Studies classrooms; the second instructed teachers (grades 3 to 12) in how to use them. *Moral Fire* represents my most concentrated effort, to date, to wishfully encroach on American Studies with all my classical music paraphernalia in tow.

Alan Lessoff, a historian who has tenaciously excavated the genealogy of "Gilded Age," has invaluably supported my work on *Moral Fire* with advice and encouragement. So have Paul Boyer and Wayne Shirley. Diane Sasson enriched and complicated my prior knowledge of Laura Langford. The Boston Symphony Orchestra and New York Philharmonic—orchestras that care about their histories—have exceptional archives and exceptional archivists; as in the past, I am indebted to Bridget Carr in Boston and to Barbara Haws and her assistant Rich Wandel in New York. My agent, Elizabeth Kaplan, and my editor, Mary Francis, valuably fortified my belief in this book.

I used to think that writers required special domestic prerogatives. My wife, Agnes, my son, Bernie, and my daughter, Maggie, long ago disabused me of this silly notion. I now more or less gratefully tolerate the distractions they variously impose.

FIGURE 1. The White City. Image courtesy of the Paul V. Galvin Library, Illinois Institute of Technology.

Prologue

Screaming Wagnerites and America's Fin de Siècle

Music and moral passion—Revisionist portraiture—Framing "fin de siècle"

Work on the present book, celebrating cultural achievements a century and more ago, coincided with a signature twenty-first-century entertainment: the twenty-ninth Summer Olympic Games, hosted by the People's Republic of China. The opening ceremonies, on August 8, 2008, were unprecedented in scale: fifteen thousand performers (including exactly 2,008 drummers) riveted an outdoor audience of ninety-one thousand, and millions more on television the world over. The four-hour production, conceived by the film director Zhang Yimou, reportedly cost $300 million—more than ten times what Athens had spent on its opening ceremonies four years previous. Defying gravity, athletes eight months in training raced around a suspended globe, some running upside down, some perpendicular to the turf below. Dancers used their writhing bodies to inscribe calligraphy on a gargantuan scroll that unfolded itself on the stadium floor. The Olympic torch was conveyed aloft by a flying sprinter while a pyre materialized to light the sky. Celebrating hoary centuries of history, shedding decades of twentieth-century subjugation and insularity, preening with futuristic technological wizardry, China showed the world a sleeping giant prodigiously awake, an archaic Golem become a sleek Goliath, rousing the new century.

The ceremonies posed a double meaning. The invention of paper, of movable type, of the compass; the sayings of Confucius; the sights and sounds of Beijing Opera and of *tàijíquán* catalogued Chinese refinement and learning. The choreographed acrobatic hordes, the lightning succession of magic tricks on the largest possible scale, each topping the one before, advertised protean resources of manpower, expertise, and cash. One decisive ingredient was the soundtrack. When Lang Lang played the *Yellow River* Concerto, when Chinese and British pop singers sang the commissioned confection "You and Me" to acres of smiling children's faces, the slick mélange of Western and Eastern ingredients reduced China to an exotic costume drama, a superficial pentatonic topping to the banal realities of Western pop and glitz.

How similar, yet different, was the White City of 1893. At the World's Columbian Exposition in Chicago, a young nation proclaimed a new dawn. "The apotheosis of civilization" showcasing "all that is beautiful, useful, wonderful," H.N. Higinbotham, president of the exposition's board of directors, called it. "We celebrate the emancipation of man," pronounced Chauncey Depew. Though Depew, president of the New York Central and Hudson River Railroad, added that the fair belonged "not to America, but to the world," the world—gaping at the artificial waterways and lagoons, at the ersatz Graeco-Roman structures and statuary—understood otherwise.[1] This, surely, was the American intent. The Chicago fair was three times bigger than the Paris Exposition of 1889, to which it favorably compared itself. More than two hundred buildings had been rapidly erected on more than six hundred acres of reclaimed swampland. Some 27.5 million visitors—about half the United States population—were logged over a period of six months. From Lake Michigan, the Columbian Exposition was a beckoning mirage. Aglow at night, its electric lights streaking the water, it was a colonnaded alabaster fantasy, a post-Venetian wonderland fabricated outside time and space.

Like the Beijing Olympics to come, the Columbian Exposition was an act of cultural reconsolidation postdating internal turmoil by three decades; no less than the Beijing Olympics, the White City possessed a double meaning. Explicitly, it inventoried American learning, science, and the arts. The Manufactures and Liberal Arts Building (reputedly the largest structure in the world, spanning more than four city blocks and incorporating a stage larger than the entire Metropolitan Opera House), the Transportation Building, the Woman's Building, the Electricity Building were crammed with evidence of New World achievement. As music director of the fair, the conductor Theodore Thomas planned "a perfect and complete exhibition of the musical Art in all its branches."[2] There would be a noontime concert every day and two evening concerts of lighter music with a split orchestra—all free of charge—plus ticketed concerts of a more serious nature. Addressing the American Historical Association at one of the fair's scholarly conclaves, Frederick Jackson Turner—in what would become famous as his Frontier Thesis—explored the American origins of self-made enterprise and daring. Binding the whole was an ordered aesthetic vision enforced by the architect Daniel Burnham in concert with the pioneering landscape architect Frederick Law Olmsted.

If Burnham, who sixteen years later would publish a landmark Chicago city plan, secured an orderly artistic template for the fair's sprawling heterogeneous contents, the countervailing display of financial and technological muscle could scarcely be overlooked. As iconic as the Statue of the Republic fronting the Court of Honor was the first Ferris wheel, a structure 264 feet high with room for sixty people in each of thirty-six cars (one of which contained a band). The mythic nocturnal illumination was a supreme feat of applied science, the first large-scale test of alternating current; all told, the fair consumed three times as much electricity as the entire city of Chicago.

Like most Gilded Age culture, the White City suffers a tarnished reputation. Louis Sullivan, whose Transportation Building contradicted the prevailing Beaux-Arts motif, famously denounced Burnham for "setting back architecture fifty years." The "Midway Plaisance" notoriously flaunted African "cannibals" and other "barbarian" species from places far away. Thomas's high-toned symphonic concerts—including one with Paderewski, whose instrument had to be smuggled in because Steinway was not one of the fair's authorized piano firms—were abandoned for lack of patronage. But by 1900 Thomas's Chicago Orchestra had triumphantly won its place in the civic pantheon of Chicago. Sullivan jealously failed to appreciate that the artificiality of Burnham's designs supported their magic; what is more, their influence endured: a "city beautiful" movement, traceable to Burnham's influence, would transform public buildings and parks in countless American cities, big and small. The racial hierarchies embedded in the Midway's living exhibits—which not so incidentally introduced Americans to Indonesian gamelan, African drumming, and other exogenous creative feats previously unknown—were of course perniciously false; but, as my example of Henry Krehbiel will show, chroniclers of the Midway have failed to adequately survey or contextualize the contemporaneous discourse on culture and race; the ideologies of Madison Grant and Adolf Hitler were decades away. Alan Trachtenberg's seminal *The Incorporation of America: Culture and Society in the Gilded Age* (1982) treats the White City as a sham façade as false as the plaster-like "staff" Burnham applied to whiten the gigantic steel-frame structures. The Columbian Exposition, he writes, "insinuated" the primacy of art and culture. Its hierarchical plan, with the Midway at bottom, ostensibly imposed "unity through subordination." It theoretically embodied a sinister reality of capitalist hegemony.

Latter-day critics of the White City are oblivious to the sheer magnitude of achievement realized by fin-de-siècle idealists. Was the White City a national brainwashing? Charles Eliot Norton did not think so; he called the fair's general design "noble, original, and satisfactory." Eugene Debs spoke of "the lofty ideal" of the fair and its "healthful influences" on working men and women for whom "the beautiful in art as well as nature" furnished "a form of worship entirely devoid of cant and hypocrisy, superior to any worship narrowed by creeds and dogmas." "I went to the fair at once," wrote Owen Wister, "and before I had walked for two minutes, a bewilderment at the gloriousness of everything seized me . . . until my mind was dazzled to a standstill." A quintessential genteel sentiment was articulated in *Century* magazine by the architect Henry Van Brunt—that the fair's quotient of "sweetness and light" could counterbalance "the boastful Philistinism of our times."[3] To dismiss such sanguine responses as naïve is to reduce men of sensibility and intellect to dupes. The same fin-de-siècle Chicago energies that realized the White City produced the Art Institute of Chicago (1879), the Chicago Orchestra (1891), the University of Chicago (1892), the Field Museum (1893), and the Newberry and Crerar Libraries (1887, 1897)—a consolidated demonstration of civic zeal in fact more unthinkable today than any of the fair's gaucheries.

NBC's Beijing commentators, straining toward high rhetoric in 2008, proclaimed a China "both outside time, and bursting every which way in a bewildering rush of transformation. They have made themselves anew, relentlessly, devotedly, so they might on these days step into history. They've submitted to an uncompromising search for mastery. . . . It is time for the universe of shimmering, still-to-be-written biographies. It is time to chase eternal youth." How much more impressive, in 1893, was James Fullarton Muirhead, the writer of a Baedecker handbook about the United States, for whom the fair's whiteness signified a fortifying purity of purpose:

> We expected that America would produce the largest, most costly, and most gorgeous of all international exhibitions; but who expected that she would produce anything so inexpressibly poetic, chaste, and restrained, such an absolutely refined and soul-satisfying picture, as the Court of Honor, with

> its lagoon and gondolas, its white marble steps and balustrades, its varied yet harmonious buildings, its colonnaded vista of the great lake, its impressive fountain, its fairy-like outlining after dark by the gems of electricity, its spacious and well-modulated proportions . . . the aesthetic sense of the beholder was as fully and unreservedly satisfied as in looking at a masterpiece of painting or sculpture, and at the same time was soothed and elevated by a sense of amplitude and grandeur such as no single work of art could produce. . . . The glamour of old association that illumines Athens or Venice was in a way compensated by our deep impression of the pathetic transitoriness of the dream of beauty before us, and by the revelation it afforded of the soul of a great nation.[4]

For millions of turn-of-the-century Americans, high culture cut a broad swath in the national experience. They drew galvanizing instruction and aspiration from the White City—as from Henry Ward Beecher and William Jennings Bryan, Thomas Wentworth Higginson and the Social Gospel. They benefited from the initiatives of individuals who undertook what otherwise would not have been attempted. My portraits are studies in heroic application. My topic is fin-de-siècle uplift.

• • •

In the course of researching my *Wagner Nights: An American History* (1994), I read that "middle aged women in their enthusiasm stood up in the chairs and screamed their delight for what seemed hours" when Anton Seidl conducted Wagner at New York's Metropolitan Opera.[5]

My first reaction was disbelief: I could not envision this wild vignette. Only with the acquisition of further knowledge did it acquire reality. I absorbed that during the Met's "German seasons"—1884 to 1891—the boxholders, who fashionably enjoyed Gounod and Bellini, ceded artistic control to zealous Wagnerites for whom *Tristan und Isolde* was a necessary catharsis. Never again would the Met be so convulsed by fraught intensities of feeling and belief. Seidl, Wagner's onetime amanuensis at Bayreuth, exuded mystery and latent power. Albert Niemann, the Met's Tristan, was the supreme singing actor of his day, a red-bearded colossus who inhabited Tristan's ravings with reckless veracity; when in act 3 he tore off his bandages, women swooned. Lilli Lehmann was a true Isolde: imperious. In her memoirs she wrote: "In the whole world there was nothing that could free greater emotions in me than [my] *Tristan* performances in New York with Niemann, where the audience sat still for minutes, silent and motionless in their places, as though drunk or in a transport, without being conscious that the opera was over."[6] At

Seidl's funeral in 1898, women without tickets clasped arms in order to force their way past policemen and into the Metropolitan Opera House.

In effect, the present book ponders the phenomenon of the Met's screaming Wagnerites and endeavors to incorporate it into a larger reading of turn-of-the-century America. The obstacles are formidable. When we think of the "Gilded Age"—of the decades between the Civil War and 1900—we think of culture as a meretricious sideshow: of the Met's "Golden Horseshoe" and Mrs. Caroline Astor, who came late, left early, and was said to resemble a walking chandelier. We think of the "genteel tradition" as framed in 1911 by George Santayana, who lethally summarized Gilded Age arts and learning as "slightly becalmed," floating "gently in the backwater," a product of "a young country with an old mentality." "[America] has enjoyed the advantages of a child carefully brought up, and thoroughly indoctrinated; it has been a wise child. But a wise child, an old head on young shoulders, always has a comic and unpromising side. The wisdom is a little thin and verbal, not aware of its full meaning and grounds; and physical and emotional growth may be stunted by it, or even deranged."[7]

More recently, historians have inflicted on this period the imagery of snobbish "sacralization" and "social control"*—of aloof institutions consciously intent on purifying culture of the quotidian, and tacitly devised to co-opt the political energies of restive masses. These are notions incompatible with the realities of Wagner at the Met.

If screaming Wagnerites standing on chairs are in fact unthinkable today, it is also because we mistrust high feeling. Our children avidly specialize in vicarious forms of electronic interpersonal diversion. Our laptops and televisions ensnare us in a surrogate world that shuns all but facile passions; only Jon Stewart and Bill Maher share moments of moral outrage disguised as comedy.

One hundred years ago, the Great War extinguished the moral fires of the late nineteenth century. One has only to read Stravinsky's aesthetic strictures of the 1930s to revisit the modernist aversion to "anarchic" sentiment. Then came the music lovers Stalin and Hitler, and in response a third wave of revulsion—post-Santayana, post-Stravinsky—toward the ostensible moral properties of high art.

That culture is girded with moral fiber was a "genteel" article of faith linked to other sanguine convictions: in the fundamental decency of civilized human nature, in the universality of moral values, in progress

*See pages 232–35.

toward a kingdom of peace and love. If—as I observe in these pages—that faith enjoyed a special resilience in the United States, its American lineage is also special. The Puritans and the Great Awakenings of the nineteenth century were pertinent manifestations of moral energy. The Transcendentalists and Abolitionists—embodying egalitarianism, idealism, and uplift—were more than pertinent. By the late Gilded Age, evangelical rhetoric saturated every American mass movement: the Knights of Labor, the Woman's Christian Temperance Union, the Farmer's Alliance, the "applied Christianity" called Social Gospel. Because they so violate twenty-first-century conventional wisdom, two aspects of this moralistic reform impulse bear stressing. The movements in question were politically progressive; WCTU president Frances Willard was a Christian Socialist. And they infiltrated progressive high culture; the Reverend Washington Gladden, who preached unionization, wrote hymns, and fought Boss Tweed, was a Wagnerite. In fact, evangelical reform links directly to the Progressive Era itself.

Wagnerism was a cultural signature of these late-nineteenth-century American decades. It pervaded intellectual discourse. Writers and painters, politicians and reformers were Wagnerites. Wagnerism in America connected to good works: "fresh air" excursions for city orphans, voting rights for women. Explicitly Christian readings of the *Ring of the Nibelung* or *Parsifal* were commonplace. *Tristan* was purged of Schopenhauerian negation. Like Henry George, peddling his "single tax" on land, or Edward Bellamy, extolling a socialist utopia, American Wagnerites were buoyant evangelical democrats.

• • •

It is little remembered that classical music in America peaked during the late Gilded Age. Reinforced by zealous Germanic immigrants, German cultural authority dictated that, both philosophically and empirically, music was "queen of the arts." For American tastemakers like Boston's John Sullivan Dwight, music superseded language; it plumbed greater depths than any other art form. And its American institutional embodiments were quickly formidable. The Boston Symphony, created in 1881, was a world-class ensemble by the time it visited New York in 1887. By 1907, the popularity and prestige of Boston's orchestra had fostered consequential "symphony orchestras" (an American coinage) in Chicago, Cincinnati, Pittsburgh, Philadelphia, Minneapolis, and St. Louis; the overdue reorganization and expansion of the New York Philharmonic followed in 1909. The Met, opened in 1883, became a nonpareil opera company with Seidl's arrival two years later. Meanwhile, the nascent search for an "American school" first crested with Antonín Dvořák, who as director of New York's National Conservatory from 1892 to 1895 vigorously pursued a mandate to instruct American composers in the cultivation of a conscious national style.

The keynote of American classical music during this epoch of singular cultural authority was meliorism. In Europe and in Russia, Debussy, Richard Strauss, Schoenberg, and Scriabin influentially purveyed sensual or aestheticist delights. Americans, however, tenaciously retained the moral criterion. Theodore Thomas, whose Thomas Orchestra plied a "Thomas Highway" of twenty-eight cities in twelve states beginning in the 1860s, called his concerts "sermons in tones." Thomas's credo, "A symphony orchestra shows the culture of community, not opera," was nationally embraced. Symphonies, especially if by Beethoven, were revered agents of uplift. Accordingly, American orchestras conferred uplifting civic identity. By comparison, opera—which more typically pedigreed "the culture of a community" abroad—was a species of theater; it bore a moral taint. Only with the advent of evangelical Wagnerism did opera in America acquire a lofty mien. To be sure, the Met's screaming Wagnerites were libidinally aroused. And, as in Europe, Wagner in America bravely embodied the "Music of the Future." But, reframed by New World conventions, the Wagner cause was at the same time explicitly wholesome.

The moral passion animating classical music in the United States at the turn of the twentieth century may be anachronistic today, but the Santayana view of a precious and "becalmed" high culture in no way describes it. Two notably iconic personalities, newly construed, make the same point about the moral thunder and lightning of the late Gilded Age. The Reverend Henry Ward Beecher is widely remembered as a blowhard exponent of "The Gospel of Gush" and for the humiliations inflicted upon him by a sexual misconduct show trial. But Debby Applegate's *The Most Famous Man in America: The Biography of Henry Ward Beecher* (2006) portrays a devotee of books and classical music, a liberal clergyman of "great, if erratic, intellect" whose inflamed abolitionism linked with the espousal of women's rights and universal suffrage. Applegate's summation reads: "What Beecher brought to American culture in an era of bewildering change and fratricidal war was unconditional love so deep and so wide that the entire country could feel his warmth, like it or not."[8]

Concomitantly, Michael Kazin's *A Godly Hero: The Life of William*

Jennings Bryan (2007) rejects the Mencken view of a mountebank "surrounded by gaping primates," contributing his "bilge of idealism" to "the simian babble of the crossroads." Kazin's Bryan is bighearted and strong, a visceral nondoctrinaire optimist whose magnetic oratory, buoyed with evangelical rhetoric and a personal aura of "god-like dignity," was politically progressive. In later times, to treat politics as a Christian crusade would signify the bigotry of the right. But Bryan was kindred not to Pat Robertson and Jerry Falwell, but to Washington Gladden and Frances Willard, Jane Addams and Lincoln Steffens.[9]

Yet another recent invitation to reconstrue the moral fevers of late-nineteenth-century America is Brenda Wineapple's *White Heat: The Friendship of Emily Dickinson and Thomas Wentworth Higginson* (2008). Though Wentworth Higginson is chiefly remembered for "bowdlerizing" Dickinson's poems after her death, he was not a timid man. In 1854, he seized a battering ram to force entry into a federal courthouse in a failed attempt to free a fugitive slave. In 1856 he armed antislavery settlers in Kansas. In 1859 he raised money and supplies for John Brown's lethal raid on Harper's Ferry. He commanded the first Civil War regiment of freed slaves, men he judged hardened by adversity into a condition of moral supremacy. He crusaded for women's rights and against immigration restriction. Of his attempt to edit Dickinson's poems, he once wrote: "I fear it is only perfunctory, and that she interested me more in her—so to speak—unregenerate condition."[10] Wineapple observes the "heartache and pain" of their correspondence and the erotic undertones of their relationship. That the volume of Dickinson's poetry Higginson co-edited in 1891 sold eleven printings says that readers were ready for it.

Henry Ward Beecher's Plymouth Church sermons, preached to three thousand souls, were but blocks distant from the Brooklyn Academy of Music, where Theodore Thomas delivered symphonic "sermons in tones" for many of the same parishioners. As Thomas would gratefully observe, women enjoyed a special place in American classical music: they constituted the majority of its listeners, avocational practitioners, and behind-the-scenes organizers. They also predominated in William Jennings Bryan's army of congregants; Bryan believed their gender morally superior.[11] His "cross of gold" speech at the 1896 Democratic National Convention was ecstatically acclaimed by delegates standing on chairs; for many, it was a peak life experience. Seidl's screaming *Tristan* audiences were a parallel contemporaneous phenomenon. Though Wineapple assumes that the erotic rapture of Dickinson's

"Wild Nights! Wild Nights!" transcended time and place, though Higginson here refused to impute sexual abandon to the virgin poetess, one could hardly find a more apt poetic equivalent of Wagner's Liebestod than Dickinson's

> Wild nights—Wild Nights!
> Were I with thee
> Wild Nights should be
> Our luxury!
>
> Futile—the Winds—
> To a Heart in port—
> Done with the Compass—
> Done with the Chart!
>
> Rowing in Eden—
> Ah, the Sea!
> Might I but moor—Tonight—
> in Thee!

Recalibrating a slightly later turn-of-the-century figurehead, Kathleen Dalton's landmark biography *Theodore Roosevelt: A Strenuous Life* (2004) challenges such axiomatic imagery as the racist imperialist, the ranting egotist, and the self-righteous poseur. Her Roosevelt is first of all a ripe and robust idealist, a heroic crusader whose passionate fixation on the morals of a nation cannot be patronized. She charts in detail his evolving, historic commitment to the rightful prerogatives of women and African-Americans. She amasses a fin-de-siècle portrait of uplift and restless achievement writ large in equal measure.

The present book produces four more turn-of-the-century candidates for revisionist portraiture. Each portrait greatly expands, and recontextualizes, a cameo drawing in *Wagner Nights* or in my *Classical Music in America: A History* (2005). Each is a study of moral empowerment. Henry Higginson, a younger cousin to Thomas Wentworth, invented, owned, and operated the Boston Symphony and built Symphony Hall. He also commanded a Civil War regiment and ran a plantation with freedmen. No less than with Thomas Wentworth, written histories are here vague and misleading: both Higginsons are misconstrued as stiff-backed patricians. My second portrait is of Henry Krehbiel, the onetime "dean" of New York music critics, whose daunting expertise in Wagner linked to important writings on culture and race. As with Beecher's notorious philandering, and Bryan's notorious prosecution of John Scopes for teaching Darwin, Krehbiel committed a blatant indiscretion when he vilified the dead Gustav Mahler. He deserves to be remembered for other things. Laura Langford, coming third, is not misremembered but ignored. It was her amazing Seidl Society that presented Coney Island's summer Wagner Nights; the rest of the year, at the Brooklyn Academy of Music, she produced more concerts than the New York Philharmonic across the river. Because he was discovered in the 1930s as an ostensible incipient modernist, because he lived into the 1950s, Charles Ives—my final subject—is not usually considered a turn-of-the-century American. But he was.

All four of my portraits are of democratic meliorists of religious temperament whose complicated lives, embodying a fluid cultural moment, remain inspirational. As exemplars of the genteel tradition, they contradict Santayana. And they rebuke conventional wisdom about the Gilded Age.

• • •

The revisionism of the present book keys on the moral fervor of four remarkable culture bearers. Its central thrust is to identify an impassioned positive strain of turn-of-the-century American high culture and call it "fin de siècle."

The term—French for "end of the century"—is of course nothing new. It is routinely applied to writers, painters, and composers in London, Paris, Vienna, and other European cultural capitals. Far less often applied to the United States, it typically refers to a dynamic moment in Old World culture, a fulcrum moment, circa 1880 to 1914, dialectically charged, tugged backward and forward, a moment of closure and of anticipatory excitement. Evoking a vibrant coda, it is freighted with decadence: escapism, aestheticism, ennui; evoking a new beginning, it connotes revolt. Mahler, Wilde, Klimt, Mallarmé are representative fin-de-siècle figures—subversives at first glance wholly exogenous to the American experience.*

Turn-of-the-century America possessed no Gustav Mahler. Its artists and thinkers did not know the turbid realms—erotic, irrational—of a

*A cultural historian who identifies an "American Fin de Siècle" somewhat in parallel with my usage is George Cotkin in *Reluctant Modernism: American Thought and Culture, 1880–1900* (1992). Cotkin writes: "Despite its spirit of rebellion and experimentation, the American fin de siècle was also marked by an attempt to maintain many assumptions essential to Victorianism . . . irony coexisted with faith, antagonism with celebration, reason with unreason" (p. 131).

Klimt or Freud. One proof is Mahler's American sojourn of 1908 to 1911. At the Metropolitan Opera, with the New York Philharmonic, he electrified and inspired. He also perplexed and exasperated. Henry Krehbiel, his New York nemesis, found Mahler's symphonies vulgar: they debased their own uplifting Romantic ideals. Eyeing Mahler's hybridity, Krehbiel wrote: "It was a singular paradox in Mahler's artistic nature that while his melodic ideas were of the folksong order his treatment of them was of the most extravagant kind, harmonically and orchestrally."[12] Krehbiel's notorious Mahler obituary proclaimed his American career a failure.

And yet Krehbiel is himself a fulcrum figure. An emblematic German-American, he equally embodies venerable Germanic traditions and nascent American strivings. American Wagnerism, as he influentially lived and espoused it, is a comparable paradox, at once subversive and wholesomely meliorist. According to conventional wisdom, the genteel values Krehbiel upheld should have condemned him to an ineffectual sidelines role. In fact, he was tirelessly proactive: no other American music critic has impacted more tangibly on the musical life he observed and inhabited.

A Krehbiel—or Higginson, or Langford, or Ives—bears no surface resemblance to a Mahler, Klimt, or Freud. But the Gilded Age and genteel tradition, while not irrelevant, only half explain them. To locate American fin-de-siècle signposts of an intense high culture in vigorous transition requires a considered act of recalibration: the extremes of fin-de-siècle decadence and revolt must be trimmed. Turn-of-the century New World tensions did not register ennui and rebellion against a backdrop of encrusted history; rather, they reflected the growing pains of a young culture. Far from evading the genteel tradition, a Krehbiel or Ives elasticized or challenged its sanguine precepts from within.

These contradictory American personalities mirrored contradictory times—of ostentatious wealth and dire poverty, of institutional growth and bitter labor unrest, of sudden progress and severe economic depression. As never before, the metropolis had become a citadel of mansions and museums, libraries and opera houses. Equally, cities signified strife and despair; according to Jacob Riis, three-quarters of Manhattan's population of more than a million lived in thirty-seven thousand tenements, "hot beds of the epidemics that carry death . . . the nurseries of pauperism and crime that fill our jails and police courts." Immigration, industrialization, urbanization accelerated the pace of change. Henry Adams observed "the disappearance of religion." Meanwhile, the nascent authority of science proposed a mechanistic, materialistic universe.[13]

As religion vied with science, art vied with business—the one a man's domain, the other overpopulated with women for whom other callings were foreclosed. Corseted, repressed, confined, housewives of the middle and upper classes succumbed to nervous prostration and other symptoms of "neurasthenia." "A weightless culture of material comfort and spiritual blandness was breeding weightless persons who hoped for intense experience to give some definition, some distinct outline and substance to their vaporous lives," writes the historian Jackson Lears.[14] "Intense experience" might take the form of free thought, or free love, or the occult sciences sampled by Mark Twain and countless others. By 1900, the New Woman was riding bicycles, playing tennis, and smoking cigarettes laced with cocaine.

While the notion of an American fin de siècle may be unfamiliar, the notion of a late Gilded Age cultural surge is not. John Higham, in a landmark 1970 essay, summarized the "reorientation of American culture in the 1890s" in terms of a "hunger to break out," to shatter "the gathering restrictions of a highly industrialized society."[15] More recently, late Gilded Age personalities once ignored or derogated—I have already mentioned Henry Ward Beecher, William Jennings Bryan, Thomas Wentworth Higginson, and Theodore Roosevelt—have been vigorously rehabilitated.

In fact, I ride a revisionist wave of some duration. Keying on Theodore Roosevelt's "strenuous life," Higham and his successors find emergent evidence of restlessness and muscle in a range of American activities, including collegiate athletics and foreign affairs. Higham's seminal picture of an 1890s "reorientation" contains points of pertinence to the present study, in particular where he discerns a "revival of buried impulses" linking to the "transcendental ecstasies of Emerson, Garrison, and Whitman," and of a "new activism" stopping short of "alienation." But *Moral Fire* differs from earlier studies in two respects. The late Gilded Age ferment I celebrate both clinches a meliorist past and anticipates a Progressive future. And previous revisionist studies omit music. The magnitude of this oversight cannot be overstated. Higham, typically, glimpses ragtime, but assumes the irrelevance of concerts and opera. Comparably, Henry May, in his invaluable and influential *The End of American Innocence* (1959), admires the potency of ragtime and jazz after 1900. But May is far from correct when he excludes classical music from his purview of the genteel tradition on the grounds that it "did not make direct statements about moral principles, did not command the same spotlight as literature or even painting."*[16] Even such a title as *The American 1890s: A Cultural Reader* (2000) has nothing to say about Theodore Thomas or Henry Higginson. If the lightning institutionalization of American classical music is ignored by such revisionists as H. Wayne Morgan, who has worked to relieve "Gilded Age" of its gaudy connotations, or Louis Menand, who has revisited the intellectual life of the late Gilded Age with infectious enthusiasm, it is because classical music has lost pertinence *today;* the result is an incomplete picture of the past.†

In the introduction to her 1999 biography of J.P. Morgan, Jean Strouse describes her befuddled discovery that Morgan was not what she had assumed him to be. Those who "won the battle over how [his] story would be told," she writes, had depicted " a ruthless predator." Strouse ascertained that many Morgan "facts," repeated by generations of chroniclers, had no basis. The bedrock of Morgan's personality and success, she concluded, was "character."[17] What is more, Morgan was an educated man who traveled widely, who spoke German and French fluently, who was not remotely a prude or philistine. Morgan's friend Henry Higginson—his exact contemporary in Boston banking circles—must be comparably redrawn. Working from sketchy information and misinformation, cultural historians have depicted him as a high-handed Brahmin, a cultural captain of industry. He was in fact a democratic philanthropist whose integrity and warmth were signatures of his success.

The late Gilded Age was the charged moment during which middle-

*Joseph Mussulman's *Music in the Cultured Generation: A Social History of Music in America 1870–1900* (1971) uniquely investigates the role of music as a moral anchor. Mussulman stresses "the atmosphere of intellectual expansiveness which the total body of literature on music exudes" during these late-nineteenth-century decades. "Neither before nor since has the literary side of American music exhibited such catholicity with respect to the backgrounds of the participants" (p. 19). The writers on classical music he explores include such central figures as William Dean Howells and George William Curtis (the preeminent columnist for *Harper's* during the second half of the twentieth century). Richard Watson Gilder, who edited *Century* (1881–1909), was a keen music lover. Bliss Perry, who edited the *Atlantic* (1899–1909), wrote *The Life and Letters of Henry Higginson.* The ubiquity of classical music in the intellectual life of the late Gilded Age is also a central theme of my *Wagner Nights: An American History* and *Classical Music in America: A History.*

†A rare exception is Lawrence Levine's *Highbrow/Lowbrow* (1989). But Levine is misleading. That he interprets Thomas as an inhibiting agent of sacralization, that he sees Higginson as a baronial overlord shows the distortive power of resilient labels and stereotypes.

class German-Americans displaced High Society boxholders as powerbrokers at the Metropolitan Opera; when Met performances of *Tristan und Isolde* were "intense experiences" received in shocked silence; when Wagner was played regularly in summertime to excited throngs at a Coney Island seaside pavilion. Many late-nineteenth-century Americans believed music mined deeper truths than words or pictures. All educated persons knew Beethoven's symphonies; Wagnerism inflected their discourse to a degree now unimaginable. Dvořák, in New York, unleashed a national controversy through his advocacy of slave songs and Indian chants as American keynotes. In Boston, Arthur Nikisch's mercurial rendition of Beethoven's Fifth ignited a firestorm challenging notions of civic ripeness. None of this activity repudiated received wisdom about art as uplift; rather, the genteel tradition, in a final dynamic phase, was stretched and reinterpreted.

. . .

One catalyst for the present book was a rereading of Lytton Strachey's *Eminent Victorians* (1918)—a landmark revisionist study surveying Cardinal Manning, Florence Nightingale, Thomas Arnold, and General Charles George Gordon. In each case, a preoccupation with piety is revisited as neurotic or sanctimonious. In parallel with Van Wyck Brooks and Lewis Mumford an ocean away, Strachey debunked the moral pretensions of a previous generation.

My "eminent Victorians"—Henry Higginson, Henry Krehbiel, Laura Langford, Charles Ives—turn Strachey on his head. I find that the relative easiness or moral complacency of present-day lives set off the prodigious individual energies and achievements of my fin-de-siècle subjects. They strive tenaciously for meaningfulness in life. Their hunger for spiritual sustenance is channeled into art, music, learning, and social action.

Turn-of-the-century, pre–World War I hybrids, they exist betwixt and between. Higginson is a financier and an aesthete. Krehbiel is a professorial German and a business-like American. Langford fluctuates between the spinet and the séance, the parlor and radical reform. Ives sells insurance and writes symphonies. In each case, a preoccupation with uplift is the motif that binds. The sequence of my portraits is chronological. "Higginson" begins in the 1860s with the Civil War, "Krehbiel" in 1893 with the World's Columbian Exposition. "Langford" peaks in the late 1890s. "Ives" hits stride around 1900.

The portraits embellish densely intersecting topics. Higginson's wife, Ida, who earnestly instructed the freed slaves on their Georgia plantation, was the daughter of Louis Agassiz, the influential Harvard anthropologist who believed blacks were biologically inferior. Krehbiel's pathbreaking studies of the relationship of race and culture advanced an ongoing national inquiry conditioned both by the Civil War and by equally inescapable Darwinian theory; at the World's Columbian Exposition, he was impressed by the music of African tribesmen others found merely primitive. Like Krehbiel, Langford served the missionary Wagner conductor Anton Seidl. Like Higginson, she was an impresario of boundless energy and resourcefulness. Ives, no less than Higginson, needed to pursue dual vocations in business and art. Higginson, Krehbiel, and Langford personify turn-of-the century high culture in Boston, New York, and Brooklyn: a study in contrasts unified by prodigious buoyant energies.

For all my subjects, the Old World was a complex frame of reference. The dismantling energies of Europe's fin de siècle paved the way for modernist revolt. As I have occasion to mention in my Summation, America's fin de siècle includes such rebellious and unsentimental creators as Theodore Dreiser and the Ashcan painters. It also includes certain Boston aesthetes who mildly mirrored turn-of-the-century decadents abroad. But, as frequently, the energies of America's fin de siècle were about *resistance* to a nascent modernist order; they had less to do with calamitous social and political disintegration than did cultural ferment in Paris or Vienna.

My expository plan is somewhat unusual. Like Strachey's, my portraits are self-contained. They strive to be lifelike. Therefore all the historiography in this book, citing writers who support or contradict my story, may be found in this Prologue and in my Summation. And it is in the Summation, rather than within the portrait chapters, that I juxtapose my subjects and infer a binding five-point template. As with Strachey, again, the subjects are chosen not as "most important," or even as a representative or comprehensive cross-section; rather, they maximize opportunities for extrapolation; ultimately, they drive a thesis. That Higginson, Krehbiel, and Langford are figures of startling accomplishment, and yet today neglected, forgotten, or misconstrued, of course greatly matters to me. The inclusion of Ives is a surprise; his prestige buttresses and amplifies what I have to say.

. . .

America's fin de siècle retained religious and puritanical values of Victorian and pre-Victorian times; further supported by the Germanic idealism of many an American thinker, it preserved the ideal of a moral criterion in art. This aesthetic crucible, challenged by such imports as Ibsen's *Hedda Gabler* or Strauss's *Salome,* proved creatively resilient.

What unifies my portraits, then, is the notion that great art can uplift. The portraits show how four individuals differently pursued this conviction via musical enterprise and experience. My thesis is that the moral criterion remained dynamic in the United States through the end of the nineteenth century—whereas abroad a looming modernism rendered it increasingly passé.

In fact, all four of my subjects outlived their charmed fin-de-siècle moment. For Higginson and Krehbiel, the new century was morally uprooted: a time of despair. Langford ended her life in despair and obscurity. Ives, long surviving his fin-de-siècle apex, withdrew into denial. But their late estrangement does not make them feeble or quaint or irrelevant to times to come. If the White City retains its frisson, it is less the Midway that excites incredulity than the white epiphany of the Court of Honor: an aesthetic dream of betterment.

FIGURE 2. Henry Higginson. Photograph by Notman, courtesy Boston Symphony Orchestra Archives.

CHAPTER 1

Henry Higginson

High Culture, High Finance, and Useful Citizenship

Civil War service—A second home in Vienna—Announcing the Boston Symphony Orchestra—John Sullivan Dwight and musical uplift—Building Symphony Hall—Choosing a conductor—"Masculine" business versus "feminine" art—Karl Muck and the Great War

> Dearest Jim,—
>
> We are in for the fight at last and will carry it thro' like men. . . . Never in my whole life have I seen anything approaching in the slightest degree to the excitement and the enthusiasm of the past week. Everything excepting the war is forgotten, business is suspended, the streets are filled with people, drilling is seen on all sides and at all times. Our Massachusetts troops were poured into Boston within 12 to 24 hours after the command was issued from here, and were the first to go on and the first to shed blood. . . .
>
> But you should have seen the troops, Jimmy: real, clean-cut, intelligent Yankees, the same men who fought in '76, a thousand times better than any soldiers living. They left their wives and children in some cases without a farewell, and *marched thro'* to Washington. We've been told of our degeneracy for years and years: I tell you, Jim, no more heartfelt enthusiasm or devotion was to be found in '76 than now. *Everyone* is longing to go. One man walked 10 miles to join a volunteer company raised and gone between Wednesday and Sunday. . . . Father gets dreadfully excited; indeed so does everyone. My best love to you, Jimmy. Yrs.
>
> H.[1]

Henry Lee Higginson, twenty-six years old, wrote to his brother James on April 22, 1861—ten days after Confederate batteries opened fire on Fort Sumter. James was in Germany. Higginson was living with his father on Chauncy Street and seeking employment. The outbreak of civil war was a timely occurrence for a young man in limbo; though hobbled by a badly sprained foot, he was soon a lieutenant and vigorously collecting men in Leominster, Shirley, Hopedale, and other towns in the Boston vicinity. By year's end, he had become captain of a regiment, drilling and instructing a variety of men from all walks of life (his ineffectual predecessor having been a barkeeper). He learned to ride and to parade. He wrote to his sister, Molly: "You can't imagine how big I feel now that I've a camp under me. A year ago this time I was learning guard-duty and squad-drill on foot; now I ride around on a big horse, have *two* rows of brass buttons on my coat . . . and am generally just as big as I can swell."[2]

In March 1862 Higginson became a major, stationed on Beaufort Island, South Carolina, but the companies under his command did not take part in a failed invasion of the mainland. He visited a teenage rebel prisoner. "I was surprised to see the little fellow this morning—young and small, with beautiful fair hair thrown back from his forehead which was high and fine, a delicately cut nose and a sweet expression about his mouth. The poor boy has a severe wound, but will recover, so the doctor thinks. I took a great fancy to him, and should much like to send his mother tidings of him. He gives his name as Hughes." Such experiences, his enforced passivity notwithstanding, quickened the heart and mind of Henry Higginson. He wrote to Jim:

> Now, Jimmy, you will feel very sorry if you have no hand in the struggle—whether we sink or swim. We are fighting against slavery, present or future, and we are struggling for the right of mankind to be educated and to think; come and do your part. Of your father's children I am the only one bearing arms; I know that I was placed exactly right for the emergency and that no one of the rest of you was so; that I went because I could n't stay at home, and have enjoyed myself highly since; that for a hundred reasons it was no sacrifice, but an enormous gratification and pleasure, and to me, as education, as experience, as occupation, as good pay for my otherwise idle time. I do not take an atom of credit to myself, but I do think that the family quota should be stronger.[3]

By December, Higginson was feeling frustrated and pessimistic, unhappy with the president, with the cabinet, with Congress, with "nothing new except the changes of generals." He had witnessed inept military leadership and endured friends slain. He was rejuvenated by a visit home in March. On the way back to Virginia, he stopped in Washington and barely missed seeing the future Beethoven biographer Alexander Wheelock Thayer, whom he had known in Vienna, and to whom he subsequently wrote while commanding an eighty-mile picket line:

> Dear Thayer:—
> . . . I tried twice in my short stay of a few hours to see you—in vain. If you could have come here, you should have seen something of our army. . . . But you must hurry back to Vienna. . . . Well, old fellow, go your own way and work out your own salvation. I am trying to work out mine, so is Jim, and so is many a good, brave man. The many little salvations will go to make that of our country and of the human race. Tell me there is no American people, is no nationality, is no distinct and strong love of country! It is a lie, and those who have said it to me in Europe simply were ignorant! We've been to school for two years all the time, and have been learning a lesson—wait and see if we don't know it and use it pretty soon. . . . My whole religion (that is my whole belief and hope in everything, in life, in man, in woman, in music, in good, in the beautiful, in the real truth) rests on the questions now really before us. It is enough to keep up one's pluck, is n't it, old fellow?[4]

Three months later, on June 17, 1863, Major Higginson was inspecting a Virginia farmhouse when a Confederate regiment suddenly bore down on his men. He ordered a charge. The enemy fled. Another Union company, under Captain Lucius Sargent, followed in pursuit. Higginson yelled at Sargent to pull back, to no avail. When he rode forward to deliver his cautionary order in person, an entire regiment of Confederate cavalry came galloping from behind. Sargent was knocked from his horse and shot. Higginson, too, was thrown to the ground. In hand-to-hand combat, he took a saber cut to his face and a bullet to the base of his spine. An enemy soldier attempted to take him prisoner; Higginson persuaded the man that he would shortly die. He crawled to a brook and drank some water, then lay down to write a death note to his father. He came within sight of a field of dead and wounded men. He was taken by train to Alexandria. His back wound, which threatened to paralyze his lower limbs, was dressed. His father was notified and came. He was sent home in a railway car crammed with slung beds; some of the men were in their death throes. In Boston the bullet lodged in his spine was found and removed. When his former comrades marched to Gettysburg, he was still being nursed by his father on Chauncy Street. Though he returned to duty in July, his recovery was slow. He felt compelled to resign from the army in August.

Writing to Thayer in March 1863, Higginson had asked to be remembered to myriad friends, both European and American, in Vienna. He continued in the same vein: "My love again to you, old fellow, and to all in Vienna or in other places, and tell them that I often and often think of them and former times with very great pleasure. My friends are still and always will be my greatest delight in life." So it was and would be. In the war, Higginson served alongside family friends and Harvard friends, including some as incipiently prominent as Charles Francis Adams Jr., the grandson and great-grandson of two presidents, who would rise to the rank of general; and Robert Gould Shaw, who would die gloriously at the head of a regiment of black soldiers. His adventures brought him into constant contact with great names and tragic waste. In the fall of 1861, barely missing action in the Battle of Ball's Bluff, he encountered the mortally wounded William Lowell Putnam—whom his uncle James Russell Lowell would commemorate in *The Biglow Papers*. Another, less dire casualty was the future Supreme Court justice Oliver Wendell Holmes Jr. In Boston not long after, Higginson visited Wendell Homes's house to tell the family that Lieutenant Holmes was "doing pretty well." In August 1862 Higginson lost two intimate friends—Jim Savage and Stephen Perkins—at Cedar Mountain: a useless encounter. Bob Shaw wrote: "It was splendid to see those sick fellows walk straight up into the shower of bullets as if it were so much rain; men, who, until this year, had lived lives with perfect ease and luxury." Shaw himself fell less than a year later while urging his African-Americans into battle from atop an exposed parapet.[5]

Communications of another sort came from Jim Higginson, by now a prisoner of war reading Virgil in confinement. "Pick me out two or three of your French books (no valuable copies) and your little black-covered fat-bellied French-English dictionary," he wrote to Henry. And again: "Allow me to call your attention to a most beautiful passage in Schiller's 'Das Lied von der Glocke' . . . 'Die schöne Zeit der jungen Liebe'—most admirable lines. Don't they meet your approval? Write to me, my boy—pity the sorrow of a jailbird." (Henry's own reading that summer included Shakespeare's *Henry VI*.) It was during the Civil War years, as well, that Higginson married while recuperating from his bullet wound. His German-born bride, whom he had known since boyhood, was Ida Agassiz, daughter of Harvard's irrepressibly eminent Louis Agassiz. Henry Adams wrote from London: "If I knew your fiancée, I should congratulate her upon getting for a husband one of the curiously small number of men whom I ever have seen, for whom I have morally a certain degree of respect. This perhaps wouldn't be quite so enthusiastic praise as one might give, but it's more than I ever said of anyone else. The truth is, a good many of my acquaintances have been getting engaged lately, and I believe yours is the only case that has made me really, sincerely glad to hear about."[6]

Completing this wartime portrait of impulsive patriotism and frustrated expectations, of democratic or elite camaraderie, of exceptional personal loss and gain, was a singularly determinant moment in Higginson's career-to-come. To his peers, Charles Russell Lowell, scion of one of Boston's great families, was a dashing exemplar of character and intellect. Five years Higginson's senior, he had already distinguished himself professionally: six years after graduating Harvard as valedictorian, he was running the Mount Savage Iron Works in Maryland. In wartime, he served as a lieutenant under Robert Gould Shaw and married Shaw's sister Josephine. He was named a brigadier general at the age of twenty-nine—and died a day later leading a charge at Cedar Creek; thirteen horses had previously been shot from under him. Brigadier General George Armstrong Custer wept at Charles Lowell's death; Major General Philip Sheridan said: "I do not think there was a quality which I could have added to Lowell. He was the perfection of a man and a soldier."[7]

Higginson would in later life daily remember Charlie Lowell. One reason was a letter—Lowell's last to Higginson, dated September 10, 1864; it embodied Higginson's lifelong credo. "I felt very sorry, old fellow, at your being finally obliged to give up, for I know you would have liked to see it out," Lowell wrote of Higginson's early retirement from the army.

> However, there is work enough for a public-spirited cove everywhere. . . . I hope, Mr. Higginson, that you are going to live like a plain Republican, mindful of the beauty and the duty of simplicity. Nothing fancy now, Sir, if you please. It's disreputable to spend money, when the Government is so hard up, and when there are so many poor officers. I hope you have outgrown all foolish ambitions and are now content to become a "useful citizen." . . . Don't grow rich; if you once begin, you will find it much more difficult to be a useful citizen. The useful citizen is a mighty unpretending hero. But we are not going to have any country very long unless such heroism is developed. . . .
>
> I believe I have lost all my ambitions old fellow. . . . All I now care about is to be a useful citizen, with money enough to buy my bread and firewood and to teach my children how to ride on horseback and look strangers in the face, especially Southern strangers. . . . I wonder whether I shall ever see you again.[8]

A quarter century later, by which time he was far the dominant figure in the institutional cultural life of Boston, Higginson gave Harvard a new athletic field, dedicated as "Soldiers Field" to Charles Lowell, Robert Gould Shaw, Stephen Perkins, James Savage, and two other of his fallen Civil War comrades: Lowell's brother James Jackson and the physician Edward Dalton. Speaking at a commemorative ceremony on June 5, 1890, Higginson also commemorated the now famous Memorial

Day address delivered by Oliver Wendell Holmes Jr. six years previous. Holmes had said: "The generation that carried on the war has been set apart by its experience. Through our great good fortune, in our youth our hearts were touched by fire. It was given to us to learn at the outset that life is a profound and passionate thing." Speaking at Harvard, Higginson aligned his purpose and content with Holmes's high example, fashioning a solemn roll call of fallen comrades in arms. The characteristic differences distinguishing Higginson's address were two: the note of intimate personal regard, and a sense of duty combining pragmatism and idealism in equal measure. Higginson recalled of Shaw: "I fell in love with this boy, and I have not fallen out yet. He was of a very simple and manly nature—steadfast and affectionate, human to the last degree,—without much ambition except to do his plain duty." Higginson remembered Charlie Lowell—"thoughtful, kind, affectionate, gentle"—for his exhortations to useful citizenry. To the young scholars at hand, he added:

> Everywhere we see the signs of ferment—questions social, moral, mental, physical, economical. The pot is boiling hard and you must tend it, or it will run over and scald the world. For us came the great questions of slavery and of national integrity, and they were not hard to answer. Your task is more difficult, and yet you must fulfill it. Do not hope that things will take care of themselves, or that the old state of affairs will come back. The world on all sides is moving fast, and you have only to accept this fact, making the best of everything—helping, sympathizing, and so guiding and restraining others, who have less education, perhaps, than you. Do not hold off from them; but go straight on with them, side by side, learning from them and teaching them. . . . Do not too readily think that you have done enough, simply because you have accomplished something. There is no enough, so long as you can better the lives of your fellow beings. Your success in life depends not on talents, but on will. Surely, genius is the power of working hard, and long, and well.[9]

• • •

Henry Higginson was of medium height and robustly built. His goatee, ample mustache, and saber scar were defining physical traits. The best-known portrait of the mature Higginson, by John Singer Sargent in 1903, evinces an aloof or even arrogant man; a cavalry cloak thrown across his knees connotes the warrior. Though in his years of service as a useful citizen Higginson could render his idealism decisively and bluntly, though his bearing was straight-shouldered and brisk, he disliked Sargent's painting for a reason. The keynote of his personality was its combination of authority and—a quality etched in his open face, and at all times vivid

FIGURE 3. John Singer Sargent's 1903 portrait of Henry Higginson. Harvard Art Museum/Fogg Art Museum, Harvard University Portrait Collection; gift by student subscription to the Harvard Union, 1903, H189; photo imaging department. © President and Fellows of Harvard College.

in his reminiscences and letters—personal affection: he liked people; he liked them to know it. As much as his banker's fortune, as much as his notions of integrity and public good, his admired simplicity of manner, a conduit for frankness and warmth, equipped him to get things done.

Doubtless pertinent is that Higginson was not born to wealth. Nor was he born in Boston—but in New York, in 1834. His father, George—who as one of thirteen children had been at work since the age of twelve—was a small commission merchant. When his business failed in the panic of 1837, he moved the family to Boston, where he found similar employment. He opened a stockbrokerage house with his cousin John C. Lee in 1848. The Higginsons lived in a series of rented homes in Boston, West Cambridge, and Brookline. At mealtimes, there was meat and potatoes five times a week, but never butter or eggs. And yet on both sides Higginson's family was connected to distinguished Brahmin clans, including Lees, Cabots, Lowells, Channings, Putnams, and Storrows. As the great Irish and German immigrations had not yet intruded, Boston was still homogenously English; it was not unusual for the Higginson abode to be surrounded by the larger homes of wealthier relatives—and the families commingled. Higginson's inseparable playmates included Charlie Lowell ("as bright as I was stupid"), with whom he skated and played pranks. He might go to church to hear cousin Thomas Wentworth Higginson—"Colonel" versus "Major" Henry Higginson, even though Henry had also in wartime advanced to the rank of colonel—preach an antislavery sermon. He might visit Dr. Holmes's Pittsfield farm on the banks of the Housatonic.

Higginson's mother was herself a Lee. She died of tuberculosis in 1849 when Henry—the second of five siblings—was fifteen. But George Higginson, who did not retire until 1874, was at all times a close companion and correspondent. The letters father and son exchanged are remarkably evenhanded: George seems more a friend and exemplar than a parent. No less than would Henry, but with far lesser means, he charitably gave away what he earned. He wept at the memory of his wife. He laughed readily and heartily. He was quick to resent and condemn conduct he thought dishonorable. Henry remembered him as "a kindly, industrious, sensible man, with a remarkable 'nose' for character, scrupulously honest, and disinterested to a high degree." George's brother-in-law Colonel Henry Lee said of him:

> Mr. Higginson was preeminent in those qualities which entitle a man to love and respect. . . . he was liberal—nay, prodigal—of his time and his money in the service of all who were "distressed in mind, body, or estate." . . . To

> enumerate his beneficiaries would be impossible, as no human being stood near enough to him to ascertain their names or number; and some surprising revelations have been made by those assisted. His habit of living, like his habit of giving, was liberal and unostentatious. An old-fashioned simplicity, in which he had been bred, he maintained through life, combined with an unbounded hospitality.[10]

At the Boston Latin School—then as now the city's elite public school—Henry Higginson remained surrounded by friends and relations. As "Bully Hig," he earned a reputation for toughness and fortitude in Boston Commons battles against roughnecks who packed snowballs with rocks. Though no Higginson in the direct parental line had ever held a college degree, Henry next entered Harvard, where his fellow freshmen (in an undergraduate population of only 304) included Alexander Agassiz and S. Parkman Blake, both future brothers-in-law. Also at Harvard with Higginson were three of the six soldiers-to-be he would memorialize at Soldier's Field: Charlie Lowell, James Savage, and Stephen Perkins. But with its dour regime of Latin, Greek, and mathematics, Harvard was otherwise not a fit; by December, it was evident that Higginson's weak eyes would force his departure.

That summer Henry Higginson, age eighteen, set out for Europe. In the Swiss Alps he engaged a guide and climbed courageously, his hands stiff from cold because he took no gloves. He explored the Aar glacier, where Louis Agassiz had done research; he vaulted deep crevices; he ascended vertical rock faces. In correspondence with his father, he pondered learning German, the "finest" language after English, and living in Paris—"the most vicious, yet the most tempting and dangerous place on earth"—to learn French. His equation of Germany with culture and learning—which would shortly grow less extreme—was, at the time, typically American. In Higginson's case, however, it was soon magnified by an avocation not practiced by his male peers at home. In London, in Milan, in Munich, in Dresden he became a devotee of the opera. He adored *Fidelio*. He was pleasingly challenged by *Tannhäuser*. He devoured Gluck, Weber, Meyerbeer, and Bellini ("but the Italian music is very meager after the German"). In the concert hall, he heard Haydn, Beethoven, Mendelssohn, Schumann. He began music lessons. He learned to play the piano.[11]

Though he returned home in 1853 and spent the better part of two years pursuing the sort of merchant business his father first knew, Henry was back in Europe three years later: in London, where he "didn't like many of the pictures" in a Turner exhibit; in Paris, where he wrote of the Madeleine: "too much gilded, too much bosh, for beauty"; in Florence, where Charlie Lowell was seriously ill; in Dresden, where he was relieved to find Lowell relocated and on the mend. Henry wound up settling in Vienna, where for two years he pursued a spartan educational regime. His weekly musical intake was nine lessons and two lectures. His dietary intake, usually omitting supper, was limited by his financial resources; he told his father: "A large portion of my yearly expenses are not for myself. . . . I sometimes curse myself for trying to help others when I've not enough money for my own real wants, but again think that money well used is not wasted." Higginson's studies included harmony, voice, and piano. He reported home that his voice was not strong enough for a hall. His keyboard studies floundered when he hurt his left arm from overuse, and likely aggravated what became a permanent injury by having it bled.[12]

In no other period is the mutual affection of father and son as vivid as during this sustained absence abroad. "Many thanks for your portrait; it is a very excellent likeness," writes Henry in May 1858. "A touch of gray in the hair and whiskers and a few wrinkles to show that you are no longer young, a half-smile and a half-joke in your eyes to signify the fun of your nature, the pleasantest mouth in the world with its very best expression . . . —it is all capital, the real old daddy." Another specimen: "You are a capital correspondent in quantity and quality; do not mind reproving me now and then (a rarity new to me so far from home), answer my questions, give me news and advice, and best of all a smile and a kiss at the end." A sampling of George's advice, on letter-writing: "Aim at simplicity and conciseness." And Henry did. "A letter should be merely a little talk on paper, and that is quite all." George at one point chided: "My dear Henry, you know I attach little importance to forms, to set rules of society, which are for the most part unmeaning, but as a matter of correct taste on your part, would it not be in better keeping to omit the terms 'old fellow,' 'old boy,' etc., when addressing me? I think so."[13]

Singular evidence of the worldly impact of the Hapsburg capital on a young Bostonian was Henry's swift acquisition of Jewish friends. "I never saw a Jew before coming here," he tells George. "But those whom I have known in Vienna are very talented, true, liberal in views of life and religion, and free-handed to a marvelous extent." George: "You are favored, for I have rarely met individuals of that race who seemed fitted in solid essentials for an intimacy of such a character. I am thankful that really worthy ones have fallen in your way."[14]

A recurrent motif of this transatlantic dialogue, in which Yankee pragmatism jostled with venerable Old World customs, was the unlikely profession in music being tested. Henry felt the need to justify his impracticality. Some years before, when first in Europe, he had ventured: "Tho' there may seem to be no positive gain in all the fine arts, they certainly can do no harm, and they may be of great use; and of music, tho' a person understanding and knowing something of it is not perhaps any more educated for practical purposes than one without it, yet it is certainly best to cultivate yourself in what you have a talent for, and it is not vanity in me to say that I have some, tho' it may be in a slight degree, for music."

The crucial letter from Henry, aged twenty-three, came in September 1857; it is a full report, reading in part:

> As every one has some particular object of supreme interest to himself, so I have music. It is almost my inner world; without it, I miss much, and with it I am happier and better. . . .
>
> You will ask, "What is to come of it all if successful?" I do not know. But this is clear. I have then improved my own powers, which is every man's duty. I have a resource to which I can always turn with delight, however the world may go with me. I am so much the stronger, the wider, the wiser, the better for my duties in life. I can then go with satisfaction to my business, knowing my resource at the end of the day. It is already made, and has only to be used and it will grow. Finally it is my province in education, and having cultivated myself in it, I am fully prepared to teach others in it. Education is the object of man, and it seems to me the duty of us all to help in it, each according to his means and in his sphere. I have often wondered how people could teach this and that, but I understand it now. I could teach people to sing, as far as I know, with delight to myself. Thus I have a means of living if other things should fail. But the pleasure, pure and free from all disagreeable consequences or after-thoughts, of playing and still more of singing myself, is indescribable. . . . and this I wish to be most clearly expressed and understood, should any one ask about me. I am studying for my own good and pleasure. And now, old daddy, I hope you will be able to make something out of this long letter. You should not have been troubled with it, but I thought you would prefer to know all about it. It is only carrying out your own darling idea of making an imperishable capital in education. My money may fly away; my knowledge cannot. One belongs to the world, the other to me.[15]

"Make no change in your plans at present," was the father's reply. "Your steady and deep-seated affection and willingness to sacrifice I needed no assurance of." But Henry was missed. The prospect of a fourth European winter seemed to George "a misjudgment, a serious error." He subsequently wrote: "I am in the dark as to the precise character of your studies. What ties have you to Vienna?" As it happens,

Henry was now ready to leave. His maimed arm undermined further study. He did not judge his musical talent in any way exceptional. And there was the looming national crisis at home, foreshadowing a new vocation for American young men. Henry's lifelong antipathy to slavery was an inheritance from both his parents. He followed closely the epochal events at hand. In 1854—during the period between his two European sojourns—Henry and Charlie Lowell, shame-stricken, joined the mob of fifty thousand following the last fugitive slave captured in Massachusetts; cousin Thomas Wentworth Higginson, ever the fiery activist, led the effort to free Anthony Burns. Henry and Charley, too, were self-described (if incipient) "radicals." "It will come to us to set this right," wrote Henry to Charlie of the Burns case.[16]

From Vienna, Henry wrote of the 1857 Dred Scott verdict denying citizenship to black Americans: "Judge Taney's decision is infamous in the last degree. . . . I do wish the North would take higher and firmer ground. It is the only course consistent with truth, and will alone save our country." He called John Brown "a real hero . . . the Southerners may curse and swear as they like; he is worth all of them out together, and his work will be accomplished in time."[17]

In November 1860—four years to the month after his arrival in Vienna—Henry Higginson returned to Boston: to a father eager to receive him; to a national conflict in which he intended to do his part.

. . .

The double rite of passage thus experienced—student years in Hapsburg Vienna, so different from the inbreedings of Brahmin Boston; eventful (if abbreviated) Civil War service, in so many respects equally remote from the Latin School and Harvard—conferred a rare breadth of experience. But as of April 1865, when Lee surrendered to Grant, Higginson at thirty was not yet ready to become a useful citizen. He lacked means, and a profession.

Adrift, he moved toward the world of business to which his father belonged. Oil speculation was rife. Some distinguished Bostonians had organized a Buckeye Oil Company to explore the Duck Creek district of Ohio. They engaged Henry Higginson as their salaried agent on site. Higginson had to transport pumping machinery, tanks, and barrels. He hired horses, he procured coal and lumber, he built a sawmill. He queried his father about bookkeeping and sought geological advice from his father-in-law. Once there were some humble living quarters, Mrs. Higginson arrived. She kept house, including a cow and chickens, and rode a horse. But no sooner had Isabel appeared than the Buckeye Company wearied of its failing Ohio venture; the Higginsons left in July—seven months after Henry began.

A second business venture left Higginson poorer than before, but is full of interest. With two friends—like himself, war veterans who had seen the South—he amassed thirty thousand dollars to purchase "Cottonham," a dormant Georgia plantation of five thousand acres, including a house, stables, and slave quarters. As Higginson put it: "We had done our best to upset the social conditions at the South, and helped free the negroes, and it seemed fair that we should try to help in their education."[18] Sherman's army had ensured that all was in disrepair. The nearest railroad was unusable. A bridge leading to the property was so rickety that two horses in Higginson's initial inspection party wound up hanging by their bellies, legs flailing in the air.

But a workforce was at hand. Many blacks had never left; others were brought in from Savannah. Higginson and his partners paid $370 per married couple, plus a house, two acres of land for corn and potatoes, and fuel for a year. The three owners worked alongside their employees, repairing, plowing, and hoeing. An optimistic surge proved short-lived. The blacks struck for higher wages. They expected to be fed and cared for. Whatever she may have made of her father's "scientific" deprecation of the African-American, Ida showed the women how to wash and iron.* She started a school where she taught reading and writing. Henry preached at the black church on Sundays. But Ida's initial enthusiasm—"they are good, active, honest people all of them"—sagged. "We none of us think that if left to themselves they would have energy enough to be really thrifty and prosperous, no matter how much help they should get in the way of lands." "Curious creatures these darkies are. I don't believe they could work, entirely left to themselves." "They are very strange people . . . Their wits and intellect seem to me far ahead of their morals." "The more I see of them, the more inscrutable do they become, and the less do I like them." "It is discouraging to see how utterly wanting in character and conscience these people seem to be, and how much more hopeful they appear at a distance than near to." Henry wrote to his father: "As for the blacks, their future is a mystery as dark as their own skins. They have understanding and quickness enough. . . . They learn quickly, comprehend easily, both as regards work and in school. But their moral perceptions are deficient, either from nature or from

*See pages 94–95.

habit or from ignorance. They know that it is wrong to steal and lie, but they do it continually."[19]

Battered by rains, the cotton crop failed. "DO NOT FRET ABOUT ACCOUNTS!!!" Henry wrote to Ida, who had returned north for a spell. "Please remember that one great reason for our coming here was the work of great importance to be done for these blacks. Money is less valuable than time and thought and labor, which you have given and will give freely. . . . Money is to be spent wisely, not hoarded forever." Upon returning south, Ida wanted to stay another year—at least until "we have . . . been of some trifling use in some way or another."[20] But there was no way. By the time Cottonham was sold for five thousand dollars, the net loss to the partners totaled sixty-five thousand dollars. Had he been a wealthy man, Higginson mused, he and Ida could have produced "some satisfactory results" over a longer period of time.

In fact, their fortunes were about to change. In February 1867, George Higginson had received an unexpected bequest, in trust to his children, fortifying the family's finances. The following January—shortly after divesting himself of his plantation—Henry became a partner in Lee, Higginson, and Company. Though he would joke that he was "taken in as a matter of charity," that he never walked to work "without wanting to sit down on the doorstep and cry," his State Street employment endured more than half a century. What kind of banker and broker was Henry Higginson? He was in his spartan office—a desk, some chairs, an iron bed with Jaeger blankets—from early morning six days of the week. He was adventurous, keenly supportive of investment in the construction of the western railroads. Compared to a Morgan or Rockefeller, he was not notably self-possessed. His high temperament made him a fallible judge of men. He suffered evident anxiety in behalf of his clients. Amid the panic of 1893, which enslaved him to his desk without surcease, his uncle and partner Henry Lee whimsically chided him to retire, "knowing that for some reason you cannot be cool, systematic, prudent, cannot be aided by partners, however faithful or competent, but partly from temperament, partly from want of early business training, must always be heated and hurried." Alluding to the Boston visit of Eleonora Duse, Lee continued:

> Why, when overtaxed, do you constitute yourself a guardian to an excitable Italian actress whom you know nothing about, who has not the most remote claim on you; why allow yourself to be made President of a superfluous Club got up by people too vacant or too ignorant to know how to live in the country?
>
> No, you are generous, you are full of benevolence inherited from father

> and mother, and in addition, you are weakly good-natured, and last but not least, you are addicted to excitement, which you foster by your overburdened feverish life, which ends in your being unstrung and depressed.[21]

Higginson's correspondents belabored similar observations and admonitions. "Will you let me exhort you most urgently to take greater care of yourself, partly by avoiding all work and all pleasure which may involve exposure to cold, or to hot emotions," Charles Eliot wrote to him in 1906. "Warmth and serenity are desirable for men of our age. . . . I submit that good sense requires a more careful way of living than comes natural to you." William James marveled at Higginson's "steam-pressure to the square inch," his "high level of mental tension," which made him "talk incessantly and passionately about one subject after another, never running dry." Higginson wrote of himself: "Lack of self-control has marked my life. When the University or a cause or a person <u>needs</u> help, I wish to bear a hand. In consequence, I bite off more than I can chew (<u>my epitaph</u>) and . . . load myself to a fretting point, often." He also wrote pertinently of Theodore Roosevelt: "Is judgment to be found coupled with such enormous energy? . . . I believe the two things to be almost always incompatible." Higginson and Roosevelt were well acquainted—not least because Roosevelt's first wife was the daughter of Higginson's banking partner George Cabot Lee (and Higginson's mother had been a Lee). They shared attitudes of restlessness, of relentlessness of intensity; Higginson's intrepid Alpine adventures and Civil War service are not irrelevant. "We had great pleasure in seeing the President," Higginson wrote of Roosevelt in 1907. "He was pleasant, jolly—indeed full of fun; talked to the students in excellent fashion . . . I agree to a dot with what he says about play and study, and also about the duty of these young men to their country. As he went along, I could not help thinking how he was saying just what was in my mind, and saying it very much better than I could. It was very wholesome talk."[22]

Like Roosevelt, Higginson could do nothing halfway. For such a man, business was necessarily more than a means to an end. Still, the end remained paramount: it was after two or three years of particular business success, coming more than a decade after he had joined his father's firm, that Henry Higginson became Boston's most useful citizen. He had left Vienna in 1860 fired with the aspiration to create an American concert orchestra comparable to Europe's finest. Having calculated that such a venture would cost him an annual personal subsidy of up to twenty thousand dollars, he placed the following announcement in the Boston press on March 30, 1881:

THE BOSTON SYMPHONY ORCHESTRA

IN THE INTEREST OF GOOD MUSIC

Notwithstanding the development of musical taste in Boston, we have never yet possessed a full and permanent orchestra, offering the best music at low prices, such as may be found in all the large European cities, or even in the smaller musical centres of Germany. The essential condition of such orchestras is their stability, whereas ours are necessarily shifting and uncertain, because we are dependent upon musicians whose work and time are largely pledged elsewhere.

To obviate this difficulty the following plan is offered. It is an effort made simply in the interest of good music, and though individual inasmuch as it is independent of societies or clubs, it is in no way antagonistic to any previously existing musical organization. Indeed, the first step as well as the natural impulse in announcing a new musical project, is to thank those who had have brought us where we now stand. Whatever may be done in the future, to the Handel and Haydn Society and to the Harvard Musical Association, we all owe the greater part of our home education in music of a high character. Can we forget either how admirably their work has been supplemented by the taste and critical judgment of Mr. John S. Dwight, or by the artists who have identified themselves with the same cause in Boston? These have been our teachers. We build on foundations they have laid. Such details of this scheme as concern the public are stated below.

The orchestra is to number sixty selected musicians; their time, so far as required for careful training and for a given number of concerts, to be engaged in advance.

Mr. Georg Henschel will be the conductor for the coming season.

The concerts will be twenty in number, given in the Music Hall on Saturday evenings, from the middle of October to the middle of March.

The price of season tickets, with reserved seats, for the whole series of evening concerts will be either $10 or $5, according to position.

Single tickets, with reserved seats, will be seventy-five cents or twenty-five cents, according to position.

Besides the concerts, there will be a public rehearsal on one afternoon of every week, with single tickets at twenty-five cents, and no reserved seats.

The intention is that this orchestra shall be made permanent here, and shall be called "The Boston Symphony Orchestra."

Both as the condition and result of success the sympathy of the public is asked.

H. L. Higginson

The simplicity of this utterance was belied by its boldness. In fact, the "full and permanent" orchestra here envisioned was not the norm "in all the large European cities." Far more typical were opera and theater orchestras whose members occasionally offered symphonic programs. And nowhere, at any time, was an orchestra of comparable stature and longevity as single-handedly shaped and supported as Higginson's would be.

• • •

The musician mainly responsible for making the concert orchestra an American specialty was the conductor Theodore Thomas, whose itinerant Thomas Orchestra toured zealously, visiting cities and hamlets of every description beginning in 1869. With a missionary's practical idealism, Thomas enforced his credo: "A symphony orchestra shows the culture of a community, not opera." That is, opera was foreign and mainly sung in foreign tongues. Also, opera was theater—like popular music, as dismissed by Thomas, it had "more or less the devil in it."

Both prongs of the Thomas credo resonated mightily in puritan New England. Symphonic speech was elevated and refined; Verdi's *Rigoletto,* whose licentious Duke goes unpunished, was banned. During decades when New York was opera-mad, feasting on Italian and French delicacies, and later fin-de-siècle decades when New Yorkers, engulfed by Wagner, swooned with high-minded erotic languors, Boston worshipped Beethoven.

The city's first signature musical institution, courteously acknowledged in Henry Higginson's 1881 proclamation, was the Handel and Haydn Society, founded in 1815; its specialties were Handel's *Messiah* and Haydn's *The Creation.* A series of local orchestras, including those of the Boston Academy and of the Musical Fund Society, ensued, to be suddenly supplanted in 1848 with the appearance of a virtuoso immigrant band: the Germania Musical Society. The Germania's Boston premiere of Beethoven's Ninth five years later drew over three thousand enthralled listeners. When the Germania disbanded in 1854, one of its prominent members, Carl Zerrahn, became Boston's leading conductor. The new orchestra of the Harvard Musical Association—also mentioned by Higginson—was entrusted to Zerrahn in 1866. With the exception of the Germania Society, all of this activity was notably self-invented. The original Handel and Haydn Society members included merchants and tailors who would "tune" their thirsty throats with wines and spirits. The early Boston orchestras similarly resembled clubs or cooperatives. The resulting music-making was distinctly democratic. It was also insular and undisciplined—a reality made palpable when in 1869 and 1870 the Theodore Thomas Orchestra rendered thirteen Boston programs, ranging from Beethoven to Wagner, with fabled power, polish, and precision.[23]

The bellwether of musical Boston for three decades beginning at midcentury was—another name acknowledged by Higginson—the critic

John Sullivan Dwight, whose *Dwight's Journal,* created in 1852, was America's premiere music magazine. Dwight was also a prime mover behind the Harvard Musical Association. He came to music as a onetime Unitarian minister who subsequently joined the Transcendentalist Brook Farm experiment; he also wrote for the Fourierist *Harbinger.* Fired by mistrust of conventional church rites, Dwight in effect reconceived "sacred" music as textless and "absolute," relocating it from the church to the concert hall; "elevating, purifying, love and faith-inspiring" symphonies, not choral masses and requiems, were appointed a paramount embodiment of ethical striving.

For Dwight, music intended for entertainment was invalid and corrupt (he called Stephen Foster's "Old Folks at Home," the best-known American tune of the later nineteenth century, a "melodic itch"). "Classical music," as he influentially defined it, excluded styles "simple, popular, or modern." He mistrusted opera, and loathed Liszt and Wagner. In years when the Thomas Orchestra eagerly championed Berlioz, Raff, Rubinstein, Wagner, Dvořák, Elgar, and Richard Strauss, Dwight embraced a tidy Germanic canon beginning with Bach and ending with Mendelssohn and Schumann. Ever espousing uplift, he denounced as "false" art "which seeks new field for originality" through "gloomy moods" having "no right to public expression," but belonging "by every modest instinct of propriety, to strict privacy, at least until the discord is resolved." His god was Beethoven, whose Adagios nearly constituted "the very essence of prayer."[24]

Though a necessary refining influence on musical Boston in its adolescence, Dwight was undeniably a snob. In terms of cultural politics, he was a democrat, preaching the universal benefits of musical uplift, whose sermons equally disclosed anxious estrangement from an immigrant rabble. Dwight concomitantly disparaged African-Americans as "simple children" who were "inferior to the white race in reason and intellect."[25] His attitudes prefigure Boston's 1890s resistance to Dvořák (who affectionately orchestrated "Old Folks at Home") and to Henry Krehbiel, whose advocacy of plantation song and other folk strains would make him a marked man in the Boston musical press.*

Dwight's earnest understanding of music as a meliorist nostrum typified the genteel tradition. For Thomas, too, concerts were "sermons in tones," a moral bulwark rooted in Beethoven. For Higginson, comparably, there was no "greater or stronger preservative against evil" than

*See pages 95–100.

music. As a young man abroad, he had resisted his father's exhortations to attend church every Sunday, preferring private Bible study. He kept a picture of Emerson on his desk. In Georgia in the 1860s, he called the Unitarian church "more tolerant than the others." In a letter of 1899, he wrote: "I believe in many tenets of socialism, else Christianity would be false and the religion of humanity would die." In 1911, to a clergy friend, he said: "I rarely go to church, but am not an entire heathen." He remained at all times religious by nature (he could not abide the "indifference" toward religion he observed in his twenties in Germany); and music was at all times for him a core article of faith.[26]

But this moral thread binding Dwight, Thomas, and Higginson, and linking Dwight and Higginson to local Transcendentalist traditions, extends no further. Unlike Dwight, Thomas did not hector; he stood tall and quiet on his conductor's pulpit. Alongside Thomas—who arrived from Germany at the age of ten and packed a pistol as a touring violin prodigy; whose body was hardened by a regime of icy baths and morning gymnastics; whose fist-pounding pugnacity was chronic—Higginson was no cultural frontiersman. Alongside Dwight, Higginson was not a hothouse New England product; refined by Viennese pleasures and Civil War rigors, he did not fear an onslaught of Irishmen and other barbarians. The democratic impulse in him was—like his antislavery scruples; like his musical affinities—a pure passion.

If Dwight and other Boston insiders spurned the mob, Higginson spurned the insiders. It was merely predictable that he would choose Europeans, not locals, to conduct his orchestra, and that he would not budge in rejecting the lassitude of venerable local musical habits. He was of course denounced as an interloping tyrant. His low ticket prices—substantially less than what the New York Philharmonic charged, or what the Chicago Orchestra would charge, beginning in 1891—were regretted as a radical innovation forcing other presenters to lower prices or seek subsidies. The players of the Harvard Musical Association vowed to undertake a longer season with more rehearsal time. Dwight called the Higginson plan "a coup d'etat, with no pretense of any plebiscite." Tightening the screws, Higginson in 1882 offered his musicians a second-year contract stipulating that during rehearsal and performance days "you will neither play in any other orchestra nor under any other conductor than Mr. Henschel, except if wanted in your leisure hours by the Handel and Haydn Society, nor will you play for dancing." The newspapers got wind of it and portrayed Higginson as a predatory monopolist. The Boston Symphony members also repudiated the new conditions of employment and appointed a delegate to air their feelings. Higginson's later account of what happened next is utterly characteristic in tone and substance:

> The delegate was pleasant and clever and laughed at my statements that the concerts would go on and that it was only a question of who would play. Therefore, on the next public rehearsal day I went to the green-room of the Music Hall and asked the men to come in after the rehearsal, which they did. I then said to them: "I made a proposition to you which you have rejected. I withdraw my proposition. The concerts will go on as they have this year, and in this hall. If any of you have anything to say to me in the way of a proposition you will make it"—and that meeting was over. During the next few days almost every man came to me and asked to be engaged. The delegate from the Orchestra was not one of them.

A sympathetic report in the *Advertiser* was as plainspoken and assured as Higginson himself:

> His plan is not for next year or a few years only. . . . To assert that this is because of a desire to autocratic control, and that Mr. Higginson is disposed to improve the occasion to gratify a fondness for arbitrary dictation, is a reckless charge so particularly wide of the truth that all who know Mr. Higginson must have read such intimations with almost as much amusement as indignation. . . .
>
> No musician can do his best in the midst of a highly trained orchestra, who has played all the night before at a ball, or who plays every alternate night under a different leader and with different associates.[27]

In fact, the artistic dictatorship Higginson would establish plainly transcended the selfish or self-righteous—accordingly, this early period of public controversy was short-lived. Events would also show that Higginson was a man quick to observe and correct his own mistakes. His orchestra's inaugural season was buoyed by startling ticket sales; for a public rehearsal of Beethoven's Ninth, the listeners overflowed onto the stage. But Georg (later "George") Henschel, the young German conductor/composer/singer whom Higginson had engaged after hearing him lead a single work for the Harvard Musical Association, proved the wrong choice. Henschel's enthusiasm, if infectious, was excessive: he lacked repose; the playing lacked refinement. Conductor-shopping in Vienna, Higginson attended a performance of *Aida* and discovered the man he now wanted: Wilhelm Gericke, who had been on the staff of the Court Opera (today's State Opera) since 1874. Though Julius Epstein, a key member of Higginson's Viennese brain trust, predicted Gericke would never sail to America, a meeting was arranged. As it happened, Gericke was feuding with Wilhelm Jahn, the director of the opera. He agreed to become the Boston Symphony's music director for five years beginning in fall 1884 at an annual salary of seventy-five hundred dollars. Interviewed by American reporters in Vienna and again in Boston, he opined that the Boston Symphony gave too many concerts (more, by far, than any Viennese orchestra) and expressed himself "dumbfounded" upon being shown the cumulative repertoire of the Harvard Musical Association—"You seem to have heard everything already; more, much more, than we ever heard in Vienna!"[28]

Gericke's Boston programs, stressing Beethoven, were less adventurous than Theodore Thomas's in New York (with the Philharmonic) and elsewhere (with the Thomas Orchestra), but less conservative than the Boston norm; Boston Symphony performances of Brahms, Bruckner, and Richard Strauss were demonstrably unpopular. Gericke himself was dignified and self-contained on the podium. He was a disciplinarian, a stickler for balance and precision. When Gericke complained that he could not obtain discipline enough, Higginson imported recruits from Vienna, including a new concertmaster: Franz Kneisel, who would also become a leading American chamber musician. The concomitant dismissals, and Gericke's intolerance for lax commitment or attendance, strained the organization; at one point, he attempted to resign. But the final outcome was strong. An ambitious touring program was added to the season, including a visit to the Midwest in 1886 and, in 1887, the orchestra's first New York concerts. At Gericke's final concert, on May 23, 1889, the audience rose and shouted, waving hats and handkerchiefs.

In less than a decade, the Boston Symphony Orchestra had become a national standard-bearer for civic culture; its example would shortly inspire the creation of important orchestras in Cincinnati, Chicago, and Philadelphia, and a dramatic expansion of the New York Philharmonic. At the end of Gericke's pivotal tenure, it numbered seventy-nine men. Its seasonal schedule had grown to 112 concerts and public rehearsals. In addition, Higginson (who in Vienna had acquired a taste for the waltzes of Johann Strauss Jr.) had in 1885 implemented a summer "Promenade" season for which the downstairs seats of the Music Hall were replaced by tables and shrubs.* Of the orchestra's loyal audience, Gericke testified that it was "one of the most cultivated and best understanding musical publics I know."[29]

*I am indebted to Brian Bell, producer of the Boston Symphony broadcasts, for this copious tabulation of local and tour performances in 1888–89. Bell also pertinently notes that, in citing "the famous '[Benjamin] Bilse Concerts in Berlin' as a model for Boston's Promenade concerts, the May 27, 1885, Boston program book cited low-cost concerts for the general populace, not the more elite popular Strauss concerts in Vienna."

Excepting a singular Boston factor, the American orchestral template thus established would endure for a century and more: multiple performances of the same program throughout the fall and spring months, a summer "pops" series, a regular schedule of out-of-town tours, a core Germanic repertoire. The singular Boston factor was of course Henry Higginson. The Boston Symphony had no board of directors, as would all subsequent major American orchestras, opera companies, and museums. Rather, its inventor, owner, and operator paid all salaries. He also covered the annual shortfall of twenty thousand dollars and more. Though he relinquished artistic policy to his conductor, the conductor served at his pleasure; as a trained musician, Higginson appropriated the prerogative to hire or dismiss each and every one of his employees. In his memoirs, Gericke wrote: "I am sure had the creator of the Boston Symphony Orchestra been another man than Henry L. Higginson, the orchestra would not have reached the age of ten years."[30]

Wilhelm Gericke returned to Europe in 1889, having declared himself "thoroughly overworked." *Dwight's Journal of Music,* having ceased publication on September 3, 1881, and the Harvard Musical Association, having in 1882 folded as a performing organization, were by that time barely a memory.

• • •

Unlike Manhattan, whose cityscape was ever changing, Boston a century ago already savored its history and preserved its historic buildings. Notwithstanding the demolition of Chickering Hall (1901–1968) and of the Boston Opera House (1909–1958), the Back Bay today retains its pre–World War I "cultural mile," including the Boston Public Library (1895), Horticultural Hall (1901), Jordan Hall (1903), the Isabella Stewart Gardner Museum (1903), and the Museum of Fine Arts (1909). With the exception of the Gardner Museum, all of these formidable edifices, not excluding the two no longer standing, were built on or near Huntington Avenue, then as now a spacious thoroughfare traversing reclaimed marshland. But if any Boston house of culture is iconically paramount, both for the specificity of its aesthetic statement and the enduring popularity of its daily functions, it is the first member of the Huntington Avenue ensemble: Symphony Hall, erected by Henry Higginson in 1900. No less than the Boston Symphony Orchestra, it defines Higginson's role as a useful citizen.

The Boston Symphony's first home was the Music Hall, erected downtown in 1852. Tightly ensconced on Hamilton Place, its plain brick exterior was noncommittal. Inside, the auditorium was rectangular and severe. The seating capacity, including two shallow galleries to the rear and sides, totaled twenty-six hundred. As de facto proprietor, Higginson appreciated that, while acoustically adequate, the Music Hall was ill ventilated and susceptible to fire. He also knew that the city planned to build an elevated railway line on the property. In 1892, with three associates, he purchased a plot of land for a new auditorium at Huntington Avenue and West Chester Park. His subsequent course of action was decisive, expeditious, and impersonally visionary.

Higginson's dual mind-set as a loyal but cosmopolitan Bostonian dictated both that the existing Music Hall shaped his thinking, and that he was equally apprised of various admired Viennese and German halls, including the Leipzig Gewandhaus erected in 1884. The Gewandhaus architects had been chosen in competition from among seventy-five applicants. Higginson held no competition; he went to Charles F. McKim of New York's McKim, Mead and White. A man of princely deportment and meticulous application, McKim had trained in Boston, New York, and Paris. His recent designs included the Boston Public Library, an Italian Renaissance palace whose every colonnade, arch, ceiling, and staircase was assiduously articulated, and the Agricultural Building at Chicago's World Columbian Exhibition, a vast four-hundred-thousand-square-foot mega-edifice classically proportioned and adorned. His response to Higginson's overture of October 17, 1892, was unequivocal: "Nothing more flattering or complimentary has ever happened to our office, and . . . we shall do our best, when the time comes, to assist you to reach the result you desire."[31]

Higginson proceeded to describe the result he had in mind. The document in question, a thousand words hastily scribbled in pencil (McKim was about to embark for Europe and there was no time to lose), forms an appropriate sequel to Higginson's Boston Symphony blueprint of 1881. It must be quoted at length:

> Boston, Nov. 27th 1892.
>
> Dear McKim:
>
> . . . 1st. The hall should hold about 2200 to 2500 people—not more; have an ample stage for an orchestra of 90 men and for a chorus of 300 singers if need be; two or three adjoining small rooms for tuning the instruments, for overcoats, hats, etc. and for the singers; have a good space for an organ which can be set into the wall. The hall must have ample exits—on several sides if may be—and ample corridors and staircases. It should be on the street level I think and have perhaps two galleries of small dimensions. I think that it should be lighted from the top only, i.e. from windows

in the top or in the highest part of the side walls. I say all this on account of quiet—to keep out sounds from the world. Of course quiet—and then full and yet delicate effects of sound are essential. For instance, our present hall gives a piano better than a forte, gives an elegant rather than a forcible return of the instruments, noble but weak—I want both. . . .

. . . Perhaps you may like to work in a small hall—700 or 800 seats—for chamber-music and lectures, &c. &c. The Viennese opera house is good for sound and for ventilation and I think the same is true of the music-hall of the Conservatory there—Gesellschaft der Musikfreunde. Gericke, Epstein, [Hans] Richter, any of these men would help you to see any building, if you use my name.

The Leipzig Gewandhaus (new) is also said to be good—very good, but I don't know. . . .

I like round-arched Norman or Lombard architecture—like some of the handsome brick buildings in Italy, and I rather incline to brick and brick ornament. I always like the severe in architecture, music, men and women, books, &c. &c.

All of which is respectfully submitted. I'd have this typewritten but then might miss you. If you care for it you'll have it typewritten. . . .

Yours,
H.L.H.

To these detailed prescriptions and predilections Higginson added one further consideration: "As I must bear the burden of the new hall, perhaps quite alone, and as I keep my purse fairly depleted all the time, I must not—cannot—spend too much money for a new hall. . . . Can you guess at the cost?"[32]

Undaunted, McKim duly had Higginson's letter typewritten and took it with him to Europe, where—while it was not the chief purpose of his trip—he conferred with the conductors Gericke and Richter, as Higginson had suggested, as well as with Paris's Charles Lamoureux. The Boston plan that McKim ultimately produced was startlingly novel. Having culled his Boston Public Library from the Italian Renaissance, he now proposed a semicircular Boston auditorium modeled after the amphitheaters of classical Greece, replete with allegorical classical statuary to the rear of the stage and in niches surrounding the raked bleacher seats. A handsome scale model was placed on display. National financial distress—the panic of 1893—put the plan on hold. Finally, on October 17, 1898, Higginson wrote to McKim on behalf of the corporation he had formed:

We feel afraid to try any experiments. While we hanker for the Greek theatre plan, we think the risk too great as regards results, so we have definitely abandoned that idea. We shall therefore turn to the general plan of

> our Music Hall and of the halls in Vienna and Leipsic [*sic*], the latter being the best of all, and . . . will ask for a plan on those lines. . . . We . . . hesitate as to whether this scheme, devoid of poetry and charm, will have enough interest to bring you in person over here and give your own thoughts and time to the completion of the work. Will you kindly tell us your wishes in the matter? We are all greatly obliged to you for the beautiful plan, which we should much like to use if we dared to run the risk. All this must seem very stupid to you, but we cannot help it.[33]

And Higginson wanted the new hall built within eighteen months.

Not only was a Greek theater not what Henry Higginson envisioned; McKim had fundamentally misgauged Higginson's understanding of useful citizenry. As a cultural leader, he had bravely and confidently undertaken the first and further steps toward creating a world-class orchestra. He would do the same for a world-class orchestra hall—but always at the same time in step with Boston. He was not remotely interested in a "Henry Higginson Hall": a monument to individual vision generously placed at service to the public. Rather, informed by what musical sophistication and worldly aplomb he had pursued and attained—Andrew Carnegie in New York could never as casually have referred his Music Hall planners to so preeminent a European musician as Hans Richter—Higginson's aspiration was to catalyze not his own but the Boston public's highest possibilities. And so it is unsurprising that the new plan McKim now submitted for Higginson's inspection resembled nothing so much as a conflation of the old Boston Music Hall and the new Leipzig Gewandhaus. Nor is it surprising, at least in retrospect, that the architect's tireless efforts to elaborate his design in pursuit of a distinctive surface elegance were at every stage ignored or courteously rebuffed by his employer.

McKim had secured his eminence partly through acute attention to decorative detail. For Higginson's new concert hall, his aesthetic plan included external statuary, a harplike finial crowning the pediment, and decorative eaves or chenaux—to his way of thinking, not ancillary but organic components without which a distinguished public building would seem naked. Higginson thought differently. Early on, on October 31, 1898, he wrote to McKim: "We have very little money to spend and shall have to ask for an exterior as plain as possible. . . . I often look at Sever Hall, Mr. Richardson's work, which is, of it all, the best looking building in the possession of [Harvard College] and which has no ornament whatsoever." The planned finial and external statues were unceremoniously excised from the McKim symphony hall. As for the chenaux,

Charles Cotting, Higginson's watchdog, advised the architect: "I have talked with the Directors, and they will not consider the chenaux for one moment . . . I am trying to save every dollar possible but of course I do not wish to cut anything out which from a practical point of view you consider necessary for the good of the structure."[34]

That these draconian "practical" economies were equally aesthetic strictures became evident during a prolonged consideration of external inscriptions. As McKim wrote on November 15, 1899, focusing Higginson's attention on certain blank spaces over the main portico and a side entrance: "We feel that nothing imparts such dignity and scholarly character, as the wise use of inscriptions, and are depending largely, in the case of your Music Hall, upon their use. They may be either commemorative, or express the value of Music in some great sentence." Some four months later, McKim wrote again: "The panel designed to carry [the Huntington Avenue inscription], and supported in arrangement by the columns below, forms an important part of the whole composition of the front (already sufficiently denuded by Mr. Cotting's ruthless economies), and if the inscription is now also taken away from us . . . , I fear the building will look, when it is finished, more like a deaf, dumb and blind institution than a Music Hall. . . . I urge you solemnly not to abandon the inscription, without which the panel intended for it will be meaningless, and the façade on Huntington Avenue unintelligible."[35]

Higginson, meanwhile, was far more concerned with how the new hall would sound. To this end, he had engaged as a consultant Wallace Sabine, who became the first professional acoustician to play a significant role in the construction of a space in which to hear music. This pioneer in "architectural acoustics" had as a member of Harvard's Physics Department spent some three years attempting to ascertain the acoustical relationship between the volume of a room, its shape, and the location of its sound-absorbing components. In fall 1898 Harvard's president, Charles W. Eliot, recommended Sabine to Higginson. Stressing the importance of angles versus curves, of raked floors and of a shallow stage, Sabine told Higginson that the scientific principles he had discerned would guarantee successful results—and Higginson, impressed by the young man's modesty, clarity, and confidence, decided to believe him. There followed a meeting with McKim in February 1899—at which Sabine, reviewing the new rectangular plan, proposed further changes. McKim, too, was impressed, and acquiesced.

The ultimate result showed a twenty-six-hundred-seat hall with two shallow rear and side balconies after the fashion of the old Music Hall (whose balconies, however, extended over the stage) and also of the Gewandhaus (which had, however, only one such balcony). Leipzig's hall was judged to boast better acoustics, but with 1,560 seats was far too small for Boston. When Sabine calculated that a proportionate increase in the Leipzig dimensions would be acoustically disastrous (resulting in a reverberation time of 3.02 seconds, versus 2.30 at the Gewandhaus and 2.44 at the old Music Hall), McKim's rectangle was greatly shortened; it was at this juncture that, with Sabine's input, the second side balcony, contradicting Leipzig, was added. Sabine was also instrumental in securing a novel feature of the final design: in effect, the Symphony Hall stage sits within a squarish wooden "soundbox" appended to the rectangle. The height of this recessed and relatively shallow space is substantially less than that of the main room. Its stage slopes upward, its ceiling downward. At Sabine's insistence, there are no drapes or boxes. And the space under the stage box is hollow. Sabine also oversaw the placement of the hall's organ, and details of the singular heating and cooling system, which drew air from the top of the building, circulated it into the auditorium via ceiling perforations, and expelled it through registers in the floor. He accepted no fee for his services, which he cherished as a decisive opportunity to test the new physical laws he had extrapolated.

It of course fell to Higginson to oversee financing and construction. The new Boston Music Hall Corporation (Henry Higginson, president) created a subscription plan and gathered some four hundred pledges. O.W. Norcross, engaged to build the building, reviewed the final specifications and could find only three hundred dollars in savings: "I think this speaks pretty well for Mr. McKim," quipped Higginson to Harvard's President Eliot. Ground was broken without ceremony on June 12, 1899. Construction proceeded without delay. Though the final cost—$771,000, including the plot—was about double the original estimate, it was by contemporary standards a comparatively modest sum (the Boston Public Library had cost over $2.5 million). The first concert took place on October 15, 1900. "No more brilliant or important event has ever figured in the musical history of Boston," reported the *Herald;* the audience, in evening dress, "represented the best brains and culture of the commonwealth." The program featured a Bach chorale followed by what was said to be the first complete American performance of Beethoven's *Missa solemnis.* Wilhelm Gericke (by then in his second stint as music director) conducted. The chorus of 250 forced the orchestra forward beyond the proscenium; the first five rows of seats

FIGURE 4. Symphony Hall from the southeast, from an early photograph, ca. 1901. Photographer unknown, courtesy Boston Symphony Orchestra Archives.

FIGURE 5. Symphony Hall interior, ca. 1901, showing two statues, Apollo and Euripides. Courtesy Boston Symphony Orchestra Archives.

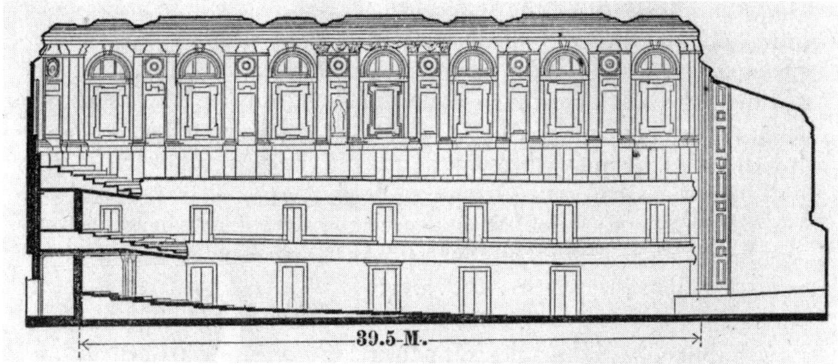

FIGURE 6. The recessed stage, as shown in Sabine's 1900 pamphlet, "Architectural Acoustics: Part 1—Reverberation." Courtesy Boston Symphony Orchestra Archives.

had to be removed. Higginson's welcoming speech, which he tellingly called a "report," singularly combined sincere modesty with honest self-assurance, dour practicality with serene idealism. It generously saluted the past and heralded the future with dignified aplomb. The new hall had "with reluctance" been mortgaged by its directors to borrow $350,000 in unsubscribed funds, Higginson said. Putting aside "the convictions and wishes of the architect," the directors had "with regret" rejected McKim's "beautiful design after the Greek theatre . . . —and they may have erred." McKim had "with absolute cheerfulness" executed a "a plan not entirely to his liking." And yet "the beauty of the hall had been won entirely by Mr. McKim, and I hope that it pleases you. I think it very handsome, and know that it is convenient and entirely safe." Higginson also acknowledged the contributions of Sabine and Norcross—and of Cotting, who "guarded our slender purse." A small room for chamber music and lectures had been sought, but proved impracticable. The old Music Hall, whatever its shortcomings, would never be forgotten, nor would those who built it. As for the orchestra itself: "Of its knowledge, its skill, its artistic qualities, its constant devotion to the best work year after year, of its consequent power to play its great repertory, I have no adequate words to speak, nor can I tell you how highly I prize our great string and wind-players, let alone our conductor, who has formed the Orchestra and led it so long, . . . I am very proud of him and of them, this band of artists, and I again thank them with all my heart, for they have done our city and our country signal and intelligent service, such as ennobles and educates a nation." And finally, this summation:

> Certain citizens of Boston build a hall, without regard to return in money, and by this act care for the happiness, the convenience, the education of the inhabitants for twenty miles around this spot; and it is fitting in a republic that the citizens and not the government in any form should do such work and bear such burdens. To the more fortunate people of our land belongs the privilege of providing the higher branches of education and of art. . . .
>
> Whether this hall can ever give so much joy to our people as the old Music Hall no one can tell. Much depends on the public, which has always been loyal and staunch to the Orchestra. I can only promise in return that it will try to do its share.[36]

As it happened, the old Boston Music Hall was not torn down after all (it survives to this day as the Orpheum). No matter: the new hall was manifestly superior in every way. With regard to the vital matter of acoustics, Higginson was of the opinion that Sabine had proved "that the Science of Acoustics exists in a definite form." Henry Krehbiel, in the *New York Tribune,* echoed this judgment. William Apthorp of the *Boston Transcript,* however, found the sound of the orchestra in its new home clear and smooth, but lacking in "body" and "fullness." George Hutchings, who built the hall's organ, had quarreled with Sabine over proper acoustical placement of the instrument; at the inaugural concert, he grasped Sabine's hand and exclaimed, "Young man, . . . I take back everything I said!"[37] As for Sabine himself, he felt he had successfully maximized sonic volume in a concert auditorium of large capacity (by existing European standards), and that criteria of clarity and reverberation had been objectively met.* (A century later, Apthorp's minority opinion is forgotten: Higginson's hall, whose coffered ceiling, open grillwork, and tall niches shun the flat surfaces faulted by all present-day acousticians, is widely regarded as a supreme acoustical space for symphonic music.)

Aesthetically, the keynote of the new hall was simplicity: a restrained color scheme of grey and gold, exposed wooden floors, a relative absence of ornamentation. Burnished organ pipes covered the back wall of the recessed stage. The small chandeliers, placed near the ceiling, were not conspicuous. The balcony railings were upholstered in crimson plush, the seats (hard, thin, removable) in dark green leather. "To those who expected magnificence or flowery adornment the hall will be something

*A present-day measurement, by Leo Beranek, records a reverberation time of 1.9 seconds at 500 Hz.—rebutting a prevalent notion, based on Sabine's calculations, that Symphony Hall has a reverberation time of 2.3 seconds. See Richard P. Stebbins, *The Making of Symphony Hall Boston* (2000), p. 216.

of a disappointment," commented the *Herald,* "but it is safe to say that no similar structure in this or any other city has been treated, from the viewpoint of decoration, in a manner so satisfying. The interior of the hall is elegant in the extreme, but it is the elegance of simplicity." The *Journal* reported that "some of the best seats in the house" were those of the second balcony, all 505 of which Higginson, following custom at the old hall, had reserved for twenty-five-cent "rush tickets" to the Friday afternoon rehearsals (then as now, really performances). A large gold medallion crowning the proscenium arch was emblazoned with the name "Beethoven"; elsewhere along the arch ten smaller gold medallions were left blank. Blank, as well, remained the exterior panels McKim had intended for inscriptions, and all but one of the sixteen interior niches he had reserved for seven-foot antique statues; as of 1900, only the Apollo Belvedere was in place, the directors having furnished no budget for this component of the architect's scheme. Remarkably, Higginson's cousin Mary Lee Elliot took these matters into her own hands in consultation with McKim, to whom she wrote on February 19, 1901: "If you would still like to have me try to get the money for the statues . . . we need say nothing to Mr. Higginson, but [could] have them put in quietly during the summer." The money was raised and the statues were installed. There was one final loose end. Higginson had predictably ignored the predictable suggestion that his orchestra's new home be called "Higginson Hall." It is not recorded who proposed the name "Symphony Hall," which entered into circulation without public discussion.[38]

Today, the plainness and functionality of Symphony Hall, inside and out, seem more than ever hallmark features: incontrovertibly, it is a place that looked old the day it was born. The tiered horseshoes of Manhattan's Metropolitan Opera House, opened in 1883, or Carnegie Hall, inaugurated in 1891, limned a different, more opulent world of culture: not communal but stratified, with boxes for the rich; lesser inhabitants were well hidden in the topmost balconies. Higginson's distaste for Carnegie Hall is a matter of record. New York views of Higginson's hall ranged from Krehbiel's approbation of its look and sound to the *Musical Courier*'s opinion that "the building . . . must be visited to learn of its cheerlessness and to feel the stern effect of architectural angularity."[39] The *Courier* likened the resulting ambience to that of a "prayer house, where ritual is considered paganism." And assuredly Higginson had honored Boston's puritan legacy, and also the legacy of John Sullivan Dwight, in realizing a concert hall that by New York or European standards evoked a house of worship.

The new hall, in sum, evinced a supreme sense of place. Though the Gewandhaus served as a partial model, the dark interior of Leipzig's hall, with its huge dangling chandeliers and densely encrusted ornamentation, was as remote from spare New England as the kaiser himself. In effect, Boston had acquired a less dowdy, less drafty version of its existing Music Hall, with enhanced amenities and acoustics. The *Transcript,* upon first inspecting the premises, even discovered "a dearly familiar look."[40] With its combination of "town-hall plainness" and "elegant simplicity," Symphony Hall managed both to retain and to celebrate feelings of cultural community, of bonded experience, that Boston and Henry Higginson held dear. It was, finally, a statement as severe, congenial, and obdurate as the man who built it and declined to bequeath to it his name.

• • •

As an embodiment of what was best about Boston, Higginson's symphony was quicker to acquire a fully appropriate home than a fully appropriate conductor. Wilhelm Gericke, who came and left twice (1884–1889, 1898–1906), proved an ideal builder and trainer. He insisted on diligence and discipline. He was experienced and skilled. The Boston press was appreciative. But the violinist Sam Franko, who quit the Boston Symphony to become Theodore Thomas's concertmaster in New York, was not alone in finding Gericke's performances "full of subtle nuances, finely balanced" and yet without "spontaneity and life."[41] Higginson gratefully supported Gericke's reformist agenda. He also had occasion to observe that Gericke, who complained of overwork, lacked the heroic capacity of a Thomas (whose commitments in New York and, later, Chicago precluded candidacy for a Boston post). In truth, Gericke was never a conductor of great international reputation. Neither was Henschel—or Emil Paur or Max Fiedler, both of whom also did Boston Symphony stints. But Higginson did manage to place two great names on his Boston podium. These were Arthur Nikisch and Karl Muck, both of whom further define what Higginson's orchestra was and was not.

Nikisch arrived in Boston in 1889 at the age of thirty-three. He was not yet Europe's idolized Svengali of the baton, concurrently conductor of the Berlin Philharmonic and of the Leipzig Gewandhaus Orchestra. But his galvanizing imprint was already self-evident. Richard Wagner, in his landmark treatise "On Conducting" (1869), impugned self-effacing "time-beating" in favor of a new breed of charismatic podium mastermind. Wagner's protégé Anton Seidl, with his mysteriously riveting "glance of steel" and supremely calibrated climaxes, introduced

Wagnerian conducting to the United States.* Nikisch—a small man with pale hands, wavy hair, and fathomless eyes—had played under Wagner in Vienna and was later Seidl's assistant in Leipzig; he introduced Wagnerian conducting in Boston.

Upon displacing the more stoic Thomas at the New York Philharmonic in 1891, Seidl fit fin-de-siècle New York: its opera mania, its immigrant tumult, its dual susceptibility to Old War eros and New World morals. And so did Nikisch. "The man is full of magnetism," reported W.J. Henderson in the *New York Times* upon traveling to Boston for Nikisch's American debut, on October 11, 1889. Henry Krehbiel, in the *Tribune,* relished "Mr. Nikisch's successful efforts in troubling the musical waters of Boston" and favorably compared Nikisch's "robust" and "vital" readings to "the love of placidity and undisturbed euphony."[42] In fact, Nikisch split Boston opinion. Either he freed the orchestra from Gericke's militaristic straitjacket, or he was too free, too sensuous, too "theatrical." As for Henry Higginson, he acknowledged the sorcerer in Nikisch. He appreciated the stature of Nikisch the musician; he even called him a "genius." But Nikisch's interpretations were not to Higginson's taste, and—crucially—Higginson mistrusted Nikisch the man. A climactic blowout was defining for both. No less than did Gericke, Nikisch discovered his Boston duties exhausting. When in 1893 he was offered the directorship of the Budapest Opera, Higginson advised him to accept; his Boston position would not be "renewed." Nikisch asked to be excused from a scheduled three-week western tour. Higginson agreed but imposed a stipulated five-thousand-dollar penalty for breach of contract. Nikisch then consented to lead the tour but only if he collected his customary two-thousand-dollar bonus. Higginson refused these terms and resorted to legal counsel. Nikisch agreed to forfeit the five thousand dollars. Higginson's side of the argument may be inferred from a letter dated April 25, 1893. He had stated his terms. He had agreed to forgive the five thousand dollars. Yet Nikisch, by belatedly pulling out of the tour, had waited "until I am in a box and without a conductor and with a lot of concerts before me." Higginson also wrote that he had received from Nikisch "several of the most remarkable letters that I have ever received, so far as insolence goes," and that the conductor, though he pled ill health, looked "as well as usual."[43]

Like the creation of the Boston Symphony Orchestra, like the building of Symphony Hall, the process by which Higginson acquired Karl

*See pages 83–85.

Muck—the conductor he ultimately favored above all others—illustrates the singular modus operandi of a useful citizen who knew what he wanted and how to obtain it. When in 1906 Gericke announced that he would not return the following fall, Higginson initiated a conductor search. The orchestra's manager, Charles Ellis, and the composer George Chadwick were Higginson's agents abroad. He also conferred frequently with his Viennese friend Julius Epstein, with the singer Milka Ternina, and with two key members of his orchestra who knew the European scene: Kneisel, the concertmaster Gericke had imported, and his onetime associate concertmaster Charles Martin Loeffler, who also happened to be one of America's leading composers. A list of twenty-five candidates was assembled—a virtual who's who of Germanic podium talent. Higginson quickly weeded out Gustav Mahler and Willem Mengelberg, whose restless interpretive predilections and progressive repertoire choices he recognized. He had no compunction about considering the Jewish Bruno Walter, but felt that at thirty Walter was probably too young.* He eventually narrowed the field to four reckonable names: Nikisch, Muck, Hans Richter, and Felix Mottl.

The ensuing negotiations were direct and businesslike. The conductors had no agents. Higginson's assessments characteristically weighed personal integrity alongside artistic prowess. Richter and Mottl proved unobtainable. Of Nikisch, Higginson wrote to Ellis: "He is just as clever as man can be, and knows all the tricks of the trade. . . . If Chadwick is with you, my kindest regards to him, and kindest regards to anybody I know who wants them. I do not know whether Nikisch would care for a pleasant message from me." To Chadwick he wrote that he feared Nikisch would (literally) gamble away any down payment and leave him in the lurch. He nevertheless made Nikisch a generous offer to return to Boston and was surprised when Nikisch said no. That left Muck, of whom Higginson wrote: "He is a good musician and would conduct admirably—though not very impressively, perhaps. I fancy he is a broader and stronger man, as well as a warmer man, than Nikisch, and I think he would keep the orchestra in better order." By June, Higginson had decided that "we are better with Muck than with anyone of the whole crew."[44]

*Fully forty years later, Arthur Judson, managing the New York Philharmonic, counseled his board that a Jewish conductor would "alienate the support of an appreciable number of important members of this community." Shunning such plausible Jewish candidates as Otto Klemperer and Erich Kleiber, the Philharmonic named John Barbirolli its chief conductor (see Horowitz, *Classical Music in America: A History* [2005]), p. 430).

And Muck—who served Boston for nine seasons (1906 to 1908 and 1912 to 1918) in fact proved a plausible fit. At forty-seven—stiffly erect and nervously alert, clean-cheeked and bespectacled—he radiated authority. He was as strict as Gericke without constraining his men (he enjoyed putting down his baton and letting them play by themselves). Fourteen years Gericke's junior, he sampled repertoire new to Boston, including Sibelius's Fourth Symphony, Debussy's *La mer,* Mahler's Fifth, and—from a sense of duty—Schoenberg's Five Pieces for Orchestra. He scheduled considerable quantities of French, Russian, and American music, known and unknown. The composers he most played were Mozart, Beethoven, Brahms, Wagner, and the early Richard Strauss (whose *Also sprach Zarathustra* seemed to him a misunderstanding of Nietzsche, and whose *Salome* he dismissed as an aberration that would not endure). During his 1906 conductor search, Higginson cautioned Ellis to warn candidates "that I do not like too much modern music, and that I do not want the extreme modern style of conducting." He continued: "I was brought up in the Vienna school (as you know) and there were plenty of men living then who had heard Beethoven conduct, as well as Mendelssohn, and knew how he wished his music given. I have known Brahms, myself, and heard his music. You know well enough what I wish, and I shall not interfere unduly with any of these men, but I don't want crazy work (such as sometimes even Nikish [*sic*] gave us . . .), and perhaps you had better tell them that I hate noise."[45]

In sum, no less than did Henry Higginson, Muck's Boston programs plied a middle course, rejecting the snobbish insularity of many a Brahmin and the radical reform being espoused by young Leopold Stokowski in Philadelphia. A comparison of Stokowski's first Philadelphia Orchestra recording, in 1917, with Muck's Boston Symphony Victor Talking Machine sessions the same year clinches this juxtaposition. In the prelude to act 3 of *Lohengrin,* Muck chooses a tempo sufficiently moderate to define the palpitating triplets; the wedding music of the middle episode is sensibly slowed down and shaped. But his Tchaikovsky is stiff. Stokowski's first recording, of Brahms's Hungarian Dance No. 5, is by comparison an act of juvenile delinquency: a playground for interpretive capers. That Stokowski and Quaker Philadelphia were never kindred failed to matter: the Philadelphia Orchestra was defined not by Philadelphia but by Stokowski. If the Boston Symphony was defined by Higginson, he and Boston became indistinguishable.

Other than Theodore Thomas's itinerant band, Higginson's was the first American orchestra to acquire an international reputation. As early as 1902 Richard Strauss called it "the most marvelous in the world." Writing from New York in 1908, Mahler urged Mengelberg to consider the vacant Boston position: "The position in Boston is the finest any musician could wish for.—It is the first and highest in this whole continent.—A first-class orchestra. A position of absolute authority. A social position that no musician can ever attain in Europe."[46] In fact, concertgoing in Boston resembled a civic obligation. The city's prominent composers—Chadwick and Loeffler, Arthur Foote and Amy Beach—were regularly performed. Chadwick sometimes conducted; Loeffler, Foote, and Beach appeared as soloists. Isabella Stewart Gardner might attend wearing a Red Sox hatband. When George Henschel bade farewell, the orchestra broke into "Auld Lang Syne"; the audience rose and sang along. For the summer Proms, patrons ate and drank at tables, and called out for the repetition of favorite numbers. Even New York was quick to concede the caliber of Higginson's constituency. Visiting Boston for Nikisch's debut in 1889, Krehbiel observed "the gentleness of the city's taste in music, the genuineness of her appreciation, the thoroughness of her understanding and earnestness of her devotion. . . . She is blessed beyond measure in the disposition of her people toward an art which makes for the civic virtues in a degree scarcely equaled by any other agent of civilization." In New York's *Musical Courier,* Otto Florsheim wrote in 1890, "Boston is more musical than any other city in the United States. . . . Take a concert like last Saturday's twentieth Symphony concert and its preceding public rehearsal. It rained all Friday and it snowed all Saturday. In New York on such unpropitious occasions all concert attendance, even that at our six Philharmonic concerts, decreases in number most materially and the atmosphere puts a damper on all musical enthusiasm in listeners and performers alike. Not so in Boston."[47]

At the Museum of Fine Arts, cultivated Bostonians would tour the galleries in deferential silence. At Symphony Hall, a defining spectacle was the frantic upstairs race of rush-ticket holders, vying for the best second balcony seats. The waiting line, where they had patiently queued, was itself a local phenomenon. "There you see people from all over this vast country, young and old, many music students, making the sacrifice of the whole day and studying while they wait," a "graduate of the rush-line" once wrote to Higginson. "Then the excitement of not knowing whether you'll get in and the joy of a seat if you do; and the brilliancy of the music from the second balcony. Oh! It's Paradise! . . . and the neighborliness of dividing your bread and butter and apple with the fellow next, if he hasn't any, and the profitable and pleasant chats it often leads to." In 1889 Higginson had occasion to bid Gericke a first farewell; he did not praise the ennobling rectitude of music after the fashion of a John Sullivan Dwight or Charles Eliot Norton, but said: "Why is the hall so crowded? Why do so many listeners of all ages sit on the steps and stand in the aisles each week and each year? They do not come there to please Mr. Gericke or me; they do not come twenty miles to show their good clothes; they come to hear the music, and they listen attentively and quietly, and go away with only a whisper of approval, perhaps, but they are happy. You and I know that very well. That audience is not from the Back Bay or from any particular set of people. They are town folks and country folks, and they come to hear the music at the hands of Mr. Gericke and his Orchestra."[48]

Undeniably, Higginson was a beneficiary of propitious conditions. In 1881, music lovers could not hear a great orchestra at home via the radio or phonograph. There were in any event no great American orchestras to be heard, other than Thomas's. Contemporary composers had not yet alienated contemporary audiences; in Boston, singularly, a local composers' community of stature was in place. Higginson seized the opportunities at hand with surgical precision. He replaced existing local orchestras with a single, exemplary band, fortified with imported talent and iron discipline. He replaced existing concert facilities with a single, exemplary hall, whose plainness of democratic decor supported a demonstrative communal exercise. He replaced existing musical leaders with a Berlin conductor not selected for his name or reputation or for any considerations expedient or financial, but because he fit specific Boston needs. His Symphony Orchestra both embodied and led the community of culture that it served.

• • •

Of Higginson's countless benefactions beyond the symphony, schools of all kinds—training grounds for useful citizenry—were frequent recipients. In particular, there was Harvard, which he had briefly attended, and from which his son Alexander—his only surviving offspring—graduated in 1898. Higginson's only college degree was honorary, conferred by Harvard in 1882. Eight years later, remembering his cherished Civil War comrades, he gave Harvard Soldiers Field. In 1893, he was named a fellow of the corporation—one of a group of five who, with the president and treasurer, formed the principal governing body of the university. Finally, he funded the Harvard Union, whose purpose was to foster a democratic camaraderie on campus.

The Madrid-born George Santayana, who viewed most things from a continental perspective, observed of the undergraduate milieu as of 1886: "The fluent and fervid enthusiasms so common among European students, prophesying about politics, philosophy, and art, were entirely unknown." Higginson sought a worldlier ambience, promoting aspirations toward public service. Speaking and writing about the Harvard Union, he resolved to challenge "habits of exclusivity and of luxury in living which have hurt our democratic university," to counteract an intolerable "sense of isolation" by promoting "the freest and fullest intercourse between the students." The existing university clubs were expensive and elitist; "we must see to it that young men entering our University stand on a footing equal in all respects." Inaugurating the Union on October 15, 1901, he admonished: "Like the Arabs, nail open your doors and offer freely to all comers the salt of hospitality."[49] In fact, the Union charged a five-dollar membership fee, subsequently raised to ten dollars. "The great majority of Harvard students can easily afford this sum," commented the *New York Times* on November 2, 1902, "but there are still a great many to whom ten dollars looks like a big sum. These men are the very ones whom the Union was intended to reach." Nevertheless, the same story reported: "Never in all its history, it is said, have Harvard men been united as they are at the present time. Never have the rich and the poor been on so equal a footing, and this state of affairs is recognized as having come about through the union."

In spirit, Higginson's initiative of course revisited his childhood and Civil War friendships, and the leisurely and expansive coffee house habits he had discovered in Vienna. "Is there a better or sweeter thing on earth than the free and close intimacy of young fellows, discussing everything on earth and in heaven, tossing the ball from one to another, lifting each other to a higher plane, as healthy, earnest boys will and thus learning to know their comrades and themselves?" he had rhetorically inquired, addressing a crowded "ratification meeting" at Sanders Theatre, proclaiming the building of "a great house on college grounds." At the dedication ceremonies two years later he said: "Looking back in life I can see no earthly good which has come to me, so great, so sweet, so uplifting, so consoling, as the friendship of the men and the women whom I have known well and loved." No less than the Boston Symphony, the Harvard Union mediated between Old World habits and New World needs.[50]

How to summarize the multiplicities of Henry Higginson? The writer and *Atlantic Monthly* editor Bliss Perry, who knew him well, observed in him "a curiously subtle combination of warrior and philosopher." Describing Higginson's public persona, Perry strung together the adjectives "picturesque," "ejaculatory," "intimate," "illogical" "noble," "whimsical," "reckless," and "delightful." The first historian of the Boston Symphony, Mark A. De Wolfe Howe, wrote: "A savor of romance, heightened by the saber-scar which the Civil War had left upon his face, was inseparable from him. There was, besides, a Yankee shrewdness, a bluntness of alternately severe and humorous speech, and withal a streak of sentiment which colored his telling words and generous deeds." Writ large upon all such juxtapositions of Higginson with himself is the abiding combination of business and art. Here is a man who on the back of a letter to George Henschel could jot "Sell for our account 3000 C. and B. 6[8] at 105" and who would interrupt his business correspondence to cable Gericke in Vienna: "Engagieren Sie niemand mehr."[51]

Extrapolating a double nature in Henry Higginson's father, Charles Francis Adams wrote: "The impression he always gave me, of ruggedness and masculinity with modesty and kindness, was altogether unique." Dr. Vincent Y. Bowditch wrote to Henry Higginson when in 1889 George Higginson died: "When I hear sneering at the Puritanism of Boston, your dear old father's face is one of a few that come up to me to put such sneers to shame and make one wish that such 'Puritanism' could be spread far and wide." Higginson replied: "Puritanism! The older I grow, the more I incline to their ideal—and the luxury and wastefulness and a thousand things send me that way. . . . Let no one sneer at ideals or enthusiasms." The puritan in Henry Higginson found memorably whimsical expression thirty-two years earlier in a letter to his sister: "James has written me a detailed account of your economy of living. It is good for you all. In the language of that great man, Dad, 'The practice is excellent.' . . . You and Frank were rapidly sinking from that high moral standard, that habit of self-denial which has formed the fine characters of your three elder brothers, of whom you are so justly proud. You were sinking into silks, velvets, Brussels carpets. . . . You are a pair of Sybarites."[52]

The Yankee plainness of Higginson's office and home; his stubby, blunt penmanship, eschewing elegance, imparting candor; the severity of Symphony Hall, inside and out; the criteria of character that condemned the gamblers and drinkers in his orchestra and impelled him to despair that "if the world consisted only of musicians, it would go to pieces at once"—all these were puritanical Boston banker traits. The business world likely aligned with Higginson's political views: though he backed the notion of a strong government, and of a central banking system, his mistrust of intervention in business and in private lives was chronic. He sided with brave individual and corporate initiatives. He did not—like Dvořák, Jeannette Thurber, and Anton Seidl in New York—call for arts subsidies, as abroad. He disliked antitrust laws and the Inter-State Commerce Commission. He regarded legislators as tardy and inefficient. He maintained no fervent party allegiance; his votes for McKinley (1896, 1900), Roosevelt (1904), Taft (1908), Wilson (1912), and Hughes (1916) more represented an exercise of civic responsibility than any emphatic mandate. Of Roosevelt, whose fire and enterprise he admired, he wrote: "Theodore talks nonsense about Wall Street" and "Roosevelt's mind is vigorous and not clear or wise." He considered "mind your own business" a sound foreign policy directive—but the Spanish-American War ignited the combatant in him. And he combated, relentlessly and successfully, the unionization of his musicians.[*][53]

On the artistic side of things, George Higginson's warmth of sentiment, leavening his puritan strictures, foretold what warmed his son. Henry's verdict in Vienna, that he had "no talent for music," applied high professional standards. He admitted to having composed "a few songs good enough for the fire on the grate." In later life, he would sit at the piano and play snatches of his own songs, and of symphonies and other favorite pieces. "It was a pleasure to hear him," his wife testified; "he had a delightful touch." In the concert hall, his ardor was boundless. "VEREHRTER HERR KAPELLMEISTER," trumpets a note to Gericke.

> "Freischütz" kenne ich vom Anfange bis zum Ende, und ich habe die Overtüre sehr lieb, aber nie wie gestern—nicht sogar in Wien—habe ich sie gehört. Jede Note, jede Phrase—alles. Das Blut ist mir in Kopf gestiegen und ich wollte nicht sprechen.
>
> High-water mark!!![†][54]

Shepherding his flock of musicians, he forbade indolence and unions; he also advised the men on investments, supported them in illness and misfortune, and established a pension fund to secure their old age. He hosted their musicales at home. He would not hear of relinquishing his personal responsibility for those he paid to make great music.

*The Boston Symphony was by far the last major American orchestra to be unionized—in 1942.

†"I know *Freischüte* inside out. I love the overture but I must say I have never heard it done as well as yesterday, not even in Vienna. Every note, every phrase—everything. The blood rushed to my head, and I didn't want to say anything."

His enthusiasm for arts and learning was unconfined by John Sullivan Dwight's condescension toward "lesser" works, or Theodore Thomas's aversion to greasepaint: he was an avid theater- and operagoer, a connoisseur of the Parisian stage, a friend to many an actor and actress (we have seen him host Duse at home).

The Brahmin milieu of uplift and idealism also inflected the complex Higginson milieu; his friendships with its leading lights were no more casual than his many others. Of his various club memberships, it was the Friday Club where he found "the best talk in the town . . . the freshest exchange of thought"; the club's other talkers included Henry Adams, Alexander Agassiz, William James, William Dean Howells, and Francis Parkman. But who besides Higginson in that group could have claimed friendship with J.P. Morgan and Andrew Carnegie—and could also in the same breath have jotted, "Harry James came in for a chat this noon. He is a good chap and agreeable"?[55]

Minus Higginson, Brahmin Boston was undeniably snobbish. Its propensities toward inbreeding and preciosity delimited the creative potential of many fine minds.* The same propensities could breed an arrogant or besieged elitism. The learned racism of a Louis Agassiz, John Sullivan Dwight, Philip Hale, or William Apthorp was a Boston liability.† The Boston notion of culture as uplift, however benignly preached as a strategy of inclusive social reform, frequently conveyed an exclusivity of tone. Charles Eliot Norton, Harvard's most celebrated professor, ran a night school for the poor and was instrumental in building model multiple-family housing for the incoming Irish. Concomitantly, he decried the influence of "the uneducated and unrefined masses" in contradistinction to people of superior "character" and "intelligence." Music, especially, was held to be morally instructive, transcending differences in language and custom that otherwise challenged the American melting pot. It was, wrote Dwight, a "heavenly influence which shall go far to correct the crudities, tone down, subdue and harmonize the loud, self-asserting individualities, relieve the glaring and forputting egotism of our too boisterous and boastful nationality"; scanning the other side of the barricades, Dwight warily eyed the Irish rabble.[56]

Higginson, too, believed in cultural uplift. But his tone was not Hale's, or Norton's, or Dwight's, and there were differences in habit and belief as well. Who among Higginson's Brahmin brethren might have attempted to

*This is the premise of Martin Green's exceptional study *The Problem of Boston* (1966).
†See pages 94–100.

run a plantation with freedmen? How many others could claim lifelong kinship with a Viennese Jew such as Julius Epstein? In theory, Dwight's Harvard Musical Association concerts might have aspired to heal and unite; in practice, they were exclusively offered to members and their guests. Higginson (who quit the HMA) never wavered from his 1881 policies of setting aside twenty-five-cent nonsubscription tickets for Boston Symphony concerts, and of charging twenty-five cents for "public rehearsals." Having frequented the twenty-cent upper-gallery seats of Boston theaters to hear Italian opera, having gone without meals as a music student in Vienna, he did not partake of the language of noblesse oblige. His hortatory vision of social harmony might take the following form:

> Democracy has got fast hold of the world, and will rule. Let us see that she does it more wisely and more humanly than the kings and nobles have done! Our chance is now—before the country is full and the struggle for bread becomes intense and bitter.
>
> Educate, and save ourselves and our families and our money from mobs!
>
> I would have the gentlemen of this country lead the new men, who are trying to become gentlemen, in their gifts and in their efforts to promote education.

Or, as at the Soldiers Field dedication we have already glimpsed: "The world on all sides is moving fast, and you have only to accept this fact, making the best of everything—helping, sympathizing, and of guiding and restraining others, who have less education, perhaps, than you. Do not hold off from them; but go straight on with them, side by side, learning from them and teaching them."[57] For someone like Dwight, Boston's high citadels of culture at best accepted lowly applicants if they seemed sufficiently scrubbed. Higginson's house of culture, by comparison, simply kept open its doors.

One aesthetic extreme of Brahmin insularity was a Francophile sensibility scented with decadence. Philip Hale was such an aestheticist: his sartorial fixture was a loose black silk tie; he turned a deaf ear to Brahms and Wagner in favor of Debussy's *Prelude to the Afternoon of a Faun* and *Pelléas et Mélisande*. Hale's counterpart at the *Evening Transcript* was Henry T. Parker, who wore a fedora, carried a bamboo walking stick, and tortured his prose with singular mannerisms of syntax and vocabulary. Higginson's prose was nothing if not blunt; unlike Hale or Parker—or Charles Martin Loeffler, court composer to Isabella Stewart Gardner, with his sensual palette and lurid programmatic fantasies; or Henry Adams, with his hypersensitive aversions to modern mores—he could never have been termed effete. And yet his most startling personal signature, confounding every stereotype of period and place, was—the recurrent motif of any truthful Higginson portrait—a "feminine" predisposition toward interpersonal affection. In old age, he wrote to Bliss Perry: "To go back to my young days, I am reading 'Faust' again, and like it. By the way, if men and women were willing to tell their thoughts and feelings freely, when on a stage, should we not have more eloquence, or at any rate more feeling, from man to man? We Yankees dislike to tell the story as we feel it, and only break out when the house begins to burn. Sometimes I wish to say: 'Hang this self-control!'"

In old age, Higginson commiserated with Henry James the younger when his uncle the novelist died:

> He had many lovers, men and women—and they will always hold him very dear—and be very grateful for his sympathy and love and for his great charm.
>
> One always wonders if a friend has had a happy life, but at least Harry made many people happy and also interested in his views of life. I hope to be included among his lovers, and that your father's and mother's children will remember me as such and as a lover of their two parents. Sometimes you have thought me extravagant in phrase about you all—but my words have been less than my thought and feelings about you all—and if they seem too strong, remember that the halo and the charm of the elders lie on your heads. Why not? Good-bye and love to you one and all.

The startling warmth, intimacy, and candor of Higginson's relationship with his father—who so restlessly endured Henry's absence in Vienna; who in wartime rushed to Virginia to join his wounded son—was self-evidently formative. "To his true comrades," Perry later remembered, Higginson "was like a lover."*[58]

Taking the measure of this man, of the equipoise binding business and art in his personal and professional attainments, one thinks, improbably, of the cantankerous Charles Ives, who contemporaneously sold life insurance when he was not composing symphonies; whose dual worlds likewise signified a complex mediation of fin-de-siècle art and life. Like Higginson, Ives balanced his unfashionably aesthetic vocation

*In *American Manhood: The Transformations in Masculinity from the Revolution to the Modern Era* (1993), E. Anthony Rotundo pertinently observes: "Presumably men had possessed 'feminine' tendencies throughout the nineteenth century, but something was encouraging their expression more strongly (or inhibiting their expression less effectively) as the century drew to a close." Less pertinent to Higginson is Rotundo's further observation: "Men in the late nineteenth century began to sort themselves out into hardy, masculine types and gentle, feminine types—a typography reinforced by William James' distinction between 'tough-minded' and 'tender-minded'" (Rotundo, pp. 264–268). Higginson defies this typology: he was both.

with worldlier, more "masculine" tasks. But the dichotomy was stressful: accommodating to "feminized" art, Ives felt the need to rail against "sissies" and "pansies." Higginson's multiple worlds spanned a harmonious orbit of authority. He was, summarized Mark A. DeWolfe Howe, "by common consent . . . the foremost citizen of Boston."[59]

. . .

In retrospect it was merely predictable that the harmonies of Henry Higginson's world would be silenced by the Great War and the national drumroll against all things German that preceded it. Boston's orchestra was not merely Germanic; literally and fundamentally, it was German. Given Higginson's defiance of the musicians' union and its restrictions on hiring and rehearsing, given the need for reform after Emil Paur's disappointing regime, Muck had quickly engaged thirty-eight new players from abroad, including twenty-seven Germans and eight Austrians. As of 1917, the hundred-man Boston Symphony contained fifty-one American citizens, of whom only seventeen were native born. There were twenty-two Germans, of whom nine had applied for naturalization, plus eight Austrians, six Dutchmen, three Frenchmen, two Italians, two Englishmen, two Russians, two Belgians, and two Bohemians.

Notwithstanding his Swiss passport, Muck himself was a patriotic German serving at the kaiser's pleasure. With the outbreak of European hostilities in 1914, he had unsuccessfully tried to enlist in the kaiser's army. Charles Ellis, meanwhile, rushed abroad to secure safe passage for Higginson's European employees. Ellis managed to retain all but three young players of fighting age. When Muck expressed reservations about returning to the United States, Higginson wrote to him via Ellis: "The feeling with regard to this war is entirely against the German Emperor, and not against the German people." That Higginson and Ellis prevailed was largely due to Anita Muck, who had grown fond of living at 50 Fenway and of such friends as Isabella Stewart Gardner. To Mrs. Muck, Higginson wrote in October 1914: "There is no question about the strong desire to have Dr. Muck return, the strong desire to keep him and make him happy." To Muck he subsequently wrote: "As for this dreadful war, you have heard my wish the other evening—peace. But on no account can we have Schoenberg. Even war is better than that."[60]

In fact, Higginson was an unwitting prisoner of his own dual views as a patriotic American who had opposed slavery and fought in the Civil War, and a passionate Europhile who retained a home abroad; who labored diligently on State Street while retaining a transcendental faith in Beethoven. Acutely sympathetic to his musicians, he would not speak out against the Axis powers. As for Muck's personal political sympathies, Higginson had long worked intimately with his conductor. Their correspondence documents an efficient business relationship built upon seeming candor and trust: we must replace our third oboist, Higginson might write: "I believe that we would better have a Frenchman or a Belgian—and I name the latter because the Brussels school is so good."*[61] In letters to colleagues and friends, Higginson insisted that, more than exemplary, Muck was actually irreplaceable. He would not countenance another Nikisch, or a Mahler or Mengelberg.† His musical needs were informed and specific; as with Symphony Hall, he maintained a principled predilection for the severe.

If Higginson's allegiance to his conductor and orchestra was unswerving, he privately denounced the kaiser as "an unprincipled man, who would rule the world for his own good and glory and that of his nation." "This man is an enemy of the world," he told J.P. Morgan (the younger) on August 5, 1914—weeks after the war began. "If he is sane, he ought to be removed, and if he is insane, he ought to be locked up. Horrible as the destruction of property will be, and destruction of life, . . . almost worse . . . is the terrible temper which has been aroused." The following month Higginson wrote at length to Colonel E.M. House, President Wilson's foreign policy advisor, urging a peace initiative and adding: "You and I have never seen anything equal to the present time, and . . . there is no occasion for it." With the sinking of the *Lusitania,* on May 7, 1915, Higginson was impatient that Wilson (with whom he was in occasional correspondence) demand "a full apology." His firm floated war bonds for the Allies. Still, he kept his views private.[62]

Once the United States declared war on April 6, 1917, however, Higginson was propelled into a maelstrom of public controversy. Leading

*And he presciently added: "I should much prefer not to have a German clarinet or oboe, because the others all are French, and because the French wood-wind has a delicate quality and is very fine. To mix the nations would not be advisable—. . . If a war were to break out between Germany and France, which is always a possibility, it would be a [illegible] to have it carried into the orchestra."

†Higginson had, however, opened negotiations with Mahler in 1908 while searching for a replacement for Max Fiedler; he considered Mahler's impending New York Philharmonic appointment "dangerous" to Boston's interests. He also believed that if he took the New York post Mahler would encounter obstacles with the musicians' union, and would have insufficient access to Carnegie Hall for rehearsals. Mahler took the New York job. Both of Higginson's predictions were accurate. See Henry-Louis de La Grange, *Gustav Mahler: Volume 4—A New Life Cut Short (1907–1911)* (2008), pp. 364–365.

the charge against the symphony's disregard for patriotic fervor was John Revelstoke Rathom, the muckraking editor of the *Providence Journal,* who wanted to know why the "Star-Spangled Banner" was not performed at the Boston Symphony's Providence concert of October 30. Rathom's crusade, typifying what Ludwig Lewisohn would term the "peculiarly unmotivated ferocity" of American war fever, daily insisted that "every German or Austrian in the United States, whether naturalized or not, unless known by years of association to be absolutely loyal, should be treated as a potential spy."[63] Boston requests for the "Star-Spangled Banner" followed. Higginson considered the national anthem both superfluous and aesthetically intrusive at Symphony Hall. But he now asked Muck to conduct it. Muck asked, "What will they say to me at home?" Higginson replied, "I do not know, but let me say this: when I am in a Catholic country and the Host is carried by, or a procession of churchmen comes along, I take off my hat out of consideration—not to the Host, but respect for the customs of the nation. It seems to me only friendly and reasonable."[64] Muck consented—and asked to resign. November 2, Higginson took the stage to announce that Muck had been asked to play the "Star-Spangled Banner" at all Boston Symphony concerts and would do so; he also announced that Muck had resigned and that "the matter is in my hands."

Isabella Stewart Gardner took matters into her hands by turning her back on the flag and leaving the hall when she first encountered her friend Dr. Muck conducting the national anthem. Troubles ensued in Baltimore, Pittsburgh, Detroit, and Springfield. Tour concerts were cancelled. Muck was rumored to be operating a clandestine radio for espionage from his summer home in Bar Harbor, Maine. Mrs. Theodore Thomas, the American-born widow of the fabled German-born conductor and now a resident of Cambridge, Massachusetts, wrote to the *Boston Herald* that those who were attacking the Boston Symphony were "shelling the one perfect and complete art creation of Boston . . . and will surely destroy this noble institution past all redemption."[65]

Henry Higginson weathered the firestorm with patience and despair. Courteously, painstakingly, he responded to letters, many abusive in tone, questioning his patriotism and good sense. To Harvard's President Eliot, he confided: "I am foolish enough to mind the nasty letters, signed and unsigned. In short, I have never learned any wisdom since I was born." To a relative, he called Muck "a typical artist who holds strong opinions about art and not very much about other things." He continued:

> Of course he is a German, and of course he sympathizes with that side, but he has done us great services which it is fair to recognize. When they talk about his having done this or that which is disloyal to us, when they say that he is pushing schemes here, they are saying what they do not know. . . . He is very shrewd and he would not give himself away on any account, no matter what he thinks of or what he wants. But I do feel very badly that the public should throw so many stones at him and at the Orchestra. . . . I am sorry to say that it has destroyed for me all pleasure in the Orchestra. We will go on with it if possible. And there comes another point. I don't know whether it is possible. If the newspapers and cavilers will stop their noise now, we can go on, and if not, I shall have to stop, and it will cost a very large sum of money. I can break all the contracts of all the men, but the poor devils have got to have something to live on, and if I won't employ them, who will? In short, it is an impossible position for them. People tell me to let them go home, but they can't go home. A Frenchman could return; the Belgians cannot . . . I tell you, dear child, I never had such a painful experience in this life.[66]

By the end of February 1918, Higginson had resolved that both he and Muck should leave the orchestra at season's end. On March 13, he wrote to the attorney general to request safe passage to Germany for Muck and his wife. Dr. Muck, he testified, "has behaved himself with absolute propriety in every respect. I have known him well and can testify to his honesty and honor."[67] Pilloried in New York by Mrs. John Jay and other watchdogs for homeland security, Muck led the orchestra's final Carnegie Hall concert of the season the next day. He was greeted with a meaningful ovation—as was Higginson when he took his downstairs center aisle seat. It was known that he was prepared to take the stage, if necessary, to defend his case.[68]

Only on March 25 was the ordeal finally taken out of Higginson's hands: having just rehearsed Bach's *St. Matthew Passion*—a supreme affirmation of spiritual triumph in dire adversity—Muck was arrested at Symphony Hall and jailed by the Boston district attorney. Boston's front-page headlines the next morning included the *Traveller*'s:

MUCK ARREST MOST IMPORTANT OF WAR

The story began:

> Department of Justice officials who have been investigating enemy aliens said today they regarded the detention of Dr. Muck . . . one of the most important since America entered the war.
>
> From other sources it was learned that this view may have a significance that cannot be gone into until official action is taken.

The same paper's page-one lead the following morning read:

SUSPECT KAISER HAD OBJECT IN SENDING DR. MUCK TO U.S.

The story implicitly portrayed Higginson as a dupe:

> So far as is known there is no direct evidence to prove when Emperor William made it possible for Dr. Muck to come to America that the move was part of the German campaign which in 1914 was to take on its cruel military aspect, but examination of German methods indicate [*sic*] clearly that Germany considered Dr. Muck could do much to make Germany popular in the United States.

On May 15 the *Traveller's* front page screamed:

MUCK INVOLVED IN PLANS FOR GERMAN REVOLT

VISITED SPOT WHERE GUNS WERE STORED

The backstory to Muck's arrest, and the rampant speculation it ignited, was that he was found to have engaged in various clandestine romantic relationships. Investigators were offended and intrigued. In particular, the district attorney had discovered a cache of letters in the Milton home of Miss Rosamond Young, an heiress who happened to be an aspirant soprano. Muck's fervent declarations of affection (which agents found "obscene") were laced with intense declarations of anti-American anger and frustration. Upon conducting in Pittsburgh, with its munitions industries, Muck wrote to Young in January 1916: "When I came upon the stage yesterday . . . and saw thousands sitting before me who have earned and are still earning millions through the murder of my people everything was red before my eyes and it took my whole strength not to yell out loud." Four months later, he wrote: "I think that I can't keep up this horrible life much longer in a country full of fanatical enemies far from my country which is struggling for its existence." He continued: "There is no stupidity cheating dumbness which cannot be perpetrated on the American people. Their ignorance and crudeness is so frightfully great that every swindle however stupid and simple is calmly believed, and upon this was based from the beginning the English campaign of baiting and lies in this country. . . . These Englishmen have known exactly how to lie and deceive the American newspaper public." The letters also documented Muck's close acquaintance with high-ranking German officials, including Count Johann von Bernstorff, the controversial German ambassador. Though Muck himself told Young, "I am doing only my duty and nothing against the holy (even Satan was once holy) laws of the so-called U.S.A.," and though no concrete evidence of espionage surfaced, Attorney General Thomas Watt Gregory approved the finding that Muck was "potentially dangerous."[69]

Having languished in a Boston cell (where Isabella Stewart Gardner characteristically defied public opinion by visiting with food), Karl Muck was interned as an enemy alien at Fort Oglethorpe, Georgia, on April 6, 1918. Under the direction of A. Mitchell Palmer (later to succeed Gregory as attorney general), his substantial American assets—forty-six thousand dollars in cash and bank accounts, plus a house and furniture—were seized. His wife, allowed to visit her husband three times a week, moved to a hotel near Chattanooga. His romantic epistles were not made public. The press, with little to go on, decided he was an actual spy.

. . .

Henry Higginson, age eighty-four, a man associated with brisk authority and staccato speech, suffered an acute physical decline in early March 1918. Subsequent to Muck's arrest weeks later, the district attorney's office shared with Higginson and Charles Ellis the conductor's love letters. The crescendo of accusations continued unabated. To Eliot, Higginson reflected: "When mud is thrown, a little usually sticks, and, at any rate, leaves a stain."[70] He reported himself incapacitated for work and unable to travel. That November, he told a business associate: "Concerning this old log, he is useless; he has made no gain for sixty days, is in bed at this minute, has a great deal of pain, and does not know whether he will ever get free from it. . . . I was so kicked and cuffed last year that I lost my temper and balance, and fretted until the machinery gave way."[71]

By this time Higginson's resignation from the Boston Symphony was well behind him. It took the form of a speech delivered at the season's closing Symphony Hall concert, on May 14, 1918. Beethoven's *Eroica* Symphony—a work whose combination of fervor with firm classical form doubtless more endeared it to Higginson than the Ninth or later Romantic works—was performed in his honor. The conductor was Ernst Schmidt, a member of the orchestra's violin section. Higginson's address was typical: crisp, concise, yet confiding. It began, "My friends: The Boston Symphony Orchestra was set up from the conviction of my youth that our country should have great and permanent orchestras," and continued, "I had hoped to have carried on the concerts during my lifetime; but this war has brought us many troubles, and, among them, the problems of the Orchestra during this season, which have exhausted my strength and nerves." Facing the musicians, he next said: "For many years we—you and I—have been good comrades—an honor and a great pleasure for me. . . . I like to think myself a member of our Orchestra, and have done my best to help you; and, on your side, you have served with an intelligence and devotion not to be forgotten by the audiences or by me. I congratulate you, and thank you for our success fairly won." Turning back to the audience, he concluded: "Our Orchestra has always been heartily supported by you and by the public throughout our country, else it could not have lived. It must live in all its strength and beauty, and now will be carried on by some friends who have taken it up; and for them I ask the same support which you have given me through all these years." Mark A. DeWolfe Howe summarized: "The tensity [*sic*] of war-time feeling and the sorrow that came from clinging too long to the trust he had placed in one who proved unworthy of it, imposed a burden he could no longer bear."[72]

Higginson had in fact repeatedly spoken of disbanding his beleaguered orchestra. His state of mind may be imagined. The Boston Symphony was his creation. It was quintessentially German. He had endured both calumny and considered criticism for supporting a conductor he had long regarded as irreplaceable. He was ultimately persuaded to cede the orchestra to a board of trustees headed by Judge Frederick P. Cabot (and also including Howe).

Boston's orchestra was now organized no differently than any other American city's. The trustees were responsible for covering deficits and choosing conductors. Higginson had intended to leave a one-million-dollar endowment, but had quietly experienced financial reversals in recent years; though some inferred stinginess and pique, he had nothing left to give. Fortunately, a group of anonymous guarantors was quickly assembled. Meanwhile, a hasty search was undertaken to identify a non-Germanic music director for the coming fall. Sergei Rachmaninoff expressed interest, but balked at the proposed pay and workload: 120 concerts.[73] A Frenchman, Henri Rabaud, was found for 1918–1919. Eighteen Germans were dismissed from the orchestra. Rabaud, mainly a composer, was replaced in 1919 by a more suitable Frenchman, Pierre Monteux. Monteux's successors would be Serge Koussevitzky, a Russian arriving by way of Paris in 1924, and Charles Munch, an Alsatian appointed as of 1949. Only with the arrival of William Steinberg in 1969 would the Boston Symphony return to German leadership.

Higginson kept a watchful eye. With his assistance, the orchestra nearly secured Britain's Henry Wood before Rabaud was found.[74] Early in Rabaud's tenure, having experienced the orchestra under both

Rabaud and Monteux, Higginson was moved to confide to Wilhelm Gericke: "I often long for a concert such as you gave us—Haydn, Mozart, Beethoven, Schubert. Only a *Wiener Kind* can play Schubert."[75]

Karl Muck, whose internment endured long past the armistice of November 11, 1918, was finally permitted to return to Germany with his wife on August 21, 1919. He told the *Boston Post:* "Germans have no place left in America, either in business or art." He also told the *Post* that, before the war intervened, he had intended to become an American citizen.*[76] But the *Post* was not done with Dr. Muck. Not long after Muck's permanent departure from the United States, a disgruntled former agent of the U.S. Bureau of Investigation sold to the newspaper copies of Muck's correspondence with Rosamond Young, illegally removed from government files. A series of page-one disclosures ensued, beginning on November 9. Muck was again falsely said to have been implicated in actual spying activities. He was also reported to have been relieved when interned because, "although a good deal of a braggart," he was "in fact a great coward . . . constantly in dread of being shot by some American fanatic." The *Post*'s excerpts from the incriminating letters included:

> I am on my way to the concert hall to entertain the crowds of dogs and swine who think that because they pay the entrance fee they have the right to dictate to me my selections. I hate to play for this rabble. . . . [In] a very short time our gracious Kaiser will smile on my request and recall me to Berlin. . . . Our Kaiser will be prevailed upon to see the benefit to the Fatherland of my obtaining a divorce and making you my own.
>
> Must we, for the sake of foolish sentiments that are imposed on us by others, foreswear the love that is divine and inexpressible by common language? No, a thousand times no! You are mine and I am your slave and so I must remain. . . . It will perhaps surprise you to learn that to a certain extent Mrs. Muck knows our relationship. She has a noble heart and her mind is broad beyond the comprehension of the swine-like people among whom we must live a little while longer.†[77]

*The impact of Muck's prolonged Boston debacle on his subsequent life remains ponderable. Arguably, his post–World War I European career, including his European recordings, does not support the electrifying impression he made in America (including a performance of the *Eroica* Symphony while interned in Fort Oglethorpe). As late as September 30, 1924, he was reported (by a San Francisco newspaper) intending to marry Rosamond Young, Mrs. Muck having died (clipping files, Boston Symphony Archives).

†Gayle Turk, in "The Case of Dr. Karl Muck: Anti-German Hysteria and Enemy Alien Internment During World War I," Harvard University thesis, 1994 (Boston Symphony Archives), questions the accuracy of the *Post*'s transcriptions of the letters.

If Muck's letters illuminate his deteriorating relationship with Boston, Higginson's letters document his deteriorating relationship with Karl Muck. Following Muck's arrest, Higginson never saw or corresponded with him again. "Whatever the Government decides is law for me," he wrote three days following Muck's internment. In private correspondence, Higginson's references to Muck emphasized personal betrayal rather than disloyalty to the nation. "To this day I have never known him to have done anything wrong so far as the United States is concerned," he wrote on June 26, 1918. "Other matters did not concern the public, although they did concern me." To the critic Philip Hale, Higginson wrote on October 29, 1918, clarifying a matter distorted in the press: "If I had believed that he had sinned in any way against our country, I should have dismissed him at once. To this day I have no reason to believe that he did so sin." Higginson's condemnation of Muck was somewhat more sweeping in a letter (to another recipient) of January 30, 1919: "I had believed that he was honest towards our country and towards me, and I am afraid he was not." He also felt impelled to complain to Victor Talking Machine that Muck's Boston Symphony recordings were not being marketed "diligently": "If by chance you are unwilling to push the records because of Dr. Muck's arrest, please remember that the music remains the same." But this handwritten letter, dated September 9, 1919, was never sent.[78]

Though German culture, learning, and science had long been held in high esteem in the United States, this crucial influence was already abating by the turn of the century. Then came the war. Charles Eliot, writing to Higginson on January 5, 1915, opined that "music is really the only subject in which Germany can still claim superiority. Her philosophy and religion have failed to work; her education has not developed in the people power to reason or good judgment; her efficiency even in war is not greater than that of her adversaries; and her ruling class is too stupid to see that their game of domination in Europe is already lost."[79]

Higginson's own view of Germany is richly chronicled by his wartime correspondence. He felt he knew Germany—"a very different place" from Austria—better than Germany knew America. He thought "many respects of the administration of civic and state affairs" to be superior to the American norm. He considered Bismarck to have been "a very remarkable and able man, and about as bad a man as ever existed." The Prussian Junker class he found dangerously bellicose. "I have heard sober people say in Germany: 'We must fight England . . . for the sake of our honor.' . . . I never heard an Englishman or a Frenchman say: 'We have got to fight Germany for the sake of our honor.'" He felt the war was unnecessary, but that its outcome was never in doubt—that America would take part and that the Allies would prevail. Above all, he felt that Americans possessed "an entirely different spirit from the Germans; they are not slaves or subjects, but are citizens, and they know it." To a Berlin friend, he wrote two months following the armistice:

> I knew that Germany had not the spirit, and that she had not the material in men to meet the other nations. You may think this arrogant, but you will find a great many of our people who would say the same thing. . . . It as one of the saddest things we ever have seen, for she stood very high indeed industrially, economically, and was making great progress as a maritime nation,—and now it is all gone. . . . I hope that presently the Germans will receive tolerably kindly treatment, and will accept with good temper what then they can get. It will be very hard indeed.

He added: "I am sorry to say we never shall see any of you again, for we never shall to go Germany. No American will be wanted there."[80]

On November 14, Higginson had surgery at Massachusetts General Hospital. Accompanied by his wife and son, he insisted on walking the four flights of stairs to the street, rather than take the elevator. The operation was performed; he never regained consciousness. The *Boston Post*'s ongoing revelations of Karl Muck's inflammatory love affair continued through December.

• • •

The incongruity of Higginson's terminal predicament bears stressing. An international orchestra based in America, performing in wartime, continued to give concerts of Beethoven and Brahms under a German conductor of imperious deportment who was known to support the kaiser. According to statements quoted in the press, Karl Muck frankly disdained the national anthem he was compelled to lead at the start of every program. So steadfast was Higginson's belief in Muck's personal integrity, so firm was his allegiance to music as a pure aesthetic realm, that he soldiered on and on with a will.

Looking back in 1920, Howe wrote that Higginson "seems to have conceived of virtually all the relations of life in terms of friendship. In his attitude toward his country, his city, his college, even toward the art of music, there was something intensely personal—just as there was in his dealings with individual men and women." His ideals of art were no less inviolable, no less pristine. The despotic music lovers Hitler and Stalin were as yet unglimpsed. Higginson was not alone, in the New World or the Old, in his conviction that—as Charles Eliot put it to him in 1918—music "sustains and consoles the human spirit in times of adversity," "transcends the limits of language or race," "ranges freely through all the civilized world and the successive generations of men." In short: Henry Higginson saw the world as a better place than it proved to be.[81]

Higginson's range of professional realms and personal acquaintances was an achievement verging on paradox. Like his creations the Boston Symphony, with its polyglot membership, and Symphony Hall, with its blended Leipzig and Boston templates, he straddled multiple worlds. A trilingual aesthete schooled more in Vienna than at Harvard, he married the daughter of a prominent European and pursued his friendships on two continents with a lover's warmth. An American businessman of puritan New England stock, he was as spartan and crisp as he was affectionate. He both espoused and embodied American freedoms.

The hybrid in Higginson was sundered by the war: its savagery and—scarcely worse, as he observed—its jingoism. Post-Versailles, America would emerge as a strong nation, a world power, but with tendencies toward arrogant isolationism and brazen cultural nationalism. Ralph Waldo Emerson, in 1837, had influentially urged American artists and intellectuals to cease listening to the courtly muses of Europe. With Europe newly fragmented and confused, the same call would acquire a cockier tone.

Late in life, Higginson was urged by a niece to write his reminiscences. In reply, he confided this overly modest yet informative summing up:

> Did I ever tell you that, if I had not been married, I proposed staying in the army, and, by this time, would have been a retired old veteran, growling at everything. I enjoyed my army life, and, on the whole, did it better than anything else—that is, I was a good regimental officer, but could not have gone above the command of a thousand men. I've not been a good business man, but have come through somehow or other. Yes, I can remember many things within my European life which were interesting to me, and some of them are so still, but they would do nobody any good, and I think they would entertain nobody.*[82]

Of the eulogies occasioned by Henry Higginson's death, none surpassed that of Boston's Tavern Club, of which Higginson had been president since 1899:

*Higginson nevertheless dictated fifty pages of reminiscences before his death.

His nature was without disguises. He endeared himself to us by his soldier-like bluntness and directness of speech, by his disregard of conventional estimates of men, by his amazing simplicities. A man of the world, in the best sense, he was nevertheless wholly without sophistication. His love of beauty was unaffected. He had no pretences. He never betrayed bitterness, except toward hypocrisy and cowardice. He had known pain and sorrow, but he kept unspoiled, to the age of eighty-five, a zest for life, the heart of youth and the gift for friendship.[83]

Of Higginson's many remarkable letters—an inexhaustible trove—none more eloquently disclosed the man than "a few words about our talk last night," written late in life to Mrs. George D. Howe:

We young folks used to consider the problems of life, and the rights and needs of men and women, and the injustices of both, also the need of refreshment and not of luxuries or even comforts. And it seemed to me that we of the young beautiful country should and could have music of the best. Hence my hopes and efforts, both for the sake of art and the sake of humanity. Do you see? But talent, or even keen perception of musical talent in others, I have little or none; nor have I ever found talent for anything, except power of work, and of recognizing friends of the best, and the enormous value of them to me. It is all second or third class, and I've been built up and lifted up to a wrong place by friends.

As to the "Eroica," I had meant to tell you how I felt about it, but it opens the flood-gates, and I can't. The wail of grief, and then the sympathy which should comfort the sufferer. The wonderful funeral dirge, so solemn, so full, so deep, so splendid, and always with courage and comfort. The delightful march home from the grave in the scherzo—the wild Hungarian, almost gypsy in tone—and then the climax of the melody, where the gates of Heaven open, and we see the angels singing and reaching their hands to us with perfect welcome. No words are of any avail, and never does that passage of entire relief and joy* come to me without tears—and I wait for it through life, and hear it, and wonder.[84]

*Writing of Beethoven's *Eroica* Symphony, Higginson could here only be referring to the culminating slow variations of the finale.

FIGURE 7. Henry Krehbiel. Courtesy New York Philharmonic Archives.

CHAPTER 2

Henry Krehbiel

The German-American Transaction

Race and the World's Columbian Exposition—The making of a music critic—Anton Seidl and Wagnerism made wholesome—Antonín Dvořák and "Negro melodies"—An activist "American school of criticism"—"Salome" and Mahler debacles—German-Americans and the Great War—Art as uplift

The grandest single exercise in American cultural inventory was the World's Columbian Exposition of 1893. No facet of the fair excited more attention than the mile-long Midway Plaisance, festooned on either side with exotic places of amusement and edification in the guise of ethnic villages: mosques and pagodas, huts of bark and straw, South Sea cabins peopled by donkey boys, camel drivers, dancing girls. The Midway's entrepreneurial mastermind was twenty-one-year-old Sol Bloom, whose enthusiasms included Bedouin acrobats and Arabian sword-swallowers. Its scholarly overseers included Otis T. Mason of the Smithsonian Bureau of American Ethnology, who called it "one vast anthropological revelation," and—in charge of all anthropological exhibits—Ward Putnam, head of Harvard's Peabody Museum of American Archaeology and Ethnology. Putnam had distanced himself from the anachronistic views of his famous Harvard teacher, Louis Agassiz, in favor of Darwinian evolution. Still, the Midway spectacle, juxtaposing an ostrich farm, animal show, and other such attractions with living exhibits of Javanese, Samoans, and other such peoples, was widely interpreted to argue a hierarchy of race.

If the Midway's most lucrative attraction was the Street in Cairo, featuring the belly dancer Little Egypt, its most notorious was the Dahomeyan

Village, featuring scantily clad Africans with swords and spears dancing to drums and bells. Americans, commented the *Chicago Tribune,* were thus afforded "an unequalled opportunity to compare themselves scientifically with others . . . tracing humanity in its highest phases down almost to its animalistic origins." The Dahomeyans were "blacker than buried midnight and as degraded as the animals which prowl the jungles of their dark land," reported *Frank Leslie's Popular Monthly.* "In these wild people we easily detect many characteristics of the American negro." J.M. Buell, in his guidebook *The Magic City,* further observed, "They have apparently relaxed none of their horrible customs, among which cannibalism is chief." He categorized the Dahomeyans as "a strong athletic people, possessing much cunning, and considerable intelligence." Like the Inuits, Indians, Tartars, and tattooed Polynesians similarly on display, they helped Americans "better to appreciate the blessings of Christian civilization and the loving direction and guidance of God."[1]

From these gawking perspectives, Henry Edward Krehbiel stood apart. Assessing the Dahomeyan war dances, he reported:

> The harmony was a tonic major triad broken up rhythmically in a most intricate and amazingly ingenious manner. The instruments were tuned with excellent justness. . . . The players showed the most remarkable rhythmical sense and skill that ever came under my notice. Berlioz in his supremest efforts with his army of drummers produced nothing to compare in artistic interest with the harmonious drumming of these savages. The fundamental effect was a combination of double and triple time, the former kept by the singers, the latter by the drummers, but it is impossible to convey the idea of the wealth of detail achieved by the drummers by means of exchange of the rhythms, syncopation of both simultaneously, and dynamic devices.

This observation, recalling the Columbian Exposition, occurs in Krehbiel's *Afro-American Folksongs* of 1914. Reporting directly from Chicago in 1893, he devoted three substantial *New York Tribune* dispatches exclusively to matters Native American. Presented by Putnam's assistant Franz Boas, a group of Kwakiutl Indians from Vancouver Island offered a series of winter dances. Krehbiel used a phonograph—a novelty he had already employed among the Iroquois of Ontario, in whose songs he had documented the use of micro-intervals—to record and transcribe their music. Like "most savage or semi-civilized peoples," he reported in a twenty-seven-hundred-word *Tribune* article with musical examples, the Kwakiutls made "ingenious use of contrasted rhythms." He cited a "Hamatsa song" in duple rhythm, accompanied in triple meter—"a common phenomenon in primitive music, but one that is rare in the highly developed Occidental art." Though his reportage is of its time—no one today would attribute to the Iroquois "so much nobility of character and real moral and intellectual gentleness" in contradistinction to "the lowest African and South Sea savages," or observe races passing "in their progress toward civilization"—Krehbiel's spirit of disinterested inquiry has not dated. His circumnavigatory prose, serene in its slow disclosure of direction and purpose, conveys such fresh intelligence as this overview of the Midway experience: "Here fraud and humbug are rich, and 'fakirs' of all kinds ply their vocation with so much impudence that the spectacle at last becomes almost amiable. The kaleidoscopic pleasure ground is classified under the head of Ethnology, however, and even if one be inclined to smile at the stamp of scientific dignity thus impressed upon it, a little reflection shows that it all depends on the visitor whether or not its significance shall be summed up in the antics of the 'fakirs.' It is easy to make a field for scientific study even out of the Midway Plaisance."[2]

The ponderous eloquence of Krehbiel's leisurely sentences and paragraphs, majestically imparting content ever acute and often fervent, mirrored the outward and inward propensities of Krehbiel the man. His pontifical tone and vast learning made him the acknowledged "dean" of New York City's music critics. He stood tall, broad-shouldered, and erect. Both his complexion and rebellious curly hair were ruddy. In luxurious girth, he was commonly observed to resemble William Howard Taft. He was also observed, by Max Smith of the *American,* flushed "with indignation when his ideals were trampled upon," and with eyes filled "with tears when they were realized." When in later life Krehbiel taught at New York's Institute of Musical Arts (later the Juilliard School), he would weep with emotion at the lectern. The tonnage of words he weekly committed to print could rise to epic heights of effusive advocacy.[3]

Krehbiel's head was weighted, and his heart suffused, with German learning and German music. It was from German art and from Richard Wagner—a contemporary pinnacle—that Krehbiel absorbed the notion that great music is nationally specific, that culture and race are bound inextricably. He assiduously documented the folk music of Jews, Slavs, Magyars, Scandinavians, and Russians. He hence understood high art not as an elite hereditary privilege, rarified and obscure, but as an emanation of folk customs admired without discriminatory qualm. "The more the world comes to realize how deep and intimate are the springs from which the emotional element of music flows," he believed, "the more fully will it recognize that originality and power in the composer rest upon the use of dialects and idioms which are national or racial in original and structure."[4] This mode of thought, democratically poised, supported another lifelong line of inquiry—into "America." It follows that "Indians" most enticed Krehbiel in Chicago, and that he wrote his book on plantation song.

Krehbiel's quest for American roots was also a product of his own tangled roots as a self-made German-American polymath. Like other children of immigrants—unlike the Boston Brahmins with whom he jousted over issues of national identity—he felt the need to investigate what it meant to be American. Born in Ann Arbor in 1854, he grew up speaking English and German with equal fluency (and later acquired a reading knowledge of French, Italian, Russian, and Latin). He studied law in Cincinnati, where his father, a Methodist preacher, settled in 1864 (and where young Henry conducted the church choir), but wound up a twenty-year-old reporter for the *Cincinnati Gazette;* his assignments included baseball games, for which he invented a new method of scoring, as well as musical events. He joined the *New York Tribune* in 1880 as a writer, reporter, and—eventually—critic.

New York City was 27 percent "German" as of 1890, according to the country-of-birth-of-mother criterion used by the Census Bureau. With Vienna and Berlin, New York's Kleindeutschland (Little Germany), situated within the Lower East Side, was one of three capitals of the German-speaking world. The late nineteenth-century influence and prestige of German learning and culture—of German music, obviously; of Germany models of scholarship; of German science, medicine, philosophy, and jurisprudence—in the United States generally, and in New York especially, is a story yet to be adequately told. It is a story in which Krehbiel was a prime mover.

An insatiable autodidact in the American manner, Krehbiel was self-taught in music, and taught himself well. He edited collections of songs and arias, and was American editor of the second edition of *Grove's Dictionary of Music and Musicians.* He translated opera librettos from German and French (including an ingenious cantata adaptation of part 2 of Berlioz's *The Trojans,* whose significance he extolled, and whose first American performance he facilitated, nearly a century before its belated canonization*). He lectured regularly and gave private lessons.

*See Henry Krehbiel, *Review of the New York Musical Season 1886–1887* (1887) for two samples of the Virgilian narratives Krehbiel wrote for the American premiere of *The Trojans at Carthage,* as conducted (in concert) by Frank Van der Stucken at Chickering Hall, Feb. 26, 1887. Krehbiel's commentary here: "No estimate of Berlioz's works is

He completed the first English-language edition of Thayer's monumental life of Beethoven. He wrote a dozen books. In addition to *Afro-American Folksongs,* these include a two-volume history of opera in America (unsurpassed by any subsequent study), the earliest history of the New York Philharmonic (for which he served as program annotator), a probing exploration of Wagnerian music drama, a survey of music for the piano, and—for laymen—a *Book of Operas* (in two volumes) and *How to Listen to Music* (reprinted thirty times). The purposes of this output ranged from refined intellectual pleasure to robust pedagogy and advocacy.

Krehbiel took for granted his esteemed membership in a community of artists. Before radio and television, automobiles and airplanes, telephones and e-mails, the daily appliances of communication and transportation were restaurants, clubs, sidewalks, streetcars, and parlors. At the finest hotel restaurants, the "free lunch counter" furnished hearty meals, for a five-cent tip, to all who purchased a cocktail, beer, or milk-and-seltzer. Artists and newspapermen there intermingled with businessmen and lawyers. At night, Union Square was a cultural hub, with Lüchow's and Fleischmann's, Steinway Hall and the Academy of Music. Elsewhere, the Lotus Club or Metropolitan Club informally hosted the musical elite. The prodigious liquid intake of Albert Niemann, the greatest Tristan of his day; the imperious conviviality of his Metropolitan Opera Isolde, Lilli Lehmann; the spontaneous communal fiddling or pianism of a Eugène Ysaÿe or Rafael Joseffy were not exceptional spectacles, but a representative species of public banter.

In such a jostling milieu, a music critic's role was participatory. William J. Henderson of the *Times* kept a weekend salon; he also wrote librettos (including one for Walter Damrosch's *Cyrano de Bergerac,* given by the Metropolitan Opera), poems, biographies, and a novel, and taught at both the College of Music and the Institute of Musical Art. Reginald DeKoven of the *World* was a successful composer of operettas. The silver-tongued James Gibbons Huneker, a café raconteur as legendary as Falstaff, taught and administered at the National Conservatory, wrote short stories and a novel, and entertained a loyal yet irreverent coterie when not reviewing concerts, plays, novels, and paintings

complete which does not take this score into account. In 'The Trojans' are to be found musical numbers which dwarf the best features of the compositions on which Berlioz's popularity rests in this country." At the same time, he found Berlioz's opera uneven in inspiration.

for a variety of newspapers and magazines. The melee of voices (many of them German), of some forty daily newspapers and of rival weekly music journals, countenanced tacit critical alliances and open journalistic wars, blatant bias (advertisements were known to purchase excellent reviews) and potent feats of opinion-making frankly informed by intimate knowledge of persons and institutions.* Under such circumstances, it is hardly surprising that, of the two dominant musicians in New York City during the final decades of the nineteenth century, one—a conductor linked to Wagner—forged a close friendship with Henry Krehbiel, and the other—a composer from Bohemia—discovered himself a recipient of Krehbiel's private counsel and influential public sponsorship.

• • •

Of Krehbiel's many colleagues in the New York musical press, some found him excessively self-assured and proud, "labored" and "overweighted with effort" in tone.[5] "The elements of criticism," Krehbiel expounded in *How to Listen to Music,* "are not matters of opinion or taste, but questions of fact, as exactly demonstrable as a problem in mathematics. . . . the questions of justness of intonation in a singer or instrumentalist, balance of tone in an orchestra, correctness of phrasing, and many other things, are mere determinations of fact." Henry Finck of the *Post,* whose facts often did not accord with Krehbiel's, said in his memoirs, "[Krehbiel] could hate like a caveman. . . . His vanity was always as big as his body." But Finck added: "We were like two lawyers who heap mounds of abuse on one another in court and then go out and lunch together." Krehbiel was a habitué of Fleischmann's, Lüchow's, and other watering hotels of the Union Square vicinity. In conversation, he was known to be jovial, witty, far less formal than in print. With Huneker, who called him "Harry," he enjoyed a long and warm friendship notwithstanding the hiatus between Krehbiel's allegiance to the Classical/Romantic past and Huneker's espousal of the proto-modernist future; in one 1904 letter, Huneker was moved to avow, "I confess nothing would wound me more than the loss of your affection or respect."

*The proactive role espoused by Krehbiel and his colleagues contradicts prevalent later notions of journalist "objectivity" and "conflict of interest." Krehbiel's detractors—notably Leonard Liebling of the *Musical Courier*—accused him of being soft on Walter Damrosch because (like W.J. Henderson) Krehbiel taught at the Damrosches's Institute of Musical Art. Krehbiel drew a line only when it came to press agents: he would not deal with them.

Richard Aldrich, who worked under Krehbiel at the *Tribune* before succeeding W.J. Henderson at the *Times,* wrote that Krehbiel "brooked little opposition"; Aldrich also wrote, "He made himself easily the first of American critics in the soundness and discrimination of his judgment [and] his deep and comprehensive knowledge." Aldrich was one of many junior critics to testify to Krehbiel's patriarchal courtesy and kindness. Gilbert Gabriel of the *Sun* felt privileged "to share the imposing geniality of a huge, handsome old gentleman with a leonine mane and a red ribbon in the buttonhole of his Prince Albert." According to Deems Taylor of the *World,* "Most of us who saw him . . . night after night called him 'Pop' and thought of him as 'Pop.'"[6]

One keynote of Krehbiel's stature as a critical writer was his gift for infusing passionate approbation with acute erudition. In the presence of greatness—typically, a dead composer or living performer—he singularly sealed the magnitude of the occasion in cold print the morning after. By way of example: an electrifying moment in the early history of the Metropolitan Opera was the New York debut of Albert Niemann as Siegmund in *Die Walküre* on November 10, 1886. Niemann was a heroic tenor gigantic in stature and legend: he had learned Siegmund from Wagner himself. But Niemann was fifty-five years old, in the twilight of a long and taxing career; and he had never been a mellifluous singer. What is more, the first act of *Die Walküre* is a portrait of young love—a duet in which the lovers, discovering themselves in one another, literally discover themselves twins. A pariah of uncertain parentage—a picture, that is, of one aspect of the protean composer—Siegmund enters Sieglinde's hut exhausted, fleeing murderous enemies. Krehbiel's long report in the *Tribune*—part of a review longer still—can barely be abridged:

> Those who go to see and hear Herr Niemann must go to see and hear him as the representative of the character that he enacts. It is only thus that they can do justice to themselves, to him, and to the art-work in which he appears. A drama can only be vitalized through representation, and the first claim to admiration which Herr Niemann puts forth is based on the intensely vivid and harmonious picture of the Volsung which he brings on the stage. There is scarcely one of the theatrical conventions which the public have been accustomed to accept that he employs. He takes possession of the stage like an elemental force. Wagner's dramas have excited the fancy of painters more than any dramatic works of the century, because Wagner was in a lofty sense a scenic artist. Niemann's genius, for less it can scarcely be called, utilizes this picturesque element to the full. His attitudes and gestures all seem parts of Wagner's creation. They are not only instinct with life, but instinct with the

> sublimated life of the hero of the drama. When he staggers into Hunding's hut and falls upon the bearskin beside the hearth a thrill passes through the observer. Part of his story is already told, and it is repeated with electrifying eloquence in the few words that he utters when his limbs refuse their office. The voice is as weary as the exhausted body. In the picturesque side of his impersonation he is aided by the physical gifts with which nature has generously endowed him. The figure is colossal; the head, like "the front of Jove himself"; the eyes large and full of luminous light, that seems to dart through the tangled and matted hair that conceals the greater portion of his face. The fate for which he has been marked out has set its seal in the chronic melancholy which is never absent even in his finest frenzies, but in the glare of those eyes there is something that speaks unfalteringly of the godlike element within him. . . .
>
> The period of Wagner's tetralogy, it must be remembered, is purely mythical. The ruggedness of the type which we obtain by such a process is the strong characteristic of Herr Niemann's treatment of Wagner's musical and literary text. It is, like the drama itself, an exposition of the German esthetic idea: strength before beauty. It puts truthful declamation before beautiful tone production in his singing and lifts dramatic color above what is generally considered essential musical color. That from this a new beauty results all those can testify who hear Herr Niemann sing the love song in the first act of "Die Walküre," which had previously in America been presented only as a lyrical effusion and given with more or less sweetness and sentimentality. Herr Niemann was the first representation of the character who made this passage an eager, vital, and personal expression of a mood so ecstatic that it resorts to symbolism, as if there was no other language for it. The charms with which he invests the poetry of this song (for this is poetry) can only be appreciated by one who is on intimate terms with the German language, but the dramatic effect attained by his use of tone color and his marvelous distinctness of enunciation all can feel.[7]

The symbolic love song in question is "Winterstürme wichen dem Wonnemond" ("Winter storms have vanished at Spring's command"), Spring being summoned by Love, with which—like the lovers—it unites. The style of singing here described (parodied by detractors as the "Bayreuth bark") privileged declamation over smoothness of emission. In the absence of recordings of the historic Bayreuth performances Wagner superintended, Krehbiel furnishes a uniquely vivid account of the kind of heightened speech, poetically fusing word and tone, that Wagner prescribed.

A season later, Krehbiel observed Niemann learning the role of Siegfried, in *Götterdämmerung*, in the East 62nd Street brownstone belonging to Anton Seidl. "The two men sat at a table with the open score before them. Seidl beat time to the inaudible orchestral music, and

FIGURE 8. Anton Seidl. Courtesy New York Philharmonic Archives.

Niemann sang *sans* support of any kind. Then would come discussion of readings, markings of cues, etc., all with indescribable gravity, while Frau Seidl-Krauss . . . sat sewing in a corner. After the performance of the drama, I sat again with Niemann and Seidl over cigars and beer."[8]

This reminiscence is in no way boastful; Seidl and Krehbiel were close friends. Seidl was also the beacon light of musical New York—

Krehbiel's model of cultural leadership, marrying the New and Old Worlds. Born in Budapest in 1850, he had served as Wagner's Bayreuth amanuensis in his early twenties and went on to precocious fame as a master Wagnerite conductor. In Manhattan, he was chief conductor at the Met beginning in 1885. When a boxholders' rebellion put an end to seven seasons of German opera, he became conductor of the New York Philharmonic.

Known in New York as "Die grosse Schweiger" ("the great silent one"), Seidl was Krehbiel's antipode in personality. "When Seidl was silent you could almost hear him thinking," Huneker quipped; Krehbiel early on observed in him "a singular combination of youth, perspicacity, calm and inflexible determination and strength of character . . . a countenance which has behind it a huge reserve force." Nor was Seidl the scholar that Krehbiel made himself become; rather he was, as Krehbiel put it, "an empiric." Drawing on the Michigan experiences of his circuit-riding father, Krehbiel further observed: "In [Seidl], impulse dominated reflection, emotion shamed logic. It was much to his advantage that he came among an impressionable people with the prestige of a Wagnerian oracle and archon, and much to the advantage of the cult to which he was devoted that he made the people 'experience' the lyric dramas of his master in the same sense that a good Methodist 'experiences' religion, rather than to 'like' them."[9]

It was a crucial point of pride and endearment that Seidl the confirmed Wagnerite swiftly became a confirmed American. He took American citizenship, spoke (fractured) English, disliked being addressed as "Herr," purchased a summer home in the Catskills, and extolled American freedoms. His silence notwithstanding, he rode the streetcar, dined at Fleischmann's, and was recognized at sight everywhere he went. He eagerly supported the American composer, and influentially championed Edward MacDowell (whose music he preferred to Brahms) and Victor Herbert (whose Second Cello Concerto he premiered, with Herbert—his frequent assistant conductor or principal cellist—as soloist).* With Krehbiel, he was a prime participant in the American Composers Concerts movement. He told Krehbiel that Wagner himself (having once

*Reviewing a Theodore Thomas concert of March 5, 1889, Krehbiel wrote: "It is not to depreciate [Tchaikovsky's Fifth Symphony], but only because there was a patriotic as well as artistic interest in the composition of Mr. MacDowell, that I confess to having derived keener pleasure from the [Second Piano Concerto] of the young American than from the experienced and famous Russian. . . . His concerto afforded a delight of no mean order. It is a splendid composition, so full of poetry, so full of vigor, as to tempt the assertion

talked of emigrating to the "fertile and more helpful soil" of the United States[10]) had anointed him his New World emissary. Seidl's most famous transatlantic precursors—an Anton Rubinstein or Hans von Bülow—had crisscrossed the young nation and returned home with fistfuls of cash. No European musician of comparable eminence had ever come to the United States and stayed. Seidl's commitment to New York was validating.

And Seidl, man and artist, radiated integrity. Krehbiel esteemed him as a pure vessel of enlightenment, a purging agent who inspired a new ripeness of reception: listeners who held their applause in thrall to deep musical and dramatic currents, not "easily pleased or attracted by curiosity alone" but predisposed to a "keen and lofty enjoyment." When, craving the glamour of expensive Italian and French voices, the Met's boxholders (who were also shareholders) announced the termination of German opera, the entrenched Wagner audience greeted the final 1890–91 performance with thirty minutes of applauding, cheering, and stamping; only the appearance of workers breaking down the sets persuaded the crowd go home. Krehbiel tabulated box office receipts to refute claims that Wagner had lost popularity. He deplored the forfeiture of a reformist audience "with intelligent tastes and warm affections," and flung this denunciation at the house's new operators: "The fickleness of public taste, the popular craving for sensation, the egotism and rapacity of the artists, the lack of high purpose in the promoters, the domination of fashion instead of love for art, the lack of real artistic culture—all these things have stood from the beginning, as they still stand, in the way of a permanent foundation for opera in New York."[11]

As Wagner's American prophet—a role he maintained as the city's busiest symphonic conductor and frequent visitor at the Met—Seidl embodied a Wagnerism fortified with moral fiber at every turn. Krehbiel's influence on the American Wagner movement, pedagogical or oracular, was scarcely less significant: he was the voluble Aaron to Seidl's taciturn Moses. These were years in which the *Ring of the Nibelung, Tristan und Isolde,* and *Die Meistersinger* received first American performances. "The critic should be the mediator between the musician

that it must be placed at the head of all works of its kind produced by either a native or adopted citizen of America." (Of the waltz movement of Tchaikovsky's "new symphony," Krehbiel—ever the cultural nationalist—wrote: "It breathes the spirit of a people who can be desperate and boisterous in their humor, but not light-hearted and careless.") See Krehbiel, *Review of the New York Musical Season 1888–1889* (1889), pp. 97–98.

and the public," Krehbiel wrote in *How to Listen to Music*. "For all new works he should do what the symphonists of the Liszt school attempt to do by means of programmes; he should excite curiosity, arouse interest, and pave the way to popular comprehension. But for the old he should not fail to encourage reverence and admiration." The same book also includes this remarkable directive: "The newspaper now fills the place in the musician's economy which a century ago was filled in Europe by the courts and nobility. Its support, indirect as well as direct, replaces the patronage which erstwhile came from these powerful ones."[12] Addressing the Wagner operas new to America, Krehbiel told his readers how Wagner culled his librettos from myth and literature, how music was applied to the stories, how the operas played at the Met under Seidl's baton. Explicating the sources of the *Ring*, Krehbiel ranged effortlessly among Greek, Roman, Norse, Egyptian, Hindu, and Persian sources. He also cited J. G. Hahn's *Sagwissenschaftliche Studien*, which extrapolated "a formula according to which the families belonging to the Aryan race have constructed their most admired tales." For *Tristan*, he surveyed English versions by Thomas Malory, Matthew Arnold, Tennyson, and Swinburne as well as Gottfried von Strassburg's thirteenth-century epic poem (and a later edition of the same by Sir Walter Scott). He pertinently noted the etymology of "Tristan" (from *triste*) and stressed how Wagner's deviations from all previous variants heightened the story and its characters. For *Die Meistersinger*, he visited Nuremberg to scrutinize the historical record and what was left of St. Catherine's Church (where the opera begins). He knew which Hans Sachs songs were authentic and which were not. He shared, in detail, a master song by Sachs with words by Pogner (also in Wagner's opera), "which, to the best of my knowledge, has never been printed or written about."

Krehbiel's interpretive exegeses of these operas (in additional *Tribune* articles) were wholly his own. For contemporary European commentators, the Wagner operas were shadowed by Schopenhauerian gloom or scented with a decadent sensualism; they brandished socialist polemics or nihilistic abandon. For Krehbiel, as for Americans generally, Wagner was about uplift. He did not attend to the Germanic nationalism of *Die Meistersinger* or to the weary pessimism of Sachs's "Wahn!" monologue. Rather, he reveled in this opera's Shakespearean "delineation of character" and added: "Although its fun is a little brutal (as becomes the place and period with which the play deals), it is not at all malicious, and is always morally healthy." As for the *Ring*, with its ambivalent ending: "Wagner's ethical conception seems to be that the era of selfishness and greed of power and gold gives place to an era of the domination of love." The downfall of the gods is "a just and righteous necessity," "a stupendous deed of morality." Of *Siegfried* (the third of the *Ring* operas), he wrote: "There is something peculiarly sympathetic to our people in the character of the chief personages of the drama. In their rude forcefulness and freedom from restrictive conventions they might be said to be representative of the American people. They are so full of that vital energy which made us a nation. . . . Siegfried is a prototype, too, of the American people in being an unspoiled nature. He looks at the world through glowing eyes that have not grown accustomed to the false and meretricious."[13] (Frederick Jackson Turner's "frontier thesis" of 1893—five years subsequent to the Krehbiel passage cited above—argued that the pioneer forged an American type combining "coarseness," "strength," "inquisitiveness," a "practical inventive turn of mind," a "restless, nervous energy," a "buoyancy and exuberance which comes from freedom."[14] He is in fact Wagner's Siegfried scrutinized through rosy American lenses.)

Where in *Tristan* and *Parsifal* Krehbiel was confronted with inescapable evidence of darker Wagner truths, he did not soft-pedal (as other American commentators did). Tristan and Isolde pursue their carnal passion in violation of Tristan's knightly duty to convey Isolde as bride to King Marke. Their tidal surrender thrilled and discomfited Krehbiel: he is the very bellwether of unjaded Gilded Age intensities. At the Met, he witnessed his companion, an experienced actress, "grow faint and almost swoon" when Niemann, as Tristan, ecstatically tore the bandages from his bloody wound.[15] The reticent New York response to this erotically crazed gesture—which Niemann did not repeat at subsequent New York performances—gauged the uncontrolled excitement it inflamed. Wagner, Krehbiel wrote of *Tristan,* should never devolve into "a mere sensual indulgence." "Reflection and comparison," conditioned by recognition of "the themes and their uses," should modulate the experience. Music may directly attack feeling, "but it is chiefly by association of ideas that we recognize its expressiveness of significance."[16] If this warning connects with New World Puritan strains, it equally connects with Friedrich Nietzsche, who decried Wagner "as a danger."

> One walks into the sea, gradually loses one's secure footing, and finally surrenders oneself to the elements without reservation: one must *swim.* In older music, what one had to do . . . was something quite different, namely, to *dance.* The measure required for this, the maintenance of certainly equally balanced units of time and force, demanded continual *wariness* of the lis-

> tener's soul—and on the counterplay of this cooler breeze that came from wariness and the warm breath of enthusiasm rested the magic of all *good* music. Richard Wagner wanted a different kind of movement; he overthrew the physiological presupposition of previous music. Swimming, floating—no longer walking and dancing.[17]

Nietzsche, the German, sensed the risk of an emotional totalitarianism. Krehbiel, being German-American, sensed risks not societal but personal.

Krehbiel's Wagner articles spawned his book-length *Studies in the Wagnerian Drama* (1904). Seidl toured widely with the Met and with his own orchestra. The Wagner movement was national, a dominant factor in general intellectual discourse during the closing decades of the century, when—as any perusal of the *Atlantic Monthly, Harper's, Scribner's,* and other genteel periodicals will confirm—classical music was a cultural common denominator more favored than the visual or theater arts, a mark of breeding more necessary to Americans than at any time since. Henry Adams attended *Götterdämmerung* in New York and reported "paroxysms of nervous excitement." Albert Pinkham Ryder went for two days without sleep or food, painting "Siegfried and the Rhine Maidens" following his New York *Götterdämmerung* experience of 1888. W.E.B. Du Bois knew the sorcery of *Lohengrin.* For Robert Ingersoll—the "great agnostic," the most popular orator of his day—Wagner told "of all there is in life." Ingersoll preached women's suffrage and birth control, and defended the rights of Jews, immigrants, and Indians; he also preached that Wagner "develops the brain" and "civilizes the heart."[18] George Curtis, who wrote "The Easy Chair" for *Harper's Monthly,* and Richard Watson Gilder, who edited *Century* magazine, were writers who notably helped to shape the life of the American mind; both supported the Wagner cause.

Like Krehbiel, like Seidl, American Wagnerism was a German-American hybrid. Buoyed by New World optimism, it furnished an intellectual tonic, a visceral shock, a gripping therapy for bookish, parched, or sequestered lives. Clinching this German-American equation, Krehbiel believed that Wagner would lead the way to an indigenous "national" opera. America's Teutonic ancestry—that is, the languages, myths, and ideas of Germany, England, and other northern European lands—conditioned a special receptivity to German opera, he believed, in contradistinction to Mediterranean French and Italian genres. German opera, he wrote, insisted on dramatic veracity. Resistant to the tyranny of wealth and fashion, it was compatible with democratic ideas. Krehbiel further prophesied that opera in America would remain "experimental" and "exotic," "until the vernacular becomes the language of performances and native talent provides both works and interpreters."[19] This latter prediction was accurate insofar as opera in English never ignited in the United States—and American composers never produced a viable operatic canon. As for the logic of Wagner as boon to a native operatic tradition, it can at least be observed that, whereas connoisseurs of Gounod and Bellini were frequently seduced by the prestige of foreign tongues, both Krehbiel and Seidl bravely espoused Wagner in English. Seidl actually embarked on a Hiawatha opera to an English-language libretto. Thus was the American discovery of Wagner entwined with Seidl's discovery of America, a transaction mediated, in the *Tribune,* by the most influential, most comprehensive explicator and chronicler of American Wagnerism.

Seidl's sudden death in 1898, at the age of forty-seven, was greeted with incredulity and dismay. For nearly a week, every metropolitan daily recounted his final hours, the cause of death (he was thought to have died of food poisoning; an autopsy revealed gallstone and liver ailments), the memorial services, the cremation. Some fifteen thousand persons applied for tickets to his funeral at the Metropolitan Opera House; some four thousand—a surging, smothering human mass in which ticketholders clasped hands with the ticketless—managed to get in, with standees packed five and six rows deep. Women outnumbered men twenty to one in the downstairs seats. The New York Philharmonic played Siegfried's funeral music. Carl Schurz, the designated eulogist, could not bring himself to speak. His place was taken by Henry Krehbiel, who read a dispatch from Robert Ingersoll. James Huneker, a gilded wordsmith not normally disposed to high sobriety, observed: "A genuine grief absorbed every person in the building. . . . The quaver in [Krehbiel's] voice, a thousand times more significant than the rhetorical phrases he uttered, set many sobbing. Alas! That Anton Seidl is dead." Krehbiel wrote of Seidl's passing, "It was a loss not to one community, but to many; not to a single artistic institution, but to art itself."[20]

• • •

During three of the dozen years that Anton Seidl dominated musical New York, one other musician—a composer—possessed higher authority. His New York sojourn of 1892 to 1895 impacted crucially on the quest for American musical identity. Both Seidl and Krehbiel esteemed him as a supreme instructor.

This was the Bohemian master Antonín Dvořák, who arrived to assume the directorship of the National Conservatory of Music on East Seventeenth Street. He had been enticed and financially ensnared by the conservatory's visionary founder, Mrs. Jeannette Thurber. Like Krehbiel and Seidl, she was determined to foster an American canon of symphonies and operas to anchor American classical music. Her school, founded in 1885 and bankrolled by her husband, was intended to persuade gifted young musicians to study at home rather than abroad, as was the custom (Thurber herself being a graduate of the Paris Conservatoire). Thurber sought Dvořák for the prestige he would confer. As she doubtless appreciated, he also happened to be an instinctive democrat, a butcher's son. And (as with Henry Krehbiel) he was both a self-made man and a cultural nationalist for whom music conveyed national character and a message, tangible or not, of locale. Unlike so many eminent composers who later wound up in the United States—with Gustav Mahler first in line—he regarded his new surroundings with intense curiosity. In fact, he was a composer who keyed on the sights and sounds of his environment; he could not have ignored the New World had he tried.

New York's press greeted famous newcomers with a predatory excitement unknown in older, more settled cities. Three months after docking, Dvořák wrote: "What the American papers write about me is simply terrible. They see in me, they say, the savior of American music and I don't know what else besides! I am to show them to the promised land of a new and independent art—in short, to create a national music."[21] Dvořák believed that deep music was rooted in deep soil. Like so many Europeans of his day, he was fascinated by America's indigenous population: Indians. He acquired a keen interest in Native American song and dance. And he encountered something else even more promising for the project at hand. On May 21, 1893, the *New York Herald* published the only immortal words Dvořák ever uttered: "In the negro melodies of America I discover all that is needed for a great and noble school of music." Seven days later Dvořák wrote, in a letter to the *Herald,* "It is to the poor that I turn for musical greatness. The poor work hard; they study seriously." Dvořák himself was born poor. As a Bohemian, he also knew what it was to belong to a Hapsburg minority. For his personal assistant at the National Conservatory, he chose the young black baritone Harry Burleigh.

Though no American ever validated slave songs as potently as Dvořák would, his insight was not unique. Jeannette Thurber, nurturing her dream of an American concert voice, packed her school with black students on scholarship. And Henry Krehbiel had embarked on an ongoing investigation of African-American folk song, the better to comprehend its potential applications. As with Wagnerism and Seidl, Krehbiel became the central champion of Dvořák and Negro melodies. He also became Dvořák's de facto artistic advisor, feeding him specimens of transcribed plantation song and Indian chant. (The Dahomeyans whose rhythms Krehbiel appreciated in 1893 were doubtless also heard by Dvořák; he visited the Columbian Exposition twice.) Krehbiel pertinently observed that Dvořák's life had been "a story of manifest destiny, of signal triumph over obstacle and discouraging environment," that he had triumphed "by an exercise of traits of mind and character that have always been peculiarly the admiration of American manhood."[22]

The crowning outcome of Dvořák's American enterprise was his "Symphony from the New World," premiered by the New York Philharmonic at Andrew Carnegie's two-year-old Music Hall on December 16, 1893. The conductor was Dvořák's closest New World friend: Anton Seidl, with whom he daily shared the second-floor round table at Fleischmann's Restaurant. In support, Krehbiel undertook an act of advocacy exceptional even for him: a twenty-five-hundred-word preview, including fourteen musical examples, whose small print blanketed half a page of the December 15, 1893, *Tribune;* it was reprinted December 16 in the *Cincinnati Gazette Inquirer* and on December 20 in the *Musical Courier*—the major national publication of its kind. As already reported in the New York press, Dvořák had dropped various hints regarding African-American and Native American points of resonance in the middle movements of his symphony. Krehbiel had the additional advantage of a visit with the composer, with whom he shared various transcribed excerpts he had chosen to cite. The result was both an exegesis of the new work and an argument for its Americanness. America's own composers had kept their distance from popular American song, whether in the form of "Negro melodies" or—an offshoot—such blackface minstrel favorites as Steven Foster's "Old Folks at Home" and "Camptown Races." Their nascent search for pedigreed credibility predisposed them toward higher musical realms. Dvořák, his credibility assured, had no such compunctions. "Swing Low, Sweet Chariot" stirred his heart; he adored "Old Folks at Home" (and in 1894 would conduct it at Madison Square Garden in his own transcription chorus and orchestra). Krehbiel, in his article, argued that the snappy rhythms and pungent scales of Dvořák's symphony were discernibly American.

Chiefly, however, he recognized and celebrated the symphony's debt to those African-American "treasures of folk music" toward which American "composers and newspaper reviewers" had "long remained indifferent." He further asserted:

> That which is most characteristic, most beautiful and most vital in our folk-song has come from the negro slaves of the South, partly because those slaves lived in the period of emotional, intellectual and social development which produces folk-song, partly because they lived a life that prompted utterance in song and partly because as a race the negroes are musical by nature. Being musical and living a life that had in it romantic elements of pleasure as well as suffering, they gave expression to those elements in songs which reflect their original nature as modified by their American environment. Dr. Dvorak, to whom music is a language, was able quickly to discern the characteristics of the new idiom and recognize its availability and value. He recognized, too, what his critics forgot, that that music is entitled to be called characteristic of a people which gives the greatest pleasure to the largest fraction of a people.

In a lecture at the Woman's University Club, delivered the previous day, Krehbiel amplified these views. America, he said, had no folk songs of its own (a common view at the time). The truest folk music derived from "a genuine naïve disposition" and "expressed the sorrow of a people." In the United States—whose native population was marginalized and suppressed, whose European immigrants were a "hotch-potch" of races whose folk expression lay in the past—these conditions were best met by the Negro.[23]

Though one of the first movement themes in the *New World* Symphony closely resembles "Swing Low," it was the second movement that Dvořák saturated with the affect and inflection of plantation song. This is the Larghetto (subsequently retitled Largo) whose yearning English horn tune he had excitedly played for his pupils, the veins of his neck throbbing red, and which William Arms Fisher would transform into the ersatz spiritual "Goin' Home" after his teacher's death. And it was this movement, at the premiere performance, that was so tumultuously applauded that Dvořák was compelled by the gesturing Anton Seidl to stand nervously erect in his Carnegie Hall box, signaling his gratitude. In fact, the symphony's first and third movements were scarcely applauded less rapturously. "The staidness and decorum of a Philharmonic audience took wings," Krehbiel reported in his review the following day. He also wrote:

> It is not to be imagined that the lovely triumph of the American symphony will close the mouths of the cavilers. It will be easy to say that it is a beautiful

> symphony, but that its character is not distinctively American. . . . Some will say that it is German in its structure, and they will have an easy contention, because the Germans having perfected the symphonic form, and Dr. Dvorak, with all his intense nationalism, being a conservative in this respect, has not deemed it necessary to smash any images in writing this work. . . . All that it is necessary to admit is the one thing for which he has compelled recognition—that there are musical elements in America that lend themselves to beautiful treatment in the higher forms of the art. . . . That [the folk music of black America] is native is proved by the fact that it is congenial to American taste, that it touches the American heart. It did last night, in spite of the conventions which rest upon a Philharmonic audience. The symphony is a beautiful work, worthy of all its predecessors from the pen of Dr. Dvorak, worthy of the aristocratic form in which it is cast, worthy of the American people. If it exerts the influence which it ought the debt which we shall owe to Dr. Dvorak will be incalculable.

W. J. Henderson, who followed Krehbiel's lead in these matters, clinched the point in a clarion *New York Times* review:

> In spite of all assertions to the contrary, the plantation songs of the American negro possess a striking individuality. No mater whence their germs came, they have in their growth been subjected to local influences which have made of them a new species. That species is the direct result of causes climatic and political, but never anything else than American. Our South is ours. Its twin does not exist. Our system of slavery, with all its domestic and racial conditions, was ours, and its twin ever existed. Out of the heart of this slavery, environed by this sweet and languorous South, from the canebrake and the cotton field, arose the spontaneous musical utterance of a people. That folk-music struck an answering note in the American heart. . . . If those songs are not national, then there is no such thing as national music.[24]

Many other facets of Dvořák's symphony proclaim its New World lineage. The opening of the Scherzo is quite obviously a whirling Indian dance with tom-tom accompaniment; the composer revealed to a New York reporter he had in mind the Dance of Pau-Puk-Keewis in Longfellow's *The Song of Hiawatha*. Above all, the unadorned musical space of the Largo evokes wide horizons. Henderson, in his review, here eloquently discovered "an idealized slave song made to fit the impressive quiet of night on the prairie" and also "the melancholy of our Western wastes." At the same time, adhering to a genre begun by Mozart, Haydn, and Beethoven, Dvořák's symphony remains European when scanned with a wider lens. For Seidl, its elegiac cast, a requiem element connecting with Longfellow's vanishing noble savage, conveyed a homesickness for the Old World—to which Dvořák, too, was undeniably susceptible. Of the New York "cavilers" about whom Krehbiel caviled, the most prominent was Huneker, who in the *Musical Courier* stressed that the symphony's "Negro" elements, rather than being cited literally, were "all greatly metamorphosed," adding, not implausibly, that "the American symphony, like the American novel, has yet to be written. And when it is, it will have been composed by an American."[25]

The entire debate was immeasurably intensified two weeks later when the *New World* Symphony was transplanted to the American Athens, where learning, social reform, and public philanthropy were enshrined, and beside which Manhattan was a polyglot bazaar, a melee of finance, commerce, and show business, a cauldron of unchecked immigrant enterprise, recreation, and vice. To demonstrate that New England proposed a different "America" was not part of Dvořák's program, or of Krehbiel's—but was not the least remarkable outcome of their preoccupation with race and national identity. In Boston, "immigrant" meant the Irish, as of 1890 numbering 149,222 out of a total population of 448,477 and a minority world apart. In New York the same year, Germans constituted the largest foreign-born population—211,000 out of 1,515,301*—and a power; a Seidl or Krehbiel, William Steinway or Carl Schurz stood equally dominant inside Deutschtum and without. According to Baedeker's 1893 guide, if children of foreign-born parents were excluded, "probably not more than one-quarter or one-fifth of the inhabitants [of New York City could] be classified as native American";[26] as ever, New York was a city of immigrants. Musical New York, keying on contemporary German thought and aesthetics, was narcotized by Wagner. Musical Boston retained loyalty to Beethoven not as a German master, but as a timeless, placeless universal icon. Preserving a pure musical bloodline transcending Romantic nationalists of more recent, more localized origin, Boston raised art on high; national soil was mere dirt.

For Louis Agassiz, at Harvard, a fixed hierarchy also sorted human types. No less than the World's Columbian Exposition, he ranked people according to color. Popular clubman, bosom friend of James Russell Lowell, father-in-law of Henry Higginson, he had deplored slavery and supported the Union cause. He also taught that blacks and whites evolved at different rates, that racial differences were deeply ingrained, and that racial interbreeding would be biologically catastrophic. Though Agassiz died in 1873, his views continued to feed Social Darwinism and

*This was eight years before greater New York was created with the addition of Brooklyn, the Bronx, Queens, and Staten Island.

anti-immigrant fears. Educated white Americans did not have to believe, as he did, that black Americans were biologically distinct in order to dismiss them as essentially exogenous. John Knowles Paine, the dean of Boston's inbred composers' community and Harvard's first professor of music, responded to Dvořák's espousal of plantation song with this statement to the press: "It is incomprehensible to me how any thoroughly cultivated musician or musical critic can have such limited and erroneous views of the true functions of American composers." George Chadwick, Boston's most performed composer, offered that "such negro melodies as I have heard . . . I should be sorry to see become the basis of an American school of musical composition." Dvořák, in the Boston view, was an uninvited interloper. Rather than the blacks and Indians he championed, he was himself a naïf.[27]

No less than Krehbiel in New York, Boston's central public arbiter of musical taste was typecast for the part. Philip Hale was eighth in line of descent from Thomas Hale, who settled in Massachusetts in or about 1638. He had attended Phillips Exeter Academy, then Yale. He studied music for five years in Germany and France. Tall, elegantly erect, in person and in print he cultivated a manner breezy, courtly, and caustic, his sartorial signature being a loose black silk tie. Ignoring Wagner, he looked to France for what was new in music and discovered Debussy. He shared the French enthusiasm for Rimsky-Korsakov and Borodin. Though he was no Oscar Wilde—he winced at Salome's lust—he supported a moderate aestheticist fringe in the vanguard of local taste.* If Krehbiel the protean German-American Wagnerite was New York personified, Hale's aplomb was buoyed by a cultural community more cohesive and venerable than that of any other American city; he would even ascribe his personal judgments to "Boston."

Hale declared himself "not excited" by the local premiere of the *New World* Symphony by the Boston Symphony Orchestra under Emil Paur on December 29, 1893. But Dvořák's New York reputation exasperated Hale. What excited him, in other words, was less Dvořák than Dvořák's sponsorship. "Mr. Krehbiel is now inclined to believe that at last we really have a great national piece of music," was a typical *Boston Journal* taunt. The symphony itself, in Hale's view, was "delightful music that can be enjoyed by men and women, and children of any or every land." As for its supposed excavation of Americana,

*See pages 221–24.

> Mr. Dvorak began to study native music after his arrival in New York. Unfortunately for the future historian we are not told how he studied it, or whether he disguised himself in his exploration so that the music would not become suspicious, frightened, and then escape. It would be a pleasure to read of his wanderings in the jungles of the Bowery and in the deserts of Central Park. . . . The composer is a modest man, and he has not even hinted at his perilous trips of the Elevated Railway or the Belt Line.
>
> After I read of these adventures . . . I was curious to hear the symphony, this symphony founded on "negro and Indian tunes," i.e., American tunes.
>
> Then I read in other newspapers statements about Dvorak and this symphony, which convinced me that the work could only be appreciated properly by an audience composed exclusively of intelligent negroes and combed and washed Indians.[28]

Hale heard nothing "American" in Dvořák's American symphony. The "Scotch snap" and pentatonic scales that New York writers cited in evidence of American raiment, he pointed out, were not unique to America. "Nor can you expect a Bohemian composer to throw off suddenly his nationality and forget it when he writes." As for Dvořák himself, he was a nationalist innocent imbued with "the spirit of Nature" and "simple and pleasing thoughts." No "struggle with the Infinite" sullied his primitive genius. When on January 1 Boston's Kneisel Quartet premiered Dvořák's Op. 96 String Quartet in F (known today as the *American* Quartet), Hale was again delighted, refreshed, and vexed. "A too frequent use of the pentatonic scale might weary after several hearings," he worried. And he worried about the influence of such music. Reviewing the first performance of Chadwick's Fourth Quartet in E minor (the same key as the *New World*), he (correctly) detected the "negrophile" Dvořák: "There is the thought of the peculiar Scottish-negro-Dvorakian thematic construction, with the suggestion of the plain-song cadences that are so often found in folk-songs. There is the thought of the heel-irritating jig, that is known from the Hebrides to Congo-land. I do not mean to say for a moment that there is any deliberate imitation of Dvorak's later music; but Mr. Chadwick has undoubtedly been influenced in spirit, and I regret this, for he is a big enough man to stand on his own legs and work out his own musical salvation." Other Boston critics "scientifically" used words like "uncivilized" and "barbaric" to describe this new, darker-complexioned chamber music.[29]

Krehbiel ventured to Boston to hear Paur's version of the *New World* for himself and also the F major String Quartet. Krehbiel found Paur's performance "diligent" and "flexible." The work was "not so well played" as in New York. Paur "had evidently taken ample pains in studying it with his band, but he misconceived the tempo of every movement so completely that the work was robbed of half its charm. It reminded one of the dinner at which everything was cold except the ice-cream." Krehbiel continued:

> The [Boston] newspaper critics in their reviews are unanimous in praising the beauty of the music and denying its right to be called American. The sarcastic and scintillant Mr. Philip Hale of "the Boston Journal," in particular makes merry of the term and thinks it wondrously amusing that anything should be called American which has attributes of or elements that are also found among the peoples of the Old World. Much of this kind of talk is mere quibbling. . . .
>
> It has not occurred to The Tribune to claim that with his symphony Dr. Dvorak has founded a national school of composition. The only thing that has been urged in the matter is that he has showed that there are the same possibilities latent in the folk-songs which have grown up in America as in the folk-songs of other peoples. . . . Music is seeking new vehicles of expression, and is seeking them where they are most sure to be found—in the field of folk-song. We have such a field and it is rich. Why not cultivate it? Why these sneers at the only material which lies to our hand? What matters if the man who points out the way be a Bohemian scarcely two years in the country? The peripatetic gypsy is the universal musician, and he makes Hungarian music in Hungary, Spanish music in Spain, Russian music in Russia, and English music in England. . . . It is characteristic of the vagueness which haunts the musical mind, let us say of Boston, in this matter that the fact that the stamp of Dvorak's individuality upon this score is cited as proof that it is not American. It would be pity if so pronounced a personality as Dvorak should conceal himself in a composition, but it would be a greater pity if the idea should prevail that in order to be American a composer must forswear himself, and follow a model which is, as yet, non-existent.[30]

Weeks earlier, on December 16, Krehbiel had written to Dvořák: "I have had no greater happiness from 20 years of labor on behalf of good music than has come to me from the consciousness that I may have been to some degree instrumental in helping the public to appreciate your compositions, and especially this beautiful symphony." Hale was granted no such satisfaction. He was not indifferent to the prospect of an American school of composition. He wrote appreciatively of the songs of Stephen Foster, and of the theater songs and dances of David Braham, as distinctly "American" in flavor. In later years, he similarly endorsed jazz. He compared the Scherzo of the *New World* Symphony with Chadwick's Scherzo in F and found the Chadwick the more American for its "dash, 'smartness,' lack of reverence and general devil-me-care"—and Chadwick's Scherzo does evince a salty

Yankee sensibility an ocean removed from Dvořák. But Hale's central point of contention with Krehbiel was chronic: Negroes and Indians, he believed, sat too low on the evolutionary scale to contribute fundamentally to American identity. He blanched at the notion that black or red Americans could be emblematic or representative Americans. His views aligned with those of white protestant cultural custodians—alienated by "barbarian" nouveaux riches, by Irish politicians and Jewish financiers, by the seeming chaos of urban, industrial America—for whom the universalized Yankee, traceable to a puritan bloodline, limned a quintessential national expression of "Anglo-Saxon" race and character.[31]

Dvořák left the United States in 1895 and died in Prague nine years later. Beginning with "Deep River," in 1916, Harry Burleigh stirred national audiences with concert transcriptions of the slave songs; in this regard, a direct line connects Dvořák and Burleigh with such later exemplars of the concert spiritual as Marian Anderson and Paul Robeson. Dvořák's prophecy that black music would found "the future music of this country" came true—the Boston view that it did not speak to all Americans was proven wrong—but in popular realms he could not have predicted, from Duke Ellington and Louis Armstrong to Gershwin and Elvis Presley.

Krehbiel's admonitions that American composers consciously cultivate an American idiom postdate Dvořák's arrival in New York; earlier, he had more patiently awaited a native school organically evolving from the cosmopolitan orientation of European-trained Americans. Burgeoning folk song research was another aspect of Dvořák's American legacy. Though Krehbiel's contribution is today little remembered by ethnomusicologists, he was in the vanguard, spurred by Dvořák's mission. Again, Krehbiel's major pertinent writings postdate Dvořák's New World sojourn. These include seven meaty *Tribune* articles, replete with musical examples and bibliographies, on the music of Hebrews, Orientals, Russians, Scandinavians, Magyars, African-Americans, and American Indians (all dating from 1899); further *Tribune* pieces on Indian music (1902), Florida song games (1902), and Russian music (1905), and the 155-page *Afro-American Folk-Songs: A Study in Racial and National Music* (1914). By the time he wrote an introduction to Josephine McGill's *Folksongs of the Kentucky Mountains* (1917), Krehbiel could report: "For some years I have talked to a considerable number of clubs, schools, and popular audiences between the Atlantic and the Mississippi River, on the subject of 'Wandering Ballads.' I seldom left a meeting without at least one contribution to my portfolios."

And he had encountered more and more young Americans singing folk songs. "Plainly, folk-song is having a real awakening, and interest in it is no longer to be merely scientific or literary, and confined to the few."

To be sure, Krehbiel's notion that black Americans were inherently "musical" is dated. But his awakening to folk song, with its attention to details of rhythm and mode, was anything but quaint, and—like the New York response to Dvořák generally—confutes conventional wisdom about racial thinking in late nineteenth-century America. Before 1900, a body of "learning" supported the notion of biologically distinct races and a cultural evolutionary scenario favoring Anglo-Saxons. A variety of "civilizing" achievements by Americans, Englishmen, and Germans buttressed the view—oftentimes more generous than snobbish—that these races would lift others toward progress; the innate inferiority of non-Western people was an assumption held by many altruistic observers. To complicate matters, the "under-civilized" primitive was associated with virtues of temperament and style offsetting "overcivilization." Not until the early twentieth century did a nascent anthropology, led by Franz Boas, cast doubt on supposedly immutable racial differences.

Krehbiel stood apart from this muddle. To a degree, his research aligns with the cult of the primitive to be found, for instance, in the confused utterances of a Theodore Roosevelt, who admired the Japanese one day and called Cubans "grasshopper people" the next. And Krehbiel was not immune to assumptions of Anglo-Saxon supremacy. But Brahmin elitists like Hale were alien to his sensibility. Racial rankings did not interest him. An egalitarian spirit of tolerance infuses his researches. His typical advice—as when he urged Jewish composers to explore such synagogue tunes as "Kol nidre" and "An Hamelech"[32]—is disinterested: pure Dvořák (and his scholarly awareness that cantors in Vienna, Paris, and Munich had used "traditional melodies in their settings of Hebrew services" is pure Krehbiel). His conviction that slave songs struck a deeper chord than other indigenous musical strains partly reflects the more belated discovery of Anglo-American folk song. And yet Krehbiel was aware of the Appalachian findings of Cecil Sharp and other collectors in the 1910s. Doubtless he found them less distinctive, more "European" in style. But his continued allegiance to Negro melodies was also an allegiance of the soul.

As late as 1910, Hale could write a Boston Symphony program note for the *New World* Symphony assaulting Krehbiel by name, tracing plantation song to white sources, and maintaining that if music which gives "the greatest pleasure to the largest fraction" is entitled to be called "characteristic" of a people, then "German folksongs are characteristic of the city of New York, and Irish folk-songs are characteristic of the city of Boston."[33] Krehbiel's *Afro-American Folksongs,* four years later, issued no such cavalier broadsides. Rather, it embodies the kind of didactic scholarship that ever absorbed him. As an open source book, it mounts a dignified plea for utilization. As a moral tract, it rebukes as "ungenerous and illiberal" those culture bearers who refused to equate "negro" with "American." Its tenor is scientific. Its substance is heartfelt.*

• • •

The critic Oscar Thompson, who succeeded W.J. Henderson at the *New York Sun* in 1937 (Henderson having moved there from the *Times* in 1902), eulogized Henderson and his generational colleagues as a distinctive "American school of criticism." Singling out Henderson, Krehbiel, Huneker, Richard Aldrich, and Henry Finck in New York, and Boston's Philip Hale, W.F. Apthorp, and H.T. Parker, he observed that they did not "draw opinions" from abroad. And he further discerned an alignment with American newspaper journalism.

Of Henderson, whom he considered "the greatest music critic America has produced," Thompson observed that he "liked to regard himself as first of all a newspaperman; he was a reporter—with a specialty, music."[34] Henderson's other specialties included yachting; his *Elements of Navigation* (1895) was used as a naval training manual during World War I. He had in fact begun at the *Times* not as a critic but as a reporter. Though he was the preeminent American authority on the singer's art, Henderson refused to call himself a "musicologist." Though no less than Krehbiel he insisted on the moral sanctity of culture, and exuded an enthusiasm and love for art that bred disaffection

*A further perspective on Dvořák's American style: he furnishes the nearest musical equivalent of the "American sublime" in American landscape art. The majestic or elegiac panoramas evoked by the *New World* Symphony mesh seamlessly with the canvases of a Sanford Gifford or Frederic Church. And Church and Krehbiel are cognates: heroic practitioners of uplift paradoxically wed to scientific reportage (of precisely categorized flowers and trees; of precisely categorized folk idioms). Their density of detail and of utterance, their combination of intense feeling with intense description and moral prescription are all mutual attributes. That Church's peak fame and influence as America's iconic landscape painter (ca. 1855 to 1870) precedes Krehbiel's period of peak influence is unsurprising: aesthetic movements in the visual arts typically precede musical aesthetics. By the time Dvořák came to the United States, Church was already an old-fashioned painter.

and disdain when hallowed standards seemed unmet, he wore his learning lightly. He cultivated a prose style notably clear, fresh, and plain.

Henry Krehbiel, whom Henderson considered the greatest music critic America had produced, wore his learning not arrogantly or even proudly but matter-of-factly, like a thick coat required by heavy weather. His prose trundled weighty words and thoughts over great distances—its very syntax was German-American—and yet, Henderson testified, "he wrote, as a newspaperman must, swiftly and pregnantly." His indefatigable scholarly energy and high Olympus of learning, whether applied to the history of opera in the United States or the mechanics of Wagnerian music drama, were remote from daily reportage. His surviving notebooks include densely scribbled researches in German and English into musical education in ancient Greece, the "Black Stone of the Mohammedans," the songs of Chief John Buck, ethnic migrations, "Anthropology vs. Philology," prehistoric European civilization, and the hymn quoted by Dvořák in his *Hussite* Overture. And yet Krehbiel the German-American began his journalistic career covering baseball games and murders in Cincinnati. In New York, he initially manned the city desk or wrote editorials. He considered himself a newspaperman—"proud of journalism as a liberal profession," "incessantly jealous of its honor and high standing," according to Aldrich.[35]

Krehbiel's German contemporaries, pondering musical affairs for the papers of Berlin or Munich, were not mobile messengers of daily events. They were professorial, thorough, methodical; their reviews did not run the morning after. Krehbiel, by comparison, was a "professor" and yet an empiricist—an American. He disdained Harvard's Francis James Child, who scanned folk song from his Cambridge armchair. To research cantorial chant, he visited synagogues. To research *Die Meistersinger,* he visited Nuremberg. Like Henderson, who went to Italy to exhume information about certain forgotten castrato singers, he went to Germany not to sit at the foot of foreign authorities, but to discover and report at first hand what he needed to know.

Though Krehbiel's *New York Tribune* was a respectable daily of modest circulation, these were the decades when William Randolph Hearst's *Journal* and Joseph Pulitzer's *World* competed for the most spectacular stories. A special weapon was "yellow journalism"—"the journalism that acts." Yellow journalists might feign insanity to expose conditions in an asylum for the poor, or solve a murder by scrutinizing corpses in a morgue—or, as happened in 1898, start a war by blaming Spain for the explosion of an American warship in Havana harbor. A major player in this colorful chapter of American journalism was James Creelman, who was shot charging a Spanish fort during the Spanish-American War and was visited in the field by Hearst himself who (as reported by Creelman) said, "I'm sorry you're hurt. But wasn't it a splendid fight?" Creelman also had certain private clients, apparently including Jeannette Thurber's National Conservatory of Music. It was almost certainly he who wrote the *Herald* story conveying Dvořák's ringing espousal of "negro melodies"—and who provocatively circulated it for comment in Boston and Vienna. (In Vienna, Anton Bruckner responded, "The basis of all music must be found in the classical works of the past. German musical literature contains no written text emanating from the negro race, and however sweet the negro melodies might be, they can never form the groundwork of the future music of America.")[36]

Krehbiel disapproved of the crudity of the *Herald*'s Dvořák campaign—but was himself a Dvořák campaigner. His notion of the newspaper as arts "patron" was an activist notion. As we have seen: when the Met claimed Wagner no longer made money, he tabulated box office receipts; when he previewed the *New World* Symphony, he met with the composer. Though he doubtless conversed with Dvořák and Anton Seidl in German, he quoted their remarks in the *Tribune* couched in a fluent English neither commanded.

"The power of the press," Krehbiel wrote, "will . . . work for good." The press was not merely activist; it was edifying, uplifting. Even music listeners were to become activists. Subtitled *Hints and Suggestions to Untaught Lovers of the Art,* Krehbiel's *How to Listen to Music* was much used in its day; the printings date from 1896 to 1924. A central source of instruction for generations of American music lovers, its 350 pages enshrine a proud definition of the critic's role: "The first, if not the sole, office of the critic should be to guide public judgment. It is not for him to instruct the musician in his art. . . . He labors to steady and dignify public opinion." To fulfill this "great mission," a "vast responsibility," the critic should be "catholic in taste, outspoken in judgment, unalterable in allegiance to his ideas, unwavering in integrity"—a mentor, that is, in equal measure pragmatic and moral.[37] Central to Krehbiel's sense of high calling as a newsman was his sense of responsibility as a public educator.

The contents of *How to Listen to Music* include key relations, sonata form, the instruments of the orchestra, and the types of opera. A typical piece of Krehbiel advice: "It is not necessary for a listener to follow all the processes of a composer in order to enjoy his music, but if he cultivates the habit of following the principal themes through a work of the higher class he will not only enjoy the pleasures of memory but will frequently get a glimpse into the composer's purposes which will stimulate his imagination and mightily increase his enjoyment." What is more, an ethically endowed criterion of beauty infiltrates Krehbiel's notion of "increased enjoyment." Distinguishing absolute music from program music, he writes that its content, "like that of every noble artistic composition, be it of tones or forms or colors or thoughts expressed in words, is that high ideal of goodness, truthfulness, and beauty for which all lofty imaginations strive." As for program music: "In determining the artistic value of the work, the question goes not to the ingenuity of the programme or the clearness with which its suggestions have been carried out, but to the beauty of the music itself irrespective of the verbal commentary accompanying it. This rule must be maintained in order to prevent a degradation of the object of musical expression. The vile, the ugly, the painful are not fit subjects for music; music renounced, contravenes, negatives itself when it attempts their delineation."

In Beethoven, Krehbiel found "soul-fortifying aspiration." In Liszt, he ambivalently experienced "a laxity of moral ideas" blended with "a profound religious mysticism." Chamber music was "chaste"; in a small room, it attained "angelic wedlock." Summarizing the highest effects of music on the non-musician, Krehbiel produced a claim that, however startling, retains plausibility: "The capacity properly to listen to music is better proof of musical talent in the listener than skill to play upon an instrument or ability to sing acceptably when unaccompanied by that capacity. It makes more for that gentleness and refinement of emotion, thought, and action which, in the highest sense of the term, it is the province of music to promote. And it is a much rarer accomplishment."

Krehbiel believed that the special intensities of American life demanded special compensatory guidance:

> We are engaged in conquering a continent; employed in a mad scramble for material things; we give feverish hours to win the comfort of our bodies that we take only seconds to enjoy; the moments which we steal from our labors we give grudgingly to relaxation, and that this relaxation may come quickly we ask that the agents which produce it shall appeal violently to the faculties which are most easily reached. Under these circumstances whence are to come the intellectual poise, the refined taste, the quick and sure power of analysis which must precede a correct estimate of the value of a composition or its performance?

At the same time, Krehbiel characteristically hugged American aptitudes and achievement. Informed by close acquaintance with the massive choral exercises of Cincinnati's May Festival, his chapter on "Choirs and Choral Music" is a veritable New World paean. Here is the avenue of praxis most accessible to the novice, a democratic performance genre "of necessity unselfish and creative of sympathy." In fact, "amateur choir-singing is no older anywhere than in the United States. . . . A little reflection will show this fact, which seems somewhat startling at first blush, to be entirely natural. Large singing societies are of necessity made up of amateurs, and the want of professional musicians in America compelled the people to enlist amateurs at a time when in Europe choral activity rested on the church, theatre, and institute choristers, who were practically professionals." There follows (of course) a learned chronology of singing societies in Germany and the United States.[38]

Krehbiel's eagerness to educate new listeners is egalitarian, democratic, American. At the same time, Krehbiel the German-American packs his pedagogy with recondite asides. His etymological acumen compels an utterly characteristic detour when introducing "chamber music," tracing Musica da Camera, Musique de Chambre, and Kammermusik to a common Greek root signifying an arch, a vaulted room, or a covered wagon. "In the time of the Frankish kings the word was applied to the room in the royal palace in which the monarch's private property was kept, and in which he looked after his private affairs. When royalty took up the cultivation of music it was as a private, not as a court, function." But what chiefly shades Krehbiel's teachings with an Old Worldly gravitas is his mistrust of the very vox populi he labors of edify. Post-Krehbiel, "music appreciation" would cheerfully assure newcomers to art that no specialized knowledge was needed. Olin Downes, who became chief music critic at the *New York Times* in 1924, vigorously exhorted listeners to "be your own music critic"—and the more converts, the better.[39]

Krehbiel did not smile or exhort. His primer was not intended for "careless seekers of diversion." "Of all the arts, music is practiced most and thought about least." The "majority of the hearers in our concert-rooms" disclose a "pitiful and anomalous" spectacle of ignorance. "It is not an exaggeration to say that one might listen for a lifetime to the polite conversation of our drawing-rooms . . . without hearing a symphony talked about in terms indicative of more than the most superficial knowledge of the outward form . . . of such a composition." Undertaking corrective instruction, Krehbiel "is willing to seem unamiable to the amateur while arguing the need of even so mild a stimulant as the book at hand. Though ideally the musician, the critic, and the public labor harmoniously," in reality the critic is locked in "irrepressible conflict" with the concert artist who reads the newspaper "with heart-burns," and with the lay listener who remains "indifferent," if not "ignorant." This reality is not a predicament, merely a condition. The critic's role is to stand his ground, keen of knowledge, lofty of purpose. He is "the Ishmaelite whose hand is raised against everybody and against whom everybody's hand is raised." He is "placed between two millstones, where he is vigorously rasped on both sides, and whence, being angular and hard of outer shell, he frequently requites the treatment received with complete and energetic reciprocity."[40]

Krehbiel charts a dialectic between elitist learning and democratic impulse. Another perspective on his German-American duality—as professor and newspaperman, scholar and remedial educator—is furnished by the only comparably popular classical-music primer of the period: *What Is Good Music?—Suggestions to Persons Desiring to Cultivate a taste in Musical Art* (1898), by W.J. Henderson (to whom Krehbiel's *How to Listen* is dedicated). Henderson's agenda is the same, but his tone is not: "The person who desires to cultivate a discriminating taste in music may acquire the fundamental knowledge in a few short months. After that, one needs only to live much in an atmosphere of good music until the acquired principles become unconsciously the moving factors underlying all attention to the art." Whereas Krehbiel surveys "the majority of the hearers in our concert-rooms" and groans, "they are there to adventure a journey into a realm whose beauties do not disclose themselves to the senses alone, but whose perception requires a cooperation of all the finer faculties; yet of this they seem to know nothing, and even of that sense to which the first appeal is made it may be said with profound truth that 'hearing they hear not, neither do they understand.'" They must come to him, must scale the high citadel of culture.[41]

. . .

German-American, too, was the labor of love of Krehbiel's late career—the first English-language edition of *The Life of Beethoven* by the American music historian Alexander Wheelock Thayer (1817–1897), a monumental biography still read and consulted (albeit as revised by Elliott Forbes in 1964), and which Krehbiel considered "the most extraordinary of all books dealing with the lives of musical composers." For Krehbiel, Beethoven's preeminence was sealed by his politics; he was "the first great democrat among musicians."[42] Thayer completed the first three of four projected volumes. Adding his own volume four, Krehbiel's 1925 edition (for which he asked and received no compensation; notwithstanding his eminence, Krehbiel was never a wealthy man) numbered 1,137 pages.

The retrospective direction of this effort, following Krehbiel's earlier immersion in more recent German and American developments, is significant: the older he got, the more he grew estranged from the present day. He was alienated by the course of music after Wagner; by Mahler, Strauss, and Debussy (not to mention Schoenberg and Stravinsky). The institutional culture of music equally offended him: even in dignified journals, he complained in 1919, "the gossip of the foyer and the dressing rooms" stood "in high esteem"; "photo-engraving, illustrated supplements, and press agents"—with whom Krehbiel, as was well known, refused to deal—had corrupted the taste of audiences and readers.[43]

In Krehbiel's judgment, the fate of Metropolitan Opera embodied this transformation. Following the demise of Seidl's German seasons, and a period of confusion, the house righted itself under the management of Maurice Grau; this was the Met's "Golden Age" of performances in Italian, German, and French purveyed by a prodigious international ensemble. But with Grau's retirement in 1903, the company was entrusted to the Austrian actor/impresario Heinrich Conried, who, as one wag put it, "knew no more about opera than the ordinary chauffeur knows about airplanes." Notwithstanding two decades of distinguished service at the Irving Place Theatre, with its world-class German company, Conried at the Met was notorious for his gaucherie and quick-buck artistry. For Krehbiel, the Conried spectacle was of "the fruits of wise endeavour and astute management" being "frittered away by managerial incapacity and greed," Conried's greediest move being to pack Enrico Caruso on stage as frequently as possible. But, as Krehbiel observed, within a few seasons it grew difficult "to keep the Caruso cult on its old hysterical plane." Conried now resorted to controversy and scandal to fill the house. Already in 1903, he had defied Cosima Wagner by staging *Parsifal,* which the Wagner family intended to reserve for the special conditions of Bayreuth. These performances earned Conried a handsome profit. The new regime's boldest and most provocative initiative, however, was the 1907 American premiere of Richard Strauss's *Salome:* an event frankly calculated to raise curiosity and anxiety to a fever pitch.[44]

Though *Salome* strikes twenty-first-century ears as a "late Romantic" effusion, early twentieth-century ears heard something different: a radical modernism packed with directionless dissonance and a riot of screaming and tingling new sounds. And what early twentieth-century eyes saw was at least as lurid. Strauss had set, verbatim, the morbid and flamboyant language of Oscar Wilde's play (as translated into German by Hedwig Lachmann), with its singular plot. Herod's teenage stepdaughter covets the crazed prophet Jochanaan. When she petulantly refuses to dance for him, Herod promises whatever prize she wants. Her dance is a striptease, shedding seven veils. She demands Jochanaan's head on a silver salver. Ecstatically, she kisses the dead lips of the prophet: a demented Liebestod. "Kill that woman!" Herod shrieks at his soldiers, and they comply.

Wilde's play was banned in England, but Lachmann's German version succeeded in Germany. Strauss's adaptation earned thirty-eight curtain calls at its 1905 premiere, in Dresden, after which it was swiftly taken up in many countries—but not England or the United States. Conried tested the *Salome* waters at a "public rehearsal" on January 20, 1907, and a benefit performance on January 22. Many in the audience fled at the beginning of the final scene. Of those who stayed to see Salome kiss the severed head, a minority offered brief and scattered applause. "The effect of horror was pronounced," a *Tribune* news story reported the next day. "Many faces were white almost as those at the rail of a ship. Many women were silent, and men spoke as if a bad dream were on them." Five days after that, the board of directors declared *Salome* "objectionable and detrimental to the best interests of the Metropolitan Opera House." It was not again seen at the Met until 1934.*

Krehbiel's four-thousand-word account of the debacle in the January 23 *Tribune*—three unillustrated columns of tiny type—calibrates the nature and magnitude of this challenge to reigning notions of art with exhaustive patience; the paragraphs average over four hundred words, the sentences more than thirty. In less leisurely times to come, no newspaper writer would attempt such density of utterance. And yet, as so often, his account resists compression; it must be sampled at something like its full length to glean the freight-train mass of Henry Edward Krehbiel at open throttle:

> A reviewer ought to be equipped with a dual nature, both intellectually and morally, in order to pronounce fully and fairly upon the qualities of this drama by Oscar Wilde and Richard Strauss. He should be an embodied con-

*But Oscar Hammerstein successfully presented *Salome* (in French with Mary Garden) at his Manhattan Opera in 1909.

science stung into righteous fury by the moral stench exhaled by the decadent and pestiferous work, but, though it make him retch, he should be sufficiently judicial in his temperament calmly to look at the drama in all its aspects and determine whether or not as a whole it is an instructive note on the life and culture of the times and whether or not this exudation from the diseased and polluted will and imagination of the authors marks a real advance in artistic expression, irrespective of its contents or their fitness for dramatic representation. This is asking much of the harassed commentator on the things which the multitude of his readers receive as contributions to their diversion merely and permit to be crowded out of their minds by the next pleasant or unpleasant shock to their sensibilities. He has not the time, nor have his readers the patience, to enter upon a discussion of the questions of moral and esthetic principle which ought to pave the way for the investigation. If he can tell what the play is, what its musical investiture is like, wherein the combined elements have worked harmoniously and efficiently to an end which to their authors seemed artistic, and therefore justifiable, he will have done much. In the case before us even this much cannot be done until some notions which have long had validity are put aside. We are only concerned with "Salome" in its newest form,—that given it by the musical composer. If it shall ever win approbation here, as it seems to have done in several German cities, it will be because of the shape into which Richard Strauss has moulded it.

Several attempts had been made to habilitate Oscar Wilde's drama on the New York stage, and had failed. If the opera succeeds it will be because a larger public has discovered that the music which has been consorted with the old pictures, actions, and words has added to them an element either of charm or expressive potentiality hitherto felt to be lacking. Is that true? Has a rock of offense been removed? Has a mephitic odor been changed to a sweet savor by the subtle alchemy of the musical composer? Has a drama abhorrent, bestial, repellent, and loathsome been changed into a thing of delectability by the potent agency of music? It used to be said that things too silly to be spoken might be sung; is it also true that things too vile, too foul, too nauseating for contemplation may be seen, so they be insidiously and wickedly glorified by the musician's art? As a rule, plays have not been improved by being turned into operas. Always their dramatic movement has been interrupted, their emotional current clogged, their poetry emasculated by the transformation. Things are better now than they were in the long ago, when music took no part at all in dramatic action, but waited for a mood which it had power to publish and celebrate; but music has acquired its new power only by an abnegation of its better part, by assuming new functions, and asking a revaluation of its elements on a new esthetic basis. In "Salome" music is largely a decorative element, like the scene,—like the costumes. It creates atmosphere, like the affected stylism of much of Oscar Wilde's text, with its Oriental imagery borrowed from "The Song of Solomon," diluted and sophisticated; it gives emotional significance to situations, helping the facial play of Salome and her gestures to proclaim the workings of her mind, when speech has deserted her; it is at its best as the adjunct and inspiration of the lascivious dance. In the last two instances, however, it reverts to the purpose and also the manner (with a difference) which have always obtained, and becomes music in the purer sense. Then the would-be dramatist is swallowed up in the symphonist, and Strauss is again the master magician who can juggle with our senses and our reason and make his instrumental voices body forth "the forms of things unknown."

It would be wholly justifiable to characterize "Salome" as a symphonic poem for which the play supplies the program. The parallelism of which we hear between Strauss and Wagner exists only in part—only in the application of the principles of characterization by means of musical symbols or typical phrases. Otherwise the men work on diametrically opposite lines. With all his musical affluence, Wagner aimed, at least, to make his orchestra only the bearer and servant of the dramatic word. Nothing can be plainer (it did not need that he should himself have confessed it) than that Strauss looks upon the words as necessary evils. His vocal parts are not song, except for brief, intensified spaces at long intervals. They are declamation. The song-voice is used, one is prone to think, only because by means of it the words can be made to be heard above the orchestra. Song, in the old acceptance of the word, implies beauty of tone and justness of intonation. It is amazing how indifferent the listener is to vocal quality and intervallic accuracy in "Salome." Wilde's stylistic efforts are lost in the flood of instrumental sound; only the mood which they were designed to produce remains. Jochanaan sings phrases, which are frequently tuneful, and when they are not denunciatory are set in harmonies agreeable to the ear. But by reason of that fact Jochanaan comes perilously near being an old-fashioned operatic figure—an ascetic Marcel, with little else to differentiate him from his Meyerbeerian prototype than his "raiment of camel's hair and a leathern girdle about his loins," and an inflated phrase which must serve for the tunes sung by the rugged Huguenot soldier. Strauss characterizes by his vocal manner as well as by his themes and their instrumental treatment; but for his success he relies at least as much upon the performer as upon the musical text. A voice and style like Mr. [Anton] Van Rooy's give an uplift, a prophetic breadth, dignity, and impressiveness to the utterances of Jochanaan which are paralleled only by the imposing instrumental apparatus employed in proclaiming the phrase invented to clothe his pronouncements. Six horns, used as Strauss knows how to use them, are a good substratum for the arch-colorist. The nervous staccato chatter of Herod is certainly characteristic of this neurasthenic. This specimen from the pathological museum of Messrs. Wilde and Strauss appears in a state which causes alarm lest his internal mechanism fly asunder and scatter his corporeal parts about the scene. The crepitating volubility with which Strauss endows him is a marvelously ingenious conceit; but it leans heavily for its effect, we fear, on the amazing skill of Mr. [Karl] Burrian, not only in cackling out the words synchronously with the orchestral part, but in emotionally coloring them and blending them in a unity with his facial expression and his perturbed bodily movements. Salome sings, often in the explosive style of Wagner's Kundry, sometimes with something like fluent continuity, but from her song has been withheld all the symmetrical and graceful contours comprehended in the concept of melody. Hers are the superheated phrases invented to give expression to her passion, and out of them she must construct the vocal accompaniment to the instrumental song, which reaches its culmination in the scene which, instead of receiving a tonal beatification, as it does, ought to be relegated to the silence and darkness of the deepest dungeon of a madhouse or a hospital.

Here is a matter, of the profoundest esthetical and ethical significance, which might as well be disposed of now, so far as this discussion is concerned, regardless of the symmetrical continuity of the argument. There is a vast deal of ugly music in "Salome"—music that offends the ear and rasps the nerves like fiddle strings played on by a coarse file. In a criticism of Strauss's "Symphonia Domestica," I took occasion to point out that a large latitude must be allowed to the dramatic composer which must be denied to the symphonist. Consort a dramatic or even a lyric text with music and all manner of tonal devices may derive explanation, if not justification, from the words. But in purely instrumental music the arbitrary purposes of a composer cannot replace the significance which must lie in the music itself—that is, in its emotional and esthetic content. It does not lie in intellectual content, for thought to become articulate demands speech. The champions of Richard Strauss have defended ugliness in his last symphony, the work which immediately preceded "Salome," and his symphonic poems on the score that music must be an expression of truth, and truth is not always beautiful. In a happier day than this it was believed that the true and the beautiful were bound together in angelic wedlock and that all art found its highest mission in giving them expression. But the drama has been led through devious paths into the charnel house, and in "Salome" we must needs listen to the echoes of its dazed and drunken footfalls. The maxim "Truth before convention" asserts its validity and demands recognition under the guise of "characteristic beauty." We may refuse to admit that ugliness is entitled to be raised to a valid principle in music dissociated from words or stage pictures, on the ground that thereby it contravenes and contradicts its own nature; but we may no longer do so when it surrenders its function as an expression of the beautiful and becomes merely an illustrative element, as aid to dramatic expression. What shall be said, then, when music adorns itself with its loveliest attributes and lends them to the apotheosis of that which is indescribably, yea, inconceivably, gross and abominable? Music cannot lie. Not even the genius of Richard Strauss can make it discriminate in its soaring ecstasy between a vile object and a good. There are three supremely beautiful musical moments in "Salome." Two of them are purely instrumental, though they illustrate dramatic incidents; the third is predominantly instrumental, though it has an accompaniment of word and action. The first is an intermezzo in which all action ceases except that which plays in the bestially perverted heart and mind of Salome. A baffled amorous hunger changes to a desire for revenge. The second is the music of the dance. The third is the marvelous finale, in which an impulse which can only be conceived as rising from the uttermost pit of degradation is beautified. Crouching over the dissevered head of the prophet, Salome addresses it in terms of reproach, of grief, of endearment and longing, and finally kisses the bloody lips and presses her teeth into the gelid flesh. It is incredible that an artist should ever have conceived such a scene for public presentation. In all the centuries in which the story of the dance before Herod has fascinated sculptors, painters, and poets, in spite of the accretions of lustful incident upon the simple Biblical story, it remained for a poet of our day to conceive this horror and a musician of our day to put forth his highest powers in its celebration. There was a scene before the mental eye of Strauss as he wrote. It was that of Isolde singing out her life over the dead body of Tristan. In the music of that scene, I do not hesitate to say again, as I have said before, there lies the most powerful plea ever made for the guilty lovers. It is the choicest flower of Wagner's creative faculty, the culmination of his powers as a composer, and never before or since has the purifying and ennobling capacity of music been so convincingly demonstrated. Strauss has striven to outdo it, and there are those who think that in this episode he actually raised music to a higher power. He has not only gone with the dramatist and outraged every sacred instinct of humanity by calling the lust for flesh, alive or dead, love, but he has celebrated her ghoulish passion as if he would perforce make of her an object of that "redemption" of which, again following Wagner but along oblique paths, he prates so strangely in his opera of "Guntram" [1894].

It is obvious on a moment's reflection that, had Strauss desired, the play might easily have been modified so as to avoid this gruesome episode. A woman scorned, vengeful and penitent would have furnished forth material enough for his finale and dismissed his audience with less disturbance of their moral and physical stomachs. But Strauss, to put it mildly, is a sensationalist despite his genius, and his business sense is large, as New Yorkers know ever since he wound up an artistic tour of America with a concert in a department store.* When Nietzsche was the talk of Germany we got "Also Sprach Zarathustra." Oscar Wilde's play, too unsavory for the France for which it was written, taboo in England because of its subject, has been joyously acclaimed in Germany, where there are many men who are theoretically licentious and practically uxorious; and Strauss was willing that his countrymen should sup to their full of delights and horrors.

To think back, under the impressions of the final scene, to the dance which precipitated the catastrophe is to bring up recollections of little else than the striking originality of its music, its piquancies of rhythm and orchestration, its artfully simulated Orientalism, and the thrilling effect produced by a recurrence to the "love music" ("Let me kiss thy mouth, Jochanaan,") at a moment before the frenetic close, when the presentation of Salome (a professional dancer, Miss Froelich, was deftly substitute for Miss [Olive] Fremstad at the Metropolitan performance) approaches the cistern in which the white flesh, black hair, and red lips of her idolatry are immured, and casts wistful glances into its depths. Since the outcome was to be what it became it would have been folly in Mr. Conried's performance to attempt to disguise

*Strauss gave two afternoon concerts at Wanamakers; he was paid one thousand dollars.

the true character of the "Dance of the Seven Veils." Miss Froelich gave us quite unconcernedly a danse du ventre; not quite so pronounced as it has been seen in the Oriental quarters at our world's fairs, not quite so free of bodily covering as tradition would have justified. Yet it served to emphasize its purpose in the play. This dance in its original estate is a dramatic dance; it is, indeed, the frankest example of terpsichorean symbolism within the whole range of the pantomimic dance. The conditions under which Wilde and Strauss introduce it in their drama spare one all need of thought; there is sufficient commentary in the doddering debility of the pleading Herod and the lustful attitude of his protruding eyes. There are fantastical persons who like to talk about religious symbolism in connection with this dance, and of forms of worship of vast antiquity. The dance is old. It was probably danced in Egypt before the Exodus; in Greece probably before Orpheus sang and

"Ilion, like a mist, rose into towers."

But it is not to be seriously thought that from those days to this there was ever any doubt as to its significance and its purpose, which is to pander to prurient appetites and arouse libidinous passions. Always, too, from those days to this, its performers have been the most abandoned of the courtesan class.

There is not a whiff of fresh and healthy air blowing through "Salome" except that which exhales from the cistern, the prison house of Jochanaan. Even the love of Narraboth, the young Syrian captain, for the princess is tainted by the jealous outbursts of Herodias's page. Salome is the unspeakable; Herodias, though divested of her most pronounced historical attributes (she adjures her daughter not to dance, though she gloats over the revenge which it brings to her), is a human hyena; Herod, a neurasthenic voluptuary. A group of Jews who are shown disputing in the manner of Baxter Street, though conveyed by Wilde from Flaubert's pages, are used by Strauss to provide a comic interlude. Years ago a musical humorist in Vienna caused much amusement by writing the words of a quarrel of Jewish peddlers under the voices of the fugue of Mozart's overture to "The Magic Flute." Three hundred years ago Orazio Vecchi composed a burlesque madrigal in the severe style of that day, in which he tried to depict the babel of sounds in a synagogue. Obviously the musical Jew is supposed to be allied to the stage Jew and to be fit food for the humorist. Strauss's music gives a new reading to Wilde; it is a caricature in which cacophony reigns supreme under the guise of polyphony. There are five of the Jews, and each is pregnantly set forth in the theme with which he maintains his contention.

This is but one of many instances of a marvelous astuteness in the delineation and characteristic portions of the music. The quality which will be most promptly recognized by the public is its decorative and illustrative element. The orchestra paints incessantly; moods that are prevalent for a moment do not suffice the eager illustrator. The passing word seizes his fancy. Herod describes the jewels which he promises to give to Salome so she relieve him of his oath, and the music of the orchestra glints and glistens with a hundred prismatic tints. Salome wheedles the young Syrian to bring forth the prophet, and her cry, "Thou wilt do this thing for me," is carried to his love-made brain by a voluptuous glissando of the harp which is as irresistible as her glance and smile. But the voluptuous music is not more striking than the tragic. Strauss strikes off the head of Jochanaan with more thunderous noise upon the kettle-drums than Wagner uses when Fafner pounds the life out of Fasolt with his gigantic stave; but there is nothing in all of Wagner's tragic pages to compare in tenseness of feeling with the moment of suspense while Salome is peering into the cistern and marveling that she hears no sound of a death struggle. At this moment there comes an uncanny sound from the orchestra that is positively blood-curdling. The multitude of instruments are silent—all but the string basses. Some of them maintain a tremolo on the deep E flat. Suddenly there comes a short, high B flat. Again and again with more rapid iteration. Such a voice was never heard in the orchestra before. What Strauss designed it to express does not matter. It accomplishes a fearful accentuation of the awful situation. Strauss got the hint from Berlioz, who never used the device (which he heard from a Piedmontese double-bass player), recommended it to composers who wished to imitate in the orchestra "a loud female cry." Strauss in his score describes how the effect is to be produced and wants it to sound like a stertorous groan. It is produced by pinching the highest string of the double-bass at the proper node between the finger-board and the bridge and sounding it by a quick jerk of the bow. This is but one of a hundred new and strange devices with which the score of "Salome" has enriched instrumental music. The dance employs a vast apparatus, but the Oriental color impressed upon it at the outside by oboe and tambour remains as persistent as its rhythmical figure, which seems to have been invented to mark the sinuous flexure of the spine and the swaying of the hips of the dancer. Devices made familiar by the symphonic poems are introduced with increased effect, such as the muting of the entire army of brass instruments. Startling effects are obtained by a confusion of keys, confusion of rhythms, sudden contrasts from an overpowering tutti to the stridulous whirring of empty fifths on the violins, a trill on the flutes, or a dissonant mutter of the basses. The celesta, an instrument with keyboard and bell tone, contributes fascinating effects, and the xylophone is used;—utterances that are lascivious as well as others that are macabre. Dissonance runs riot and frequently carries the imagination away completely captive. The score is unquestionably the greatest triumph of reflection and ingenuity of contrivance that the literature of music can show. The invention that has been expended on the themes seems less admirable. . . . There is no escape from the power of the music when it soars to grandiose heights in the duet between Salome and the prophet, the subsequent intermezzo and the wicked apotheosis. It overwhelms the senses and reduces the nervous system of the listeners to exhaustion. . . .

[As Salome,] Mme. Fremstad accomplished a miracle. A sleek tigress, with seduction speaking in every pose, gesture, look and utterance, she grew steadily into the monster which she was when she sank under the shields of the soldiers while the orchestra shrieked its final horror and left the listeners staring at each other with starting eyeballs and wrecked nerves.

The first thing to command attention in this masterpiece of opprobrium is its descriptive aplomb; Krehbiel's disgust does not deafen his capacity to appreciate the score's sonic amazements. Secondly: even in the throes of turbulent distemper he retains the coolness of judgment to discern the pabulum of Jochanaan's stentorian phrases. As for the question, "Is it art?": Krehbiel renders no final verdict—he appoints his readership the jury. Evidence is offered that Strauss is a meretricious "sensationalist," that his "business sense is large." In the *Grove Dictionary of Music and Musicians* (2001), the music historian David Murray observes of Strauss and *Salome:* "It is unlikely that he pondered over the 'morality' of the piece; he simply turned it into an opera, with acute faithfulness and all the professional resource which had been awaiting such an opportunity. . . . Strauss was less concerned to fathom any 'deeper meaning' it might have than to exploit its operatic potential." These are Krehbiel's points—and he is unforgiving.

. . .

In December 1907—less than a year after the premiere of *Salome*—musical New York greeted another controversial visitor from twentieth-century Europe. This was Gustav Mahler from Vienna: a city whose fin-de-siècle throes dwarfed the challenging erotic and intellectual turbulence of American Wagnerism. For Vienna, new music was Mahler and Arnold Schoenberg, new art Gustav Klimt and Egon Schiele. Sigmund Freud, riddled with fears and phobias, was excavating his dreams. And Mahler himself—as the embattled reformist director of the Vienna Opera beginning in 1897, as the composer of vast symphonic trajectories striving for pious reverie amid droll jokes and sinister asides—was a Janus in turmoil, bent in homage to Beethoven yet revered as prophet of the new by Schoenberg and his progeny. It was Heinrich Conried who lured Mahler to New York with a salary offer he could not refuse. At Conried's Met, he encountered casts superior to Vienna's, an acceptable orchestra, and laughably old-fashioned stagings he at once set out to transform. The excitement with which he was greeted was equaled by the acclaim for his first assignment: *Tristan und Isolde,* on January 1, 1908. Krehbiel wrote: "It was easy to recognize in Mr. Mahler's work last night that he is a master of his art."

Mahler's own eager first New World impressions are informative. To Adolf Roller, whose Secessionist designs had famously refreshed Vienna's *Tristan* and *Fidelio,* he confided: "The audiences here, and all the factors affecting the artist . . . in contrast with 'our people' in Vienna

[are] unsophisticated, hungry for novelty, and in the highest degree eager to learn. . . . Only one thing is respected here: ability and drive!"[45]

When Mahler found himself displaced at the Met by an Italian juggernaut led by Giulio Gatti-Casazza and his ferocious colleague Arturo Toscanini, he wound up in 1909 at the helm of a musical organization far smaller and less established: the New York Philharmonic. A group of millionaires had just taken over, resolute to challenge the symphonic standards of Boston and Chicago. These "guarantors," headed by Mrs. George R. Sheldon, expanded the season from eighteen to forty-six concerts and arranged for the orchestra's first tour. Mahler had never known such unwanted supervision as they would provide. As Alma later put it, "in Vienna my husband was all powerful. Even the Emperor did not dictate to him, but in New York, to his amazement, he had ten ladies ordering him like a puppet."[46]

Mahler's relationship with Henry Krehbiel proved equally onerous. Krehbiel, too, was accustomed to perquisites of power and respect. Seidl had honored him with his friendship. Dvořák had accepted his counsel. Mahler asked nothing of Krehbiel; he had his own agenda. "It will be my aim to educate the public," he told a reporter, "and that education will be made gradually and in a manner which will enable those who may not now have a taste for the best later to appreciate it." If such a plan seemed patronizing, Krehbiel answered in kind. Of Mahler's version of Beethoven's Fifth, in December 1909, he reported that Mahler "phlebotomized" the first movement's mini-cadenza for solo oboe (which normally invites a free play of expressive nuance) "by giving it to two oboes and beating time for each note . . . in a rigid andante." He further complained: "Into the cadence of the second subject of the third movement, Mr. Mahler injected a bit of un-Beethovenian color by changing the horn part so that listeners familiar with their Wagner were startled by hearing something very like Hagen's call from 'Götterdämmerung.'"[47]

For Mahler the composer, the differences between modern instruments and those of Beethoven's day dictated rescorings. Aesthetically, too, Mahler was a creature of his Vienna, not Beethoven's. His readings of nineteenth-century repertoire abounded in the sudden dynamics, edgy phrasings, and biting staccatos of his own symphonies, whose complex narratives intermingled Romantic uplift and modernist despair. Krehbiel had no use for such music. Its signature mixture of celestial and quotidian strains ("some of them borrowed without acknowledgement"), its "extravagant" elaboration of "melodic ideas of the folksong order" offended his understanding of rarified art. When in December 1909 Mahler as conductor of the Philharmonic programmed his own First Symphony, Krehbiel as annotator of the Philharmonic requested permission to reprint a letter in which Mahler explicated certain programmatic elements in the work. Mahler responded by prohibiting Krehbiel from writing anything at all. For the Philharmonic program book, Krehbiel in fact wrote:

> In deference to the wish of Mr. Mahler, the annotator of the Philharmonic Society's programmes refrains from even an outline analysis of the symphony which he is performing for the first time in New York on this occasion, as also from an attempt to suggest what might be or has been set forth as its possible poetical, dramatic, or emotional contents. . . . Mr. Mahler's conviction, frequently expressed publicly as well as privately, is that it is a hindrance to appreciation to read an analysis which with the help of musical examples lays bare the contents and structure of a composition while it is playing. . . . All writings about music, even those of musicians themselves, he holds to be injurious to musical enjoyment.

Reviewing the performance, Krehbiel had this to say:

> There is abundant evidence in Mr. Mahler's compositions that in constructing them he follows extra-musical suggestions. The [first] symphony has no justification without a programme. . . . More than the public the composer would have benefited had he told what train of thought, or sequence of emotions, he conceived to be at the basis of his symphony. It was not dignified by being left to make its appeal unaided; it would have not been degraded had an extra-musical purpose been ascribed to it. . . . Mr. Mahler's refusal to take advantage of his opportunity presents him in the light of a composer convinced that his music carries its own message; it compelled a multitude of his hearers to wonder what he bases his conviction upon.

In the symphony's noisy finale, Krehbiel added, Mahler disclosed himself "a prophet of the ugly."*[48]

By summer 1910, Mahler was in conflict with the guarantors over his salary. The following season, the guarantors formed a program committee to supervise repertoire. Mahler had arrived in New York with a heart condition. His health now greatly deteriorated. A themed "Italian" program on February 2, 1911, proved his final Philharmonic concert.

*W. J. Henderson, reviewing Mahler's First, wrote of the finale: "The conclusion of the movement reverts to the manner of its beginning . . . and suggests that when the weather is bad in Tyrol it is beyond the powers of language to characterize" (*New York Sun,* Dec. 19, 1909).

His death in Vienna, on May 18, provoked the most notorious fulmination of Krehbiel's long career, a fifty-inch obituary beginning:

> Gustav Mahler is dead, and his death was made to appear in some newspaper accounts as the tragic conclusion of unhappy experience in New York. . . . He was paid a sum of money which ought to have seemed to him fabulous from the day on which he came till the day when his labors ended, and the money was given to him ungrudgingly, though the investment was a poor one for the opera company which brought him to America and the concert organization which kept him here. He was looked upon as a great artist, and possibly he was one, but he failed to convince the people of New York of the fact, and therefore his American career was not a success.

Krehbiel's precepts included:

> It is a fatuous notion of foreigners that Americans know nothing about music in its highest forms. Only of late years have the European newspapers begun to inform their readers that the opera in New York has some significance. Had their writers on music been students they would have known that for nearly a century New Yorkers have listened to singers of the highest class—singers that the people of the musical centers of the European continent were never permitted to hear. Mr. Mahler . . . never discovered that there were Philharmonic subscribers who had inherited not only their seats from their parents and grandparents, but also their appreciation of good music. He never knew, or if he knew he was never willing to acknowledge, that the Philharmonic audience would be as quick to resent an outrage on the musical classics as a corruption of the Bible or Shakespeare. He did not know that he was doing it, or if he did he was willing wantonly to insult their intelligence and taste by such things as multiplying the voices in a Beethoven symphony.[49]

The Mahler-Krehbiel feud documents arrogance mutually unmasked. Krehbiel's "vanity as big as his body," of which Henry Finck complained, is here on naked display. Mahler's vanity was of a different variety: a self-absorption in new surroundings indistinguishable from hubris.

In an open letter to "the music critic of the *New York Tribune,*" the pianist Ossip Gabrilowitsch wrote: "No *critic* would be so eager to throw a pail of mud on a fresh grave. Only an enemy would do that."*[50] That Krehbiel treated Mahler as an enemy may be traced to two others who had treated Krehbiel as a friend. Dvořák had characteristically assisted

*Henry Finck, who would have known, later commented: "No doubt, Krehbiel felt he had gone too far. He did not resent the polemics of the young Russian pianist, but continued to treat him fairly, on his merits." Finck, *My Adventures in the Golden Age of Music* (1926), p. 192.

him in preparing a preview of the *New World* Symphony. Seidl had characteristically invited him to witness an intimate *Götterdämmerung* rehearsal with Albert Niemann. Krehbiel acknowledged Dvořák and Seidl as supreme Old World authorities—and they offered respect and interest toward Americans in return. Mahler, who was known to have engaged a member of the Philharmonic to spy on his colleagues for evidence of disloyalty to the embattled conductor, was as vulnerable and mercurial as Seidl had seemed priestly and remote, or Dvořák empathic and messianic. His emendations to Mozart, Beethoven, and Schumann, his gargantuan symphonies with their folk ditties and hidden programs appeared to embody no authority save his own pregnable will.

In Krehbiel's eyes, Mahler's blasphemies broached "a question of what might be called moral aesthetics."[51] That Mahler knew himself to be a composer of stature put him on an easy footing with Beethoven: he interacted creatively with the Fifth Symphony; he felt no impulse to worship. But for Krehbiel, Mahler was no Beethoven: his interpretations were profanations.

• • •

Art as uplift is an idea with venerable Germanic roots. Luther influentially espoused the wholesome effects of music, and so of course did Bach. If Mozart and Beethoven were by comparison less conventionally religious, they nonetheless imbibed the humanist ideals of German philosophers, and so did Americans of the late Gilded Age. Henderson's *What Is Good Music?* even cites Immanuel Kant:

> [Kant] holds that "the Beautiful is that which, through the harmony of its form with the faculty of human knowledge, awakens a disinterested, universal, and necessary satisfaction." By disinterestedness in relation to beauty, Kant means freedom from gratification of sensual appetite or preconceived conceptions. The Beautiful gives pleasure, not because it satisfies any physical appetite or corresponds to any extant idea, but because in and through itself it imprints its own Ideal upon the soul, which, by its faculty of knowledge, is capable of receiving it.

Matthew Arnold's criterion of "high seriousness" also impacted significantly on late nineteenth-century American culture bearers; his *Culture and Anarchy* was widely read, and Arnold himself prominently toured the United States as a lecturer in the 1880s. The *New York Post*'s Henry Finck, in whose writings the discourse of Krehbiel and Henderson was typically simplified, simply wrote: "Music can impart only good impulses."[52]

In the history of American classical music, Boston's John Sullivan Dwight—a Germanophile whose translations of Goethe were among his important accomplishments—was a key progenitor of such "genteel" thinking. Dwight insisted on the ennobling properties of great symphonies—chiefly meaning Beethoven's, which he considered "religious." "I hazard the assertion, " Dwight wrote, "that *music is all sacred,* that music in its essence, in its purity, when it flows from the genuine fount of art in the composer's soul, when it is the inspiration of his genius, and not a manufactured imitation, when it comes unforced, unbidden from the heart, is a divine minister of the wants of the soul. . . . To me music stands for the highest outward symbol of what is most deep and holy, and most remotely to be realized in the soul of man."

Dwight's Bible was Germanic and ended with Mendelssohn and Schumann. He disliked opera. Theodore Thomas, whose itinerant Thomas Orchestra spread the gospel for symphonic music coast to coast, called "master works" a "character-building force" and "uplifting influence." He espoused Beethoven above all other masters, mistrusted *Tristan,* and denounced popular music as having "more or less the devil in it." A fundamentalist, he deferred to the score as holy writ. Mahler, in New York, transgressed this bedrock of American musical values unawares.[53]

Dwight was a onetime Unitarian minister. Thomas called concerts "sermons in tones." And Henry Krehbiel, a preacher's son, spoke from the pulpit in his *New York Tribune* reviews. And yet—like Seidl and Dvořák, like American Wagnerism—Krehbiel reinterprets the genteel tradition of Dwight and Thomas in its last and ripest phase. He is as worldly and impassioned as Dwight is desiccated. He makes Thomas—a time beater alongside Seidl, who displaced him in New York—seem parochial. He also charts the limits of fin-de-siècle genteel energies. *Salome* and Mahler marked the border of the acceptable. The opposition they engendered illustrated that the project of German musical idealism, as transplanted to the United States, was ribbed—and therefore heightened and prolonged—by a lingering puritanism.

What is more: in Krehbiel's case, *Salome* and Mahler signify a turning against the Germanic, shading the later identity of this archetypal German-American. By 1900, Berlin and Vienna, pressed forward by social and political currents inherent to Europe, had blown open a new musical page unknown in America. When in his Mahler obituary Krehbiel criticized "fatuous" foreigners who ignored American achievement, who overrated Roller's Secessionist stage designs ("not accepted here as inspired revelations") and who in their enthusiasm for Mahler's Eighth Symphony failed to question the propriety of joining a church hymn to Goethe's *Faust,* part 2; when in his *Salome* review he called German men "theoretically licentious and practically uxorious" for "joyously" acclaiming Strauss's hedonism, he was documenting and further disclosing an act of separation mirroring a twentieth-century sea change in German-American identity.

In the larger scheme of things German-American, New York's German-language Stadttheater, home to opera and operetta, tragedy and farce, to venders hawking beer, had by the turn of the century been superseded by Carnegie Hall and the Metropolitan Opera House. Anglos like the diarist George Templeton Strong had been interlopers in Deutschtum; *Die Meistersinger* at the Met, three decades later, was a German-American affair, with downtown singing societies supplementing the chorus and a double constituency (Germanic and not) crowding the auditorium. The bearded Leopold Damrosch, Polish-born and Berlin-educated, was in 1885 succeeded at the helm of his New York Symphony by his clean-shaven son, Walter—who proceeded to marry the daughter of a leading Republican Party politician and to conduct in the living rooms of Vanderbilts. Compared to his New York predecessors Theodor Eisfeld and Carl Bergmann, Theodore Thomas, though born in Essen, was an American: like Walter Damrosch, he arrived in the United States as a child; like Walter, he married—his second marriage, in 1890—into an important American family. Seidl arrived in New York a German and died a New Yorker supported by the city's civic and political leaders, writers and businessmen, Germans and Anglo-Americans.

Krehbiel's story partakes of this larger German-American odyssey. His meliorist Wagnerism, his combination of scholarship and daily journalism, his very prose—its circumlocutions, its tireless sentences and paragraphs—were German-American. Had he been a little older, he might have written reviews in German for the *Staats-Zeitung.* By the 1880s, it became possible to mediate between uptown and down. Krehbiel therefore inhabits a pivotal stage in the dispersion and cross-pollination of New York's world-class musical high culture. Clinching this evolutionary trajectory, and postdating Thomas and Seidl, was the Great War against Germany and Austro-Hungary: amplified by organized sallies of hysterical anti-German propaganda, it compelled and inspired German-Americans to become Americans only. German works and artists were widely discarded by American orchestras and opera houses. In New York, the Philharmonic abandoned Strauss and other living German composers. At the Met, German-language performances were banned, and neither Beethoven nor Wagner were given.

The German enemy incited no more patriotic American response than that of Henry Krehbiel. He called the kaiser's war effort "the most monstrous crime of a millennium." Though the ban on Wagner seemed philistine to him—"the beautiful and good in art" had "neither geographical nor political boundaries"[54]—he supported Gatti-Casazza's dismissal of six German singers, including the popular Johanna Gadski. When the Met returned to Wagner in February 1920, it was with a new *Parsifal* translation by Henry Krehbiel, appointing English the language of redemption. Long a proponent of opera in English, Krehbiel had nevertheless once expressed ambivalence about losing "some of the bone and sinew of the drama" were Wagner given in translation.[55] Now, in the shadow of punishing treaty terms imposed at Versailles, "Sei heil, entsündigt und entsühnt!" became "Be whole, forgiven and absolved!"

But Krehbiel the postwar American was at the same time increasingly stranded in postwar America. His insistence on immutable, inviolable aesthetic criteria distanced him even from his generational colleagues—not only the renegade Huneker, who could appreciate the luminous sonic properties of Schoenberg's atonal *Pierrot Lunaire* (though finding it "ugly") as early as 1912, but his old nemesis Philip Hale, who as early as 1911 had made a cause of Debussy's *Pelléas et Mélisande.* Through its final 1924 edition, Krehbiel's *How to Listen to Music* recognized nothing beyond "Classical" and "Romantic" works. "What is Romantic to-day becomes Classic tomorrow. Romanticism is fluid Classicism. It is the emotional stimulus informing Romanticism which calls music into life, but no sooner is it born, free, untrammeled, nature's child, than the regulative principle places shackles upon it; but it is enslaved only that it may become and remain art."[56] Krehbiel was unable to admire Stravinsky past *The Firebird.* Upon auditioning Schoenberg's Five Pieces for Orchestra in 1921, he declared the composer "an acousmatic, who accepts what he thinks are aesthetic evangels without the power, willingness or desire to inquire into their rationality, his hallucination being that whatever enters his mental ear is significant, or true." Longing for the past, he penned an essay—"The Curse of Affectation and Modernism in Music"—bemused by the noise of traffic and machines, and by Einstein's view that there was "no such thing as a straight line in the universe."[57] It was a fitting swan song: one month later, on March 20, 1923, he was dead at the age of sixty-nine. Aldrich, Finck, and Henderson were among the pallbearers at his funeral.

The *Tribune*'s obituary coverage, filling an entire page, was headed "Entire Music World Mourns for Krehbiel." No previous writer had so robustly impacted on New York's musical community. Never again would the passing of an American critic so resemble, in its ceremonies and acknowledgments, the death of a head of state. Condolence wires and letters came from London, Paris, Berlin; from Paderewski, Rachmaninoff, Mengelberg. Olive Fremstad, the preeminent singing actress of the day, told the *Tribune:* "This is such a shock to me I cannot speak more. I have known him through my entire musical career." Aldrich wrote, "It is not too much to say that he had set musical criticism in the United States on a plane that it had never occupied before, in respect of technical knowledge, breadth and penetration of view, critical faculty and power of expression." Henderson said, "Above all things he had an unending enthusiasm. He loved music. He lived with it and on it. It was almost the bread of his daily life."[58] Krehbiel was also memorialized, at a New York Public Library event, by Harry Burleigh.*

The following spring Aldrich quit the *Times;* in a retrospective column, he remarked that "it is a task to listen to new things at best; and when the result seems to be that the new things are poor stuff, discouragement comes too easily." Finck left the *Post* the following season and wrote: "Richard Aldrich [retired] chiefly because, as he himself told me, he could no longer endure the torture of listening to the preposterous cacophonies of the so-called futurists or modernists in music and because of the boredom of writing about them. . . . I may as well say it now as later—one of the chief reasons why I gave up writing criticisms for a daily paper was the same as Aldrich's."[59]

That Henderson was the last survivor of the genteel Old Guard was just: for him, the apex of music was not Beethoven but Wagner; his stamina for the new exceeded that of the others. Venturing into modern music, he is Krehbiel tweaked toward a grudging tolerance. He found *Pierrot* undeniably "interesting" (1925). Webern's Symphony, if "not good music," was "a whole circus of fun, and that is what most of the audience at a concert of cubist art expects" (1929). Berg's *Wozzeck* was "absorbing . . . gruesome . . . ghastly . . . filled with sinister power. But

*Burleigh's talk was titled "Mr. Krehbiel as I Knew Him." Krehbiel had written enthusiastic Prefatory Notes for the first edition of Burleigh's settings of five poems of Laurence Hope (among his highest achievements as a composer of art songs). W. J. Henderson supplied similar notes for other Burleigh publications. I am grateful to Jean Snyder for this information.

it is not opera" (1925). Stravinsky's *The Rite of Spring,* "undoubtedly a masterpiece of modernist music," was in places ugly, "but the purpose of the ugliness is understandable" (1924). The same composer's *The Soldier's Tale* seemed "empty pretense" (1928); but his *Apollo* was "chaste, dignified, restful," "genuinely beautiful" (1928). Henderson's insistence that art be meliorist never degenerated into prattle, but his heart was not in the new works he agreed to accept. On July 4, 1937, while writing an article about Josef Hoffmann, he put a gun to his head and pulled the trigger. He was eighty-one. His friend Aldrich had died five days before.[60]

In John Sullivan Dwight and Theodore Thomas, genteel adherence to the beautiful dictated mistrust of high emotion. For Krehbiel and Henderson, beauty and emotion readily coexisted; what they mutually mistrusted in Richard Strauss was lack of feeling. Whatever they might have said, preserving honored precepts of beauty, they chiefly experienced uplift not in their minds but in their hearts.

• • •

By the time of his death, Henry Krehbiel was twice an anachronism. If no longer a German-American, Krehbiel the self-made, self-taught newsman retained a barnacled scholarly mien out of touch with the streamlined aesthetic fashions of a new century. As a genteel culture bearer, he retained, unflinching, his iron criterion of uplift. No such aesthetic anchor would stabilize art in times to come. The modernists would be quick to ridicule their forebears, and Hitler and Stalin, music lovers both, would forever discredit the view that art could only be benign.

But if great music was demonstrably no guarantee of goodness, its humanizing properties were in late nineteenth-century America demonstrably evident. That Albert Niemann bearing his wound as Tristan caused some to swoon, that Salome's apostrophe to a severed head offended sensibilities does not condemn genteel audiences as dogmatic or inane. More obviously, these examples—and many others—illustrate the high degree to which art in the public arena once seemed to matter. For a charmed moment, musical New York embraced an elevated Wagner ideal purged of cant, and espoused an ecumenical vision of America transcending bias. It was a moment beautiful, true, and good.

FIGURE 9. Laura Langford. The *Brooklyn Daily Eagle*.

CHAPTER 3

Laura Holloway Langford

Servitude, Disquiet, and "The History of Womankind"

"The Ladies of the White House"—A tangled past—From theosophy to Wagnerism—Musical missionary work—"Earnest, manly women"—Reforming the Shakers—A life in limbo

According to the fifteen-page prospectus for the Seidl Society's 1894 Brighton Beach season, issued June 2, there would once again be fourteen concerts weekly—two a day—at Coney Island's Brighton Beach resort. Anton Seidl would again conduct an orchestra so seasoned that its repertoire included "OVER FIVE HUNDRED different works, by nearly ONE HUNDRED COMPOSERS." The season would begin "with a characteristically beautiful program" on June 30 and conclude, ten weeks later, on September 3. A Beethoven symphony would be featured every Friday night for eight weeks running (the Ninth Symphony being omitted). New works by Goldmark, Godard, Grieg, and Dvořák would be heard. "The Classic Masters" would be represented by Beethoven and Mozart, the Romantics by "Schumann, Schubert, Weber and others." The Americans Edward MacDowell, Frederick Converse, and Harry Rowe Shelley would be included. More earnest fare would be leavened by "light popular music": "Pleasure seeking people who are appreciative of music which delights the ear, as well [as] serious students and teachers alike recognize the charm, and enjoy the grace and delicacy which Mr. Seidl infuses into such composition." Above all, "the Repertoire of the Concerts will include the most gigantic works by Richard Wagner"—hefty doses from *Tannhäuser, Lohengrin, Die Meistersinger, Tristan und Isolde, The Ring of the Nibelung,* and *Parsifal.* Tickets for subscribers would cost only twenty-five cents per concert. What is more, pursuing its conviction that "women are indeed the Music of life," the society—whose members were exclusively female—would pursue its "philanthropic work" in support of Brooklyn orphans and women of all classes and conditions, escorting them to the seashore free of charge for rest, relaxation, and enrichment "with the sympathy of Music, recognizing with Wagner 'that its spirit, like that of Christianity, is Love, and that it excites within us, as soon as we are filled with it, the highest ecstacy [*sic*] of illimitability.'"[1]

All of this was business as usual. An additional, novel feature of the 1894 summer season would be a series of four concert-length lectures on Wagner's *Ring*, written by Seidl himself—"the first instance that lectures have been delivered to the accompaniment of a FULL ORCHESTRA."* That the lectures would be read "by the President of the Seidl Society" proved of chief interest to the *Brooklyn Daily Eagle*, which two days later published a two-thousand-word report under the following headline:

THE WAGNER TRILOGY

Anton Seidl's Lectures at Brighton Beach This Summer

A Novel Idea of Interpreting the Great Composer's Masterpieces—The President of the Society Describes the Work Which Will Be Done in the Music Pavilion by the Sea.

The article took the form of an interview with the president in question: Mrs. Laura Holloway Langford, who called the lectures "the greatest educational feature of the season's work," and continued: "My little part will be all the more smilingly performed because I appreciate the value of Mr. Seidl's exposition of Wagner's method and ideas."

The *Eagle*'s reporter ventured: "This one feature of the season, while looked upon as the most novel and attractive of all, has been commented upon with some anxiety, lest the size and openness of the music hall at Brighton may prove too much for the vocal powers of even a man." Langford retorted: "No; the acoustic properties of the music hall are well nigh perfect."

"But what if wind and tide are against you?" the reporter persisted.

"Wind and tide will not affect the music at the beach this summer and the precautions that will be made for the music will enable a

*In fact, the Seidl Society had itself presented such a lecture four years before—see page 146.

speaker to be heard with clearness and distinctness. . . . The wall of the building on the ocean side will be padded."

"Will not that be a costly and difficult thing to do?"

"We women, who are going to do it with the help of a man and a ladder and sufficient material, have not considered it a difficult matter." . . .

"What promise have you of the success of the season?"

"The natural and inevitable result of persistent hard work, combined with the allied factors of public interest in orchestra concerts; a growing desire on the part of all sorts and conditions of people to improve themselves, musically and otherwise, and thus increase their enjoyment of life. . . . The four years of profit and pleasure afforded by Mr. Seidl and his orchestra there makes the prospect now one of almost sure success. . . . The benevolent work of the society is always upheld by generous hearts and willing hands."

. . .

That before creating her Seidl Society, Laura Holloway Langford had long worked as an editor for the *Daily Eagle* was doubtless a factor contributing to the paper's always copious reportage of Seidl Society activities—reportage that helped to make Langford a potent object of public admiration (as reported by *Eagle* writers amazed by her power and energy) and irritation (as elsewhere reported by writers more discomfited than amazed).

Culling from stories in the *Eagle* and from an 1888 article in *The Ladies' Home Journal and Practical Housekeeper,* the historian Diane Sasson has extrapolated a pertinent biographical picture.[2] Langford claimed to have been born Laura Carter in 1848 on a picturesque plantation near Nashville. Her aristocratic father, Samuel Jefferson Carter, was said to have been a relative and close friend of Andrew Johnson; he traced his lineage to the "Carters of Blenheim," to the "first families of Virginia," to the "Greenmary Court" of "King Carter." Her mother, Anne Vaulx Carter, was a Quaker who reportedly "spent many hours upon her knees praying for her children and for her husband." The plantation was frequented by "the most cultivated and distinguished men." Its hundreds of slaves were never sold or whipped; rather, their treatment was "civilizing and Christianizing." Laura attended the Nashville Female Academy. But this idyllic existence was devastated by the Civil War. It was Laura who persuaded the family to move north, where Samuel invested "the price of the plantation" on Wall Street—and lost his fortune.[3]

In Nashville, Andrew Johnson often walked Laura to school. In an 1875 reminiscence, she recalled that he would

> ask her questions concerning her lessons, and tell her how little he knew as a little boy. She never seemed to be pleased with any counsel he would give her as to her duties as a grateful little girl, and once he was so struck by her silence that he asked her if she was proud that she was a little girl and could go to school. "No," was her determined reply, with a flash of the eye and a toss of the head. "Not glad, my child, what more would you have?" "I would be a boy," she said. "And why a boy, little girl?" "Because I could be like you and Pa, and be smart and know heaps; and then sometime maybe I would be Governor."

Johnson replied, "My daughter, if you are ever to be Governor, you must first learn to control your temper." Langford added, "Many years after, when he was President, he said that the first time that he ever thought of a woman in other than a domestic capacity was when that child, full of ambition and dissatisfaction with her condition, startled him with the assertion that she wanted to be Governor of Tennessee."[4]

According to Langford, Johnson also proposed the idea that became her first book: *The Ladies of the White House; or, In the Home of the Presidents.*

> President Johnson had never heard that the White House was burned; said it was only sacked by the British, and was left uninjured. Mrs. Holloway then fresh from school—contradicted her host, and a merry argument was carried on over the matter. Early the next morning she consulted the congressional library, and, armed with her proofs, sought the president and triumphantly showed him what history had to say on the subject. He good-naturedly admitted she was right, made her a low bow, and said to her: "Why do you not write the history of the White House and tell us all about the events that have transpired here?" Mrs. Holloway agreed to do it, if she could get the families of the presidents to help her with facts, when President Johnson offered to help her gather material.[5]

Early married and widowed as Laura Holloway, she lived in the White House as a "favorite of the National Executive" while writing *The Ladies of the White House.* She then moved to Brooklyn—not yet a borough of Manhattan, with its immigrant melee, but an independent city of churches. As an associate editor of the *Daily Eagle,* she was a prominent socialite and prolific writer. Despite a "delicate, nervous, and highly sensitive nature," she supported a dozen family members, even enabling her parents to buy back "the old home in Tennessee"—"and her father and mother, who had always pined for their native air, passed their last days in comfort there, and were buried beside their friends of the sunny South."[6]

This genteel self-portraiture was reinforced by *The Ladies of the White House,* first published in 1870, and a second such volume: *The Mothers of Great Men and Women* (1883). These tomes—more than six hundred pages apiece—are innocent of the larger play of history; rather they are moral lessons. Beethoven's "morbid sensitiveness" and "helpless melancholy" were assuaged by his susceptibility "to woman's sympathy." Of his mother, who died when he was sixteen, Holloway writes in *Mothers of Great Men and Women:* "Her spirit must have hovered near him as a guardian angel to sustain his courage." She reasons:

> Every record we have of Ludwig von Beethoven shows . . . his extreme sensitiveness to the kindness or unkindness of others toward him. He must have suffered exquisite torture at beholding the brutal conduct of his father and his reminiscences of his mother, though summed up in a few brief sentences, prove beyond a doubt that it was to her sympathetic ear that he confided his sorrows and aspirations, and that it was upon her bosom that he hid his tears. . . . No mother can need a higher tribute than that he paid to her memory. "She was to me such a good and loving mother, the best of friends. Oh, who would be so happy as I, could I still speak the sweet name 'mother,' and have her hear it?"

And music itself succored Beethoven. It "is not only a delight but a medicine," writes Holloway.

> What a soothing refreshment is music in the domestic circle after a day of toil! It is the greatest aid to reflection and calms down the sudden and foolish impulses. It is the most tranquilizing of all sedatives; the gentlest of all stimulants; the most humanizing of all recreations. It is an accompaniment to wisdom and sheds light upon the darkness of the soul. It is a founder of peace on earth and good-will among men.

Holloway here quotes Luther: "Satan hates [music] because it drives away temptation and evil thoughts." Turning to Mendelssohn—a Gilded Age paragon of gentleness, nobility, and integrity among composers, of intellectual breadth and productive achievement*—Holloway adduces the influence of Leah Mendelssohn: her "perfect propriety," "cordial hospitality," her "calm" and "happy" Christian motherhood. "Her one weakness appears to have been excessive nervous excitability, leading

*See Joseph Mussulman, *Music in the Cultured Generation: A Social History of Music in America, 1870–1900* (1971).

at times to peevishness and to unreasonable demands; but as a rule she held herself well in hand, and was a spring of delight to her household and friends."[7]

Of the First Ladies profiled in Holloway's first and best-known book, the heroine of the 1881 edition is—a First Lady postdating the initial edition of 1870—Lucy Webb Hayes, the first president's wife to acquire something resembling a college degree. Born in Lexington, Kentucky, in 1833, Lucy Webb was the daughter of a physician of strong moral conscience; he freed the slaves he inherited from his aunt. The family moved to Ohio, where Lucy attended the Cincinnati Wesleyan Female College; the topic of her graduation speech was "The Influence of Christianity on National Prosperity." With her lifelong sense of Christian duty, she adopted her parents' Abolitionist convictions. She took a keen interest in reform schools, orphanages, and asylums during her husband's tenure as governor of Ohio and as president of the United States (1877–1881). Earlier, during his Civil War service, she visited his encampments, helping in tent hospitals, sewing, and cooking. In Washington, Mrs. Hayes was known for attending to individual cases of need among the city's slum-dwellers, disbursing as much as a thousand dollars monthly in funds donated by herself and by supportive cabinet members. With her vibrant contralto, she enjoyed singing hymns and also played the piano and guitar; among the musical performers she invited to the White House was the African-American soprano (and "Queen of Staccato") Madame Selika, who came with Frederick Douglass. She was the first First Lady to maintain a schedule of appearances distinct from her husband's.

"Her eyes are large and expressive, and deepen in color from gray to black as the feelings are wrought upon," writes Holloway in her much-reprinted history. "All her features are expressive, and her face is a most pleasing and animated one. She has a gay and sunny temperament, hence her face is the mirror of much that is bright and beautiful. She owes much of her good looks and her happiness to her wonderful health, for she is as splendid a specimen of physical womanhood as the country can boast, and her presence is a tonic to weaker women."

"Thoroughly kind in expression," Mrs. Hayes's speech abjured gossip and carefully gauged "the feelings of others." "Ardently attendant to the duties and requirements of a Christian life," she was steadfast in her "loyalty and faith in her husband," whose success was largely due to his wife's "intelligent appreciation of his aspirations." The "sweet simplicity" of her life, even in Washington, was such that she "avoided all manner of extremes in dress," eschewing diamonds and "low-neck or short-sleeved dresses." "She never gave a dinner or an evening party that was not on a scale of elegance compatible with her position." She fastidiously abstained from influencing her husband's appointments and policy decisions. "Applicants for office were turned over to the secretary, and through the years of her stay in the White House she succeeded in avoiding this source of annoyance."

History has dubbed Lucy Hayes "Lemonade Lucy" for enforcing her husband's ban on liquor at the White House. Holloway cites a letter by a Reverend Dr. Read: "Noble stand for a noble Christian woman! God be praised for such a grand, heroic woman to occupy the highest social position in the nation at this time! It is an answer to prayer." In refusing to serve wine, Holloway writes, Lucy Hayes

> exhibited rare courage, because it was not only an unpopular step, but it was one that placed her in contrast with her predecessors in the position she was holding—a circumstance which was her chief regret. As to the right of a woman to take the authoritative stand she did, she did not stop to consider, for she was in her own home even if in the Executive Mansion, and the public had no more right to dictate what she should drink than what she should eat or wear. . . . It was this evidence of her moral power, more than the mere fact of her being a temperance advocate, that drew the women of this country about her. And taken all in all, she is one of the finest representatives of her sex who has held the place she has filled. This is the verdict of the women of this country, who by thousands signed the testimonials sent her, and united in presenting to the nation her portrait, as a manifestation of their gratitude for worthy representation. It is the first instance of the kind in the history of any nation, and it marked the prestige of a people who are every year becoming more renowned throughout the world, and more and more an example of the advancing power of civilization.[8]

A preface to the 1881 edition of *The Ladies of the White House* salutes "the moral influence that has been exerted by the untarnished reputations and the social qualities of the women who have successively filled the posts of Hostess of the Presidents' House" and adds, "At a time when the women of this country are commanding the attention of the civilized world by reason of their higher education, superior mental attributes, and exalted social status, such a book is of exceptional value." The volume's tone of genteel approbation is only mildly disturbed by Holloway's obvious advocacy of a greater role for women, and her annoyance that "not a few strong, gifted natures have been content to lead automaton lives in that famous old mansion." Especially in the United States, she observes, wives of "public men" are "left behind" and "doomed to slavery of the most repulsive kind during the best years of life." She discerns "stronger traits of character" among First Ladies "of the Revolutionary period." After the presidency of John Quincy Adams, they became "social queens and nothing more"—and "some were too little used to the world to care for even this." Mrs. Hayes, by comparison, signaled "the new woman era."[9]

From the perspective of many new women, however, Lucy Hayes was herself too much a "social queen and nothing more." Far from advocating women's suffrage, she agreed with her husband that "maternity is inconsistent with the like discharge of citizenship."[10] She would not join the Women's Christian Temperance Union. Her visits to the Kentucky Asylum for the Blind or the National Deaf Mute College betokened gestures, not ongoing relationships.

What was known of Laura Holloway—what she wrote and said about herself—resonated with her genteel portraiture of Lucy Hayes. And yet Holloway was not the southern belle she seemed. And her volumes of politely hortatory nonfiction document a different person from the worldly impresario and restless spiritualist she amazingly became. Henry Adams called the American woman "still a study." To study the complex trajectory of Holloway's several careers is to glimpse the fate of women of high capacity and aspiration in a fin-de-siècle moment—a moment that furnished no adequate personal models, unless self-invented.

• • •

In actuality, as Diane Sasson has shown, Laura Carter was born in 1843, not 1848. Her father, Samuel Jefferson Carter, was from southern Virginia, not the Tidewater region of "King Carter's plantation." Her mother, Anne Vaulx, belonged to a prominent Tennessee family. Laura received an orthodox Calvinist religious education. The Nashville Female Academy, from which she graduated in 1860, was known as the nation's largest "school for young ladies." According to the principal, the Reverend Collins D. Elliott, its rigorous academic curriculum, including languages and the arts, was fortified "according to God's word." The "sweetly submissive and sublimely trusting lady heart" was there protected from "strong-minded" women who might infect students with "mannishness." Reverend Elliott once fired a teacher who suggested that educated young women might forego marriage. Laura's graduation essay was titled "Martyrdom for Truth."[11]

Her home life, however, was less genteel. Samuel Carter raced horses and managed hotels. He also supplied Governor Andrew Johnson with "pure whiskey." He owned eleven slaves. The family responded to the Civil War with divided loyalties on both sides. When northern troops arrived in Nashville in 1862, Carter was cordial to the officers who lodged and dined at his St. Cloud Hotel. But one of the vignettes in the "Anecdotes of Andrew Johnson," published in *Century* Magazine, records Laura's arrest for spitting on Union soldiers from the hotel porch.

> General Dumont immediately sought Johnson and said: "Governor, I hated to make this arrest on account of you and her father. But she has been indulging in all sorts of contempt, and I thought it about time to check her. When I told her she ought to behave herself while you were a guest at the hotel, she defied you, and said she would yet dance on your grave."
>
> "Oh, you mustn't mind these little rebels," responded Johnson. "There is no harm in Laura."[12]

This tangled tale grows more tangled: in June 1862, Laura Carter married a Union officer: Junius B. Holloway of Richmond, Kentucky. Like the Carters, the Holloways were slave-owning Unionists. The marriage proved precipitous. Holloway was captured by Confederate forces, then paroled, then dismissed from the Union army, then arrested as an accused Confederate guide. Laura had to intercede with Governor Johnson on his behalf. Their only child, George, was born in Nashville in 1864. Because Laura kept all this a secret, it is impossible to reconstruct the dissolution of the marriage. In 1871, she told Johnson, "The very name I bear is not my own and I despise it." She subtracted five years from her age to erase her marriage years. She presented herself in the north as a childless widow.[13]

Meanwhile, Samuel Carter emerged in the new South as a Tennessee state assemblyman—a "scalawag." He urged acceptance of Emancipation as "an accomplished fact." The Confederate rebellion, he said, had been "madness and folly," a "disastrous experiment . . . however much I may have been attached personally to individuals engaged therein." But he opposed allowing former slaves to vote or to testify in court. He was defeated by a more conservative opponent in 1865.[14]

The Carters left Nashville for New York the same year. To generate some income, Laura undertook chronicling the nation's First Ladies. Apparently, President Johnson's private secretary wrote letters to the living ex-presidents in support of the project. Holloway's purported connection to "first families of Virginia" buttressed these solicitations. She may have resided at the Johnson White House for a period of weeks—

not for years, as she later claimed. She finished her book in late 1869. By 1870, she had moved the family to Brooklyn—an independent city until it merged with Manhattan, Queens, Staten Island, and the Bronx in 1898—and had become a newspaper editor, first for the *Daily Union,* later for the *Daily Eagle.*

In Brooklyn, Holloway also helped to create a Southern Women's Bureau "to assist Southern Women who desire to be educated in the various Professions and Arts and also for whose who are already sufficiently cultured to accept positions of trust and responsibility, and a pecuniary return therefor [*sic*], and to benefit the thousands of our women who . . . have been left in circumstances which require the utmost efforts of brains and hands to secure the comforts of life." An endorsement from the *Phrenological Journal and Science of Health* added that "through this bureau it is presumed progressive ideas will be disseminated in the South, and that much good may grow out of it." At the first meeting, on June 7, 1870, Holloway was elected corresponding secretary. Sixteen days later, she offered a talk on "Women's Labor in the South." According to the *New York Times,* she "dilated on the oft-told story of man's inhumanity to woman, and announced that the day was at hand when women would assert their rights and secure their proper position in the world." She excoriated opponents of women's rights as "tame, stay-at-home, slaving women who had no thought beyond their kitchens." The *Daily Eagle* called her lecture a "harangue . . . against the tyrant man. . . . Her hottest indignation was directed against the 'namby-pamby, good women,' who remain 'unspotted from the world.'" Holloway was observed "urging the shrieking sisterhood" to "write victory on their banners." Female readers of the *Eagle* were advised to avoid the bureau "and try to become good women." A published version of the talk, titled "The Women of the South," decried the "baleful influence" of slavery on women "accustomed always to be served by the hands of inferiors, and educated only in those trivial accomplishments that are said to adorn the drawing-room."[15]

The Southern Women's Bureau was short-lived. Its last meeting, on December 8, 1870, again featured a Holloway lecture: "Perils of the Hour," this time praised by the *Eagle* for eschewing "the phantasies of the strong–minded," and for condemning "those artificial chimeras which find their sole aim and end in cosmetics and fantastic dress," in favor of "the honor and usefulness of women in the domestic circle." Henry Ward Beecher, who was there, called this "the most eloquent lecture ever delivered on the women in America."[16]

With the expiration of the Women's Bureau, Holloway found other causes and forums. In 1869, her head had been "read" by the phrenologist Samuel R. Wells, who identified benevolence as her strongest characteristic. Holloway's article "Personal Independence in Women," published in *The Phrenological Journal and Science of Health* in 1874, urged individual initiative to counteract "social bondage." In 1871 and 1872, Holloway persuaded Brooklyn businessmen to give youngsters in their employ "two holidays during the summer without loss of salary . . . provided said days are spent at the seashore, and under the care of those having charge of the working children's picnics"; her "fresh air fund" raised money in support. Holloway's "An Old Grudge—A New Fuss," printed by the *Eagle* in 1876, argued for women's suffrage on the grounds that feminine meekness and love were more Christ-like than the masculine propensity to "shed blood and enslave." By this time, Holloway's parents had moved back to Tennessee—but not to their old homestead, as Laura later claimed. Samuel died in 1873, Anne Vaulx in 1874. As for her son, George, the 1880 Federal Census reported him living in Brooklyn with two Chinese who ran a laundry. Two years later, he entered West Point.[17]

Taking stock of this saga—of loyalties northern and southern, of propensities rebellious and submissive—no coherent picture emerges. Laura Carter reviled Union soldiers and married one. She omitted Abolitionism from her admiring portrait of Lucy Webb Hayes, but blamed slavery for condemning southern women to surrogate lives. She frequently—but by no means invariably—submitted to aristocratic or Victorian conventions of language and thought, yet was one of the first women to work fulltime for a major newspaper. She was equally a woman of daunting energy and the poised possessor of a deep and cultivated speaking voice laced with the languors of the South. As of 1884—the year she left the *Eagle*—and 1885—the year of the last of her hortatory books—she had not nearly integrated these contradictory currents of her life and times.

. . .

Following the death of his eighteen-month-old son in 1885, William James frequented a Beacon Hill psychic named Leonora Piper. Mrs. Piper would go into a trance and reveal knowledge of James's family. James's psychological investigations already included attending séances and reporting on mediums. He studied Mrs. Piper and even hypnotized her; at length, he concluded that she possessed "supernormal powers." His wife, Alice, attempted to "develop" latent capacities that might help her to become a medium herself. His brother, Henry, was also receptive to communications from "the other side."[18]

These susceptibilities were not unusual A short list of luminaries who pursued credulous interest in occult experience around the turn of the century would include Elizabeth Barrett Browning, Thomas Edison, Sigmund Freud, Horace Greeley, Victor Hugo, George Bernard Shaw, Alfred Russel Wallace, and W.B. Yeats. Gustav and Alma Mahler, in New York in 1909, attended a séance as companions of the financial and cultural philanthropist Otto Kahn, a man of shrewd intellect and sophisticated taste. A table levitated; a mandolin flew through the air.[19] The Mahlers pondered this experience for days.

The spiritualist movement of the late nineteenth century, and attendant fascination with the paranormal, is today chronicled as a symptom of dissipating religion and encroaching modernity. The malaise Nietzsche termed "weightlessness" partnered the growing prestige of natural science. Intense religious cravings were common among middle-class women. Deprived of such earlier domestic duties as spinning and quilting, discouraged from studying mathematics or science, shunning the male contagions sex and money, they suffered an enforced passivity. "Neurasthenia" was the usual diagnosis for nervous prostration. The remedial strategies ranged from homeopathy, dress reform, and women's suffrage to mysticism and Eastern religion.[20]

Laura Holloway's quest at various stages embraced spiritualism, vegetarianism, phrenology, Buddhism, Vedanta, and Shakerism. She also acquired prowess as a clairvoyant. In the years immediately following her resignation from the Brooklyn *Eagle,* her religious and reformist energies were channeled into a ready and waiting vessel: the theosophical movement initiated by the redoubtable Helena Petrovna Blavatsky. Madame Blavatsky, with whom Langford studied in London in 1884 upon departing America "in search of health and rest," was an obese Russian of distinguished birth. She smoked incessantly, wore ill-fitting red robes, and transfixed disciples with bulging magnetic eyes variously accounted blue, grey-blue, or azure. A torrent of intellectual energy, she claimed to synthesize all the world's great religions, with particular emphasis on the wisdom of the East. The three goals of her anarchic international Theosophical Society were "the formation of a universal human brotherhood without distinction of race, creed, sex, caste, or color; the encouragement of studies in comparative religion, philosophy and science; and the investigation of unexplained laws of nature and the powers latent in man." Blavatzky's own unexplained powers included levitation, clairvoyance, and telepathy. She traced her authority to Master Morya, who visited her in Tibet and whose own master, the Lord of the World, came from Venus. Her prolific writings, often dictated to her telepathically, constitute a potpourri of esoteric wisdom.[21]

In the United States, to which she relocated in 1873, Madame Blavatsky denounced mere spiritualists as simpletons and frauds. Her higher hocus-pocus was embroidered with copious allusions to Buddhism and Hinduism. Though at all times shadowed by controversy and scandal, and occasionally exposed for pulling a fast one, she possessed the aplomb to confess deceit with a winning wink and chuckle that were not always appreciated. In 1878, beleaguered in America, she moved on to India, where theosophy sided with Hindu nationalists against Christian missionaries. Her wanderings, documented and apocryphal, eventually took her to London, where her teachings resonated with the radical ideals of Fabian socialism, and where she died in 1891.

Holloway was admitted as a fellow of the New York branch of the Theosophical Society in 1884; her certificate of membership was signed by Blavatsky, William Quan Judge, and Theosophical Society cofounder Henry Steele Olcott.[22] Blavatsky and theosophy align with three motifs in Holloway's later life. First, there was the madame herself: her powers of self-invention, her nerve, confidence, and feistiness. Second was the life force of a potently eclectic spiritual brew, bursting conventions of thought and behavior. Third there were the political implications of a movement internationalist, pacifist, socially progressive, and chiefly speaking to women.

If Blavatsky catalyzed a liberating new life for Holloway, Holloway was eventually known as a "failed" disciple. Meanwhile, she returned to Brooklyn in October 1884 and resumed her remunerative life as a genteel journalist, producing such inspirational volumes as *Famous American Fortunes and the Men Who Have Made Them* (1885), *Adelaide Nielsen: A Souvenir* (1885), and *Howard: The Christian Hero* (1885).* The sixty-page Adelaide Nielsen booklet, for instance, is a self-described "labor of love" illustrating "the degree to which [Nielsen] possessed the power of recuperation." An illegitimate child, a run-away, a barmaid, she regenerated as a famous actress. Offstage she was "a very lovable and loving woman," "sweet and reverent; strong and earnest of

*It was also reported in the press that during these years Holloway wrote fiction under a pseudonym.

soul." Of her early death at the age of thirty-two, Holloway writes that "doubtless it was best" to have expired "in the fullness of her prime."

Holloway's final, 541-page book, *The Woman's Story, as told by twenty American women* (1888), is not one of her mega-efforts. Rather, it is a compendium of short fiction by twenty authors, each of whom chose for Holloway "their best sketch work." Holloway's own contribution is a one-page preface noting that women are "the largest contributors" to American fiction, and brief biographies of each writer. Coming first, Harriet Beecher Stowe is identified as "the foremost American writer of her day, hence her story ["Uncle Lot"] has the place of honor in this collection." Holloway also writes: "Mrs. Stowe always speaks of [*Uncle Tom's Cabin*] as having been revealed to her, and very recently she declared that she did not write it, that God gave it to her." Of the remaining nineteen authors, only Louisa May Alcott, represented by "Transcendental Wild Oats," remains a name today. Holloway characteristically writes: "Miss Alcott was a noble woman, well educated and cultivated. . . . Her devotion to her kindred was a beautiful trait in her character."[23] In short, the book is an oddly cloistered performance, recapitulating the 1870s gentility of *Ladies of the White House.*

More than ever, Holloway's nature and calling were a tangle of contradictory talents, predilections, and needs: a combustible but latent potion. A catalyst yet more powerful than Helena Blavatsky was required.

• • •

Anton Seidl was cloaked in sphinxlike self-possession.* His flowing raven hair was combed straight back from the forehead. His sculpted features were Gothic. He dressed carefully in black or white suits. Born in Budapest, trained in Germany, he was rumored to be an atheist, and an illegitimate son of Franz Liszt. No less than Liszt, he exuded an allure both priestly and erotic. Unlike Liszt, he was not a candidate for romantic French or Italian liaisons. He and Mrs. Seidl were well ensconced in an East 62nd Street brownstone, and in a Catskill cottage known to friends as "Seidl Berg."

At the Metropolitan Opera, or with his New York Philharmonic, Seidl on the podium remained remote, poised, and mysterious. He never smiled; he did not even shake hands with soloists. "A baton incarnate," James Gibbons Huneker called him. "He riveted his men with a glance of steel." Only the musicians, reading his face, witnessed the sleeping

*See pages 83–85.

volcano of Seidl's personality sprung to life. Only a coterie knew his slow and laconic speech; or his scathing ironies, embellished with sweet, damning smiles. "He made enemies easily, friends slowly; his very failings were virile, his virtues masculine," Huneker wrote. "He was a man to his ensphered soul!" Few knew that Seidl was in the habit of giving away clothes to needy strangers, or of touring with his orchestra without salary. Immersed in his work he might go twenty-four hours without food. His mentality was missionary; he sacrificed himself.[24]

Next to Seidl, Madame Blavatsky was a mountebank reeking of tobacco. And Seidl's guru was no vague Tibetan Master, but a mentor deceased and yet tangible, respectable yet subversive: the single most dominant artistic force in fin-de-siècle America. Richard Wagner encompassed Buddhism, Christianity, and myth in a powerful syncretic creed without claims to telepathy or magic. He concocted not a watery stew of books and miracles, but a revolutionary repertoire of enduring musical theater works. And Wagnerism was wonderfully malleable. If abroad Nietzsche, D'Annunzio, Baudelaire were decadent or otherwise dangerous Wagnerites, in America the Wagner contagion ensnared a multitude of milder aesthetic, social, and intellectual reformers.*

Seidl was New York's leading musical personality for a dozen years, having immigrated in 1885. As a young man, he had lived with Wagner and his family in Bayreuth, an indispensable amanuensis who copied scores, assisted at the Festspielhaus, and—as a kind of surrogate son—supplied daily companionship to the voluble and hyperactive composer. As Wagner's appointed conductor, he introduced the *Ring* throughout Europe in 1882 and 1883. Next—two years following Wagner's death—came the New World, where as chief conductor at the Metropolitan Opera he led first American performances of *Das Rheingold, Siegfried, Götterdämmerung, Die Meistersinger,* and *Tristan und Isolde.* Beginning in 1891, he conducted the New York Philharmonic. He also regularly appeared in Brooklyn beginning in 1888, when he was engaged to conduct at Brighton Beach.

The logic of this last assignment was questionable. Though not yet home to Steeplechase, its most famous and enduring amusement park, Coney Island was already New York's "Sodom by the Sea," hosting beer gardens, shooting galleries, and sideshows. Its east end, however, was dominated by the luxurious Brighton Beach, Manhattan Beach, and Oriental Hotels, each a fashionable watering hole on the Euro-

*See pages 86–89.

pean model. The Manhattan Beach music pavilion, fronting the hotel's manicured lawn and ornate verandas, featured America's most popular bandmaster: Patrick Gilmore. At Brighton Beach, Herman Colell—a business associate of the redoubtable Oscar Hammerstein, an impresario of gargantuan ambition and achievement—persuaded the owners to build a three-thousand-seat music pavilion of their own. Colell failed to obtain Johann Strauss Jr. or the Garde Republicaine Band of France, or the Coldstream Guards from England; he instead engaged Anton Seidl with members of his Metropolitan Opera orchestra. When their twice-daily concerts, brandishing symphonic and operatic excerpts at inexpensive prices, were ignored by hotel and racetrack patrons partial to marches and waltzes, the disillusioned hotel management offered no support; Seidl's seaside concerts, according to the *Musical Courier,* were "given to those only who chanced to know that they were taking place, because some one had spoken of them or because they happened to run down for a breath of salt air and were amazed to find a species of enjoyment the like of which Coney Island ne'er knew before and probably will not know again." In 1889, Seidl agreed to return for a thousand dollars less, but the hotel remained inattentive; no manager for the concerts was appointed. Seidl was unyielding; in the opinion of the *Musical Courier,* he "did not comprehend the significance of the movement he was making. He championed and artistically conducted the enterprise with the sincere conviction that the great moving bulk of the people were pining for an opportunity to embrace high-class musical performances among their summer recreations." Seidl himself told the press: "I will confess frankly that I do not content myself with the approval of the fashionable musical public; my chief aim is, rather to attract to the concerts . . . the music-loving masses who wish to cultivate their taste, and who, lacking both time and means to attend the classical concerts given during the winter season, will now be afforded the opportunity of listening . . . at an outlay which lies within the reach of all." And he complained that his sponsors had failed to properly promote his programs of Beethoven and Wagner.[25]

This was the stranded call for help that Laura Holloway, herself stranded, answered with every fiber of her being. The Brighton Beach concerts were accessible only to women with escorts. Holloway proposed to the Brighton Beach Railroad that arrangements be made for women and children to attend the 1889 summer season. The railroad, hungry for concertgoers, agreed to reserve special cars for this purpose, with comparable amenities at the hotel and pavilion. This became the germ of the Seidl Society, founded by Holloway in early 1889. The constitution and bylaws, published that year, spoke of "securing to its members and to the public increased musical culture," and "of promoting musical interest among women generally." The society aimed "to reach all classes of women and children and by its efforts in their behalf to prove the potent influence of harmony over individual life and character." Membership was offered, for five dollars annually, to "any woman of good standing." Meetings would be held monthly.[26]

The initial membership of the Seidl Society was two hundred. Five hundred women attended the first annual dinner. For the 1889 Brighton Beach concerts, tickets were sold to members for twenty-five cents each—about one-quarter the minimum price of admission to comparable events in Manhattan. Transportation to Coney Island cost an additional fifty cents. The trainloads of Seidl Society women rescued the Seidl concerts—attendance rose 50 percent over 1888. Seidl was emboldened to give entire symphonies, including Beethoven's third, fifth, sixth, seventh, and eighth. Meanwhile, the society brought several thousand working girls, and poor or orphaned children, to the seashore for recreation and culture. It also sponsored lectures at the hotel. The 1889 speakers included Susan B. Anthony, who rebutted the notion that "the object of woman's life is to help man"; Grace B. Dodge, the New York City schools commissioner, whose topic was "how to elevate the character of working girls"; and Henry Krehbiel, who lectured on *Parsifal*.[27]

That Krehbiel's lecture inspired the Seidl Society to offer a *Parsifal* Entertainment as its first concert production the following spring illuminates Holloway's method: she did what needed to be done. Notwithstanding the Wagner rage, *Parsifal* had not been mounted in America: the Wagner family disallowed staged performances outside Bayreuth. Walter Damrosch had led two concert performances in Manhattan in 1886—performances inadequately prepared, cast, and conducted. For Seidl (who would return to Bayreuth in 1897 to lead *Parsifal*), this last Wagner opera was his master's supreme achievement. For many Americans, as well, it marked an apex: the highest manifestation of the meliorist Wagner. The prominent art critic Mariana Van Rensselaer, one of many Americans who joined the Bayreuth pilgrims for the first *Parsifal* performances in 1882, wrote in *Harper's* that *Parsifal* was "the deepest in theme and completest in execution" of Wagner's works; she was transported. Charles Dudley Warner, also at Bayreuth, called *Parsifal* "a modern miracle play" and—a foretaste of Mark Twain's reportage from Bayreuth nine years later—added: "It is of course possible that the crowds of Bayreuth were victims of a delusion, and of skillful contrivance. I can answer for many of them that they would like to be deluded again in just that way."[28]

Wagner's Bühnenweihfestspiel—his festival play for the consecration of a stage—preaches renunciation of the flesh as a means of redemption. Its sources include myth, religion, and philosophy. In the New York press, W. J. Henderson discerned "a sermon on the necessity of personal purity in the service of God," a "religious drama" in the tradition of Aeschylus. Henry Krehbiel (who was not untroubled by Wagner's avowal of self-denial) stressed pertinent Greek and medieval roots. For many American Wagnerites, however, the likeness of Parsifal to Christ, of Kundry to Mary Magdalen, and of the culminating Holy Grail sacrament to the Last Supper were defining. A minority opinion therefore damned *Parsifal* as a blasphemy; for the majority, its rites were specifically and triumphantly Christian. "Parsifal is no other than Christ," explicated the *Brooklyn Daily Eagle.* It "was written with the events in the life of Christ in . . . mind," wrote John P. Jackson of the *New York World.* The liberal theologian Washington Gladden, an advocate of applied Christianity, witnessed *Parsifal* at Bayreuth and found "a source of refinement and moral invigoration," invoking "great religious ideas . . . with tremendous power." The Seidl Society's *Parsifal* presentation likewise stressed Christian readings. At the same time, the eclecticism of Wagner's spiritual vision doubtless appealed to Holloway herself. Blavatsky's affinity for Buddhism, her mistrust of sex, her appropriation of the mythology of the Knights Templar are pertinent to *Parsifal* as experienced by Holloway.[29]

All these currents fed—indeed, mandated—the singular Palm Sunday *Parsifal* Entertainment of March 31, 1890: an event at once religious and secular; sensory and genteel; intellectual, spiritual, and social. The preliminaries included a Seidl Society lecture entitled "*Parsifal,* the Finding of Christ through Art" and a new spring style: the *Parsifal* toque. The venue was the Brooklyn Academy of Music (not the present BAM, but its Brooklyn Heights predecessor, a favorite site for uplifting lectures and charity balls, in a fashionable neighborhood epitomized by the late Reverend Henry Ward Beecher's affluent Plymouth Congregational Church). The decor, specially commissioned, featured carpets, watercolors, engravings, streamers, and—onstage—a white and silver cathedral scene; a proscenium banner conveyed the word PARSIFAL in flowered green letters and also a medieval "S"—the Seidl Society's insignia. The packed house—an audience exceptionally distinguished in bearing, attire, and pedigree—included ex-president Grover Cleveland and his wife; the Brooklyn mayor Alfred Chapin, and his wife; Mr. and Mrs. J.P. Morgan; and the Reverend Beecher's successor, Dr. Lyman Abbott. Grover Cleveland was one of many listeners observed following a libretto. Reporters took note of "the number of eager, intelligent faces, especially of the ladies." As for Wagner's music, about three-quarters of the score was heard beginning at five o'clock in the afternoon and ending at ten, with a catered dinner midway through. The Good Friday Spell made an overwhelming impression. Lilli Lehmann, who sang Kundry, recalled: "The place was transformed into a temple."[30]

No man had ever thought to conceive anything like the *Parsifal* Entertainment. Overnight, Laura Holloway became a singular hortatory force in the cultural life of New York City and its environs.

. . .

Two months later, Laura Carter Holloway married Colonel Edward Langford, secretary and treasurer of the Brooklyn Brighton, Coney Island Railroad Company. He was a well-preserved Civil War hero and former deputy police commissioner. Both bride and groom, wrote the *Daily Eagle,* were "well-known in Brooklyn social circles." Though the *Eagle* did not disclose how the newlyweds had met, it may be assumed that the railroad's Seidl Society arrangements—including not only the train cars, but the facilities for unescorted woman at the railroad-operated Brighton Beach hotel—had been undertaken with Colonel Langford's participation. In addition to affirming the Seidl Society/Brighton Beach relationship, the marriage affirmed Holloway's social pedigree, heretofore buttressed by such fictions as one perpetuated in the *Eagle*'s wedding announcement: that she was "a cousin of Andrew Johnson." Laura Langford now belonged to an actual distinguished family—including the eminent Wagnerite critic W.J. Henderson, who happened to become her brother-in-law.[31]

Though attendance at the Brighton Beach music pavilion increased in 1890, though the emphasis on new music—Chabrier, Dvořák, Massenet, Mascagni, Saint-Saëns, Richard Strauss—ambitiously intensified, the enterprise still seemed chimerical to many. Others "disposed at first to scoff," testified a letter writer in the *New York Mirror,* remained "to pray." The railroad company elected not to engage Seidl in 1892 and 1893—a decision possibly influenced by the national financial crisis of 1891. When the Brighton concerts resumed in 1894, the Seidl Society supplanted the railroad/hotel as the presenting organization. The season now assumed its most tenacious form. Subscription seats cost as little as

FIGURE 10A. Brighton Beach program cover. Courtesy Brooklyn Historical Society.

fifteen cents, more commonly twenty-five—"ridiculously little," in the opinion of the *Musical Courier.* The repertoire included symphonies by Haydn, Mozart, Beethoven, Schubert, and Dvořák. Novelties by Berlioz, Liszt, and Saint-Saëns were commonplace. Wagner was performed, on average, more than twice daily. Wagner nights filled the three-thousand-seat pavilion to capacity. These seashore audiences were observed to be quieter than those in New York's winter concert rooms. The *Eagle* wrote: "All the social and intellectual factors of Brooklyn life are present . . . and the crowd there is unlike any gathered anywhere outside of Bayreuth. The Seidl concerts are the attraction. . . . When [they] are underway the grounds are deserted and the place wears a quiet Sunday afternoon aspect, amazing to strangers whose ideas of Coney Island have been gathered from accounts of the West End." Posted notices read: "Talking during the performance is a breach of politeness not common to Seidl audiences. Real lovers of fine music are considerate of their neighbors and always thoughtful of the courtesy due the conductor and the orchestra." Smoking was forbidden except in the last row of the upstairs gallery. Decorum was further ensured by Seidl Society ushers wearing "S" badges: "women of pleasant, modest demeanor but withal earnest and painstaking in their work." When admonitions failed, policemen were efficiently summoned.[32]

If all this was women's work, so too was the society's larger summer agenda, organized with missionary thoroughness and precision. In 1894, the hotel opened a restaurant in the Bathing Pavilion Building—a site near the train station and not far from the Music Hall. According to a Seidl Society announcement, "Ladies who remain over at the Beach between the Concerts will find the Pavilion dining rooms the best place to obtain delightful food, wholesome cooking, and at really modest prices. . . . The arrangements for the accommodation of ladies are altogether good." A Seidl Society Bicycle Rest, nearby, was available for overnight storage; tires were inflated free of charge. The society held free religious services at the Music Hall every Sunday morning at eleven—"Eminent Divinities of the various denominations will officiate. Members and friends of the Seidl Society are cordially invited to attend." The society offered singing lessons. Among the society's summer lecturers were Henry S. Olcott, president of the Theosophical Society ("The Power of Music in Psychic Development"), and the suffragettes Susan B. Anthony and Elizabeth Cady Stanton. Stanton told two hundred Seidl Society members that theirs was the first women's club known to her "organized on a basis of complete equality." She also said: "I think if you would make Mrs. Holloway commissioner of streets in New York they would not be dirty long. She could clean out New York City in less than three months." Henry Krehbiel offered lectures with musical examples performed by Anton Seidl at the piano. W.J. Henderson's talk on orchestration undertaken in 1890 "because many Seidl Society members confessed to their ignorance of various instruments" was said to be the first such musical lecture—in America or Europe—accompanied by a full orchestra (Anton Seidl conducting). The Wagner lectures Langford read in 1894, with their live symphonic excerpts, were an outgrowth of this singular activity.[33]

The society's special concerts included an 1896 "Free Cuba" benefit for Cuban soldiers wounded in the war with Spain; Seidl orchestrated Louis Moreau Gottschalk's "La Gallina" for the occasion. "Worker's" or "People's" Concerts, for which tickets were distributed at Brooklyn churches, featured waltzes, overtures, cornet and violin solos, and such ostensibly lighter Wagner as the act 1 finale of *Lohengrin.* A reporter at one such event observed "many Germans, apparently mechanics in the better paid trades" who "who understand music better than their wives do, thus reversing the rule of the regular Seidl and Philharmonic audiences." Working women with babies were invited to avail themselves of a "children's pavilion" with child care, a nursery, and a playroom.[34]

Children's matinees were a defining feature of every summer season. With the support of the railroad/hotel, these included the train ride to Coney Island, beach time, lunch, and an afternoon concert. Thousands—from the Hebrew Orphans Asylum, the Brooklyn Orphans Asylum, and other such institutions—took part annually. An "inflexible" rule required Seidl Society members to identify and accompany young "protégés." Tents with cots were provided for tired bodies—and also milk, ice cream, chewing gum, and candy. A typical "children's festival" program, given August 3, 1896, listed:

Nicolai: Overture to *The Merry Wives of Windsor*

Delibes: Pizzicato from *Sylvia*

Humperdinck: *Hansel and Gretel* excerpts

Bizet: Seguidilla and Toreador March from *Carmen*

Auber: Overture to *Fra Diavolo*

Wagner: *Tannhäuser* March

"America" (with singing by the Seidl Society Choir and the audience)

Though Seidl required an assistant conductor at Brighton Beach, he invariably led the concerts for children. "I think it is beautiful," he said in anticipation of the 1895 children's festival. "So many children to sing together will be an inspiration for the orchestra, and after the happy time they will go home and dream of the sweet songs they have sung and heard."[35]

Presumably, this "philanthropic" work was a chief topic at the annual Seidl Society summer luncheon—an event closed to the press because it was closed to men. (Of the 1891 luncheon, the *Eagle* reported: "No man was admitted even to look at the decorations of the table, but it is understood that these were suitably dainty.") Another Seidl Society news report, filed from Brighton Beach in 1889, pithily observed: "One of the ideas of this organization is to prove that women can enjoy themselves alone."[36]

Beginning in fall 1890—eight months following the success of the *Parsifal* Entertainment—the society also presented a "winter season" at the Academy of Music. The 1890–91 schedule of eleven concerts (October to March) far exceeded the New York Philharmonic's concurrent schedule of six concerts (November to April) across the river. The initial program, on October 20, was all-Wagner, beginning with the *Lohengrin* Prelude and closing with the Liebestod from *Tristan*. The second program was all-Liszt. The season's contemporary music included Grieg's *Peer Gynt*, Saint-Saëns's *Omphale's Spinning Wheel*, and Strauss's *Don Juan*. The closing event, on March 19, was a Grand *Parsifal* Concert including music not heard at the *Parsifal* Entertainment. As the Metropolitan Opera Chorus took part, it was possible to give act 3 in its entirety; the Prelude and act 2 excerpts were also heard. An announcement read: "The Seidl Society has spared no outlay or effort to have the most notable musical event in the history of Brooklyn." The Family Circle at the Academy of Music was entirely reserved for "working women who love music," every member of the society having been invited to submit two names and addresses of women "who work for their own support and are considered suitable candidates for this courtesy." Reviewing the penultimate concert of the 1890–91 season, the *Eagle* summarized:

> Speaking in all earnestness, it ought to be said in dignity, in beauty, in loftiness of aim and fullness of fulfillment the concert had not had its equal in either New York or Brooklyn this season. . . . The 10 concerts of the Seidl Society have been phenomenally successful. They have quickened the artistic spirit of Brooklyn and opened a new era in its musical life. . . . They have also demonstrated most strikingly the capacity of women to labor in larger

> and nobler fields than ordinarily occupy their attention in the department of art.[37]

After that, the Seidl Society presented up to sixteen concerts seasonally at the Brooklyn Academy. Popular prices were maintained. Fundraising (to pay off the annual deficit) stressed donations of twenty-five cents to a dollar. "Larger contributions will of course be accepted, but if the desired sum should be raised by the donation of small amounts the society feels that it had accomplished a great work in reaching so many people." Only Seidl conducted. His "Metropolitan" or "Seidl" Orchestra comprised players he regularly engaged. The cathedral setting for the *Parsifal* Entertainment was retained for all concerts, with the addition of palms at the base of the columns. The hall was darkened—a practice far less common than today. As in summer, the society sponsored lectures, both on Wagner and a variety of nonmusical subjects. A Seidl Society Chorus—both women and men—was formed. As in summer, children's matinees might feature a Weber overture, a Liszt Hungarian Rhapsody, or the Intermezzo from Mascagni's *Cavalleria rusticana*. Though there were no seashore excursions, the society would for instance host Thanksgiving dinner for the Howard Orphan Asylum (Brooklyn's poorest). "There were about one hundred and twenty of these orphans," reported the *New York World*.

> Every one of them was occupied dispatching a large plate of turkey, cranberry sauce and vegetables, and seemed too busy to take any notice of strangers.
>
> Beautiful women dressed in handsome silks, which were covered with aprons, waited on them. These women were members of the Seidl Society, and they would not allow any of the colored attachés of the asylum to do any of the work. For three days previous they had been busy preparing for the feast, and were assisted by two professional cooks from New York. All the cakes and delicacies were made by the women themselves.[38]

The Seidl Society was never shy about calibrating the magnitude of its achievement. Langford called the society a "new departure in the history of women's clubs." A typical self-description of the Brighton Breach concerts read:

> There is no place in the world where concerts approaching in artistic merit those given by Mr. Seidl and his Metropolitan Orchestra, can be heard at the nominal cost of 25 cents, and there is no other organization in this country that gives concerts of equal merit throughout the year—winter and summer—as the Seidl Society. Its object is to further a national interest in music, and to enable the people to hear the best music and amid the most congenial

surroundings. The great success of the Winter Concerts—their exceptional artistic merit and decorative accessories—have spread the name and fame of the Seidl Society over every city in the Union. . . . The Seidl Society works for success . . . it is a woman's organization whose ideal of usefulness is to set an example of practical work and public enterprise, and to advance widespread interest in music.[39]

As a Seidl Society mouthpiece, the *Daily Eagle* praised "the energetic and ever enthusiastic workers who are trying with much diligence and patience to make Brooklyn the music center of the nation." The *Eagle* also observed: "The capacity of the members of this society to hustle and sell concert tickets is what baseball managers call phenomenal." As of 1894, the *Eagle* marveled that the Seidl Society had "maintained itself . . . with a perseverance almost of the Calvinistic saints until its name is everywhere known and famous. Business men would not assume such responsibility in the hope of accumulated wealth. They can scarcely be blamed, for business is business. But an organization of women will sometimes courageously assume risks from which mere men will shrink." Kenyon West, a writer of ephemeral distinction, celebrated the Seidl Society in 1894 for Lyman Abbott's New York *Outlook*—an article reprinted by the *Eagle,* and again by the Seidl Society. It read in part:

There is one aspect of the higher life of Brooklyn which is not receiving the praise it deserves. In one respect she can hold herself head and shoulders above other cities, and that is because of the concerts which are held every summer at Brighton Beach. These concerts owe their existence to the self-sacrificing efforts of a few noble and clever Brooklyn women, who have formed themselves into a society for the cultivation of musical taste among the masses. . . . Here we have the opportunity of hearing the finest music in the world, rendered by one of the best orchestras in the country, conducted by one of the greatest conductors the world has ever seen, a man famous on two continents. What do we pay for the concerts? Twenty cents apiece, occasionally forty cents! I can buy as many tickets for the whole season as I have time to use, and they will cost me no more than the price charged for one seat in the opera house during the winter. It seems to me that when the Music Hall at Brighton is not well filled, it shows a singular disregard of great opportunities for culture, for recreation, for refreshment of the spirit, for the uplifting of the soul. . . .

The great difference between this Seidl Society and many others is that its object is not self interest, it is pure benevolence. It is plain that such music cannot be furnished at such a price without some people putting their hands in their pockets and giving largely. Is this not as good as endowing a library? . . . I have often thought that if some rich men would endow the Metropolitan Opera House in New York, and make it possible for these great singers and musical artists to be heard by the great mass of music lov-

> ers, of hungry, thirsty, aspiring men and women, who now cannot afford even a glimpse of the inside of the Opera House, . . . it would be as noble an act as the founding of the Astor Library, or the building of the Chicago University, or President Low's gift to Columbia.[40]

The director of the music school at Indiana's DePauw University, in an 1891 letter to the *Musical Courier,* exclaimed: "What the managers mean by not advertising these concerts properly throughout the country is more than I can comprehend. Here is one of the best orchestras in the world . . . giving two unsurpassed concerts every day for two months or more, rendering the best music and the latest of imported scores. . . . I hope to listen to about 60 concerts before I leave." If the Manhattan press was less attentive and more circumspect, the *Musical Courier* once exclaimed, "Goodness knows what they do it for. Ordinary women would rather put the energy into new bonnets and send the money to the missionary Huyler. But these women are extraordinary, and some time after they are all dead the town will be putting up a monument to them as public benefactors, perhaps with a bas-relief representing Herr Seidl waving his baton and a chorus of adoring angels about him."[41]

"SEIDL'S GREAT ORCHESTRA" did find its way into Broadway's first electric sign, a Coney Island advertisement in five colors. But no Seidl monument was ever erected. Nor did "the name and fame of the Seidl Society" spread "over every city in the Union"; the society's penchant for self-praise documents a hunger for recognition—and, at Brighton Beach, for patrons—never satisfied. And yet Langford, today forgotten, was one of the most astonishing operatives in the history of American classical music. The claims she made were merely just. Very likely, no contemporaneous concerts of comparable distinction, in the New World or Old, so promoted new music—the "Music of the Future" of Wagner and Liszt. Inspired by Bayreuth, the ambience of the society's concerts—the darkened hall, the diligent ushers, the "decorative accessories"—was also singular. So was the zealous democratic philanthropy of the entire enterprise. No one more fervently understood than Seidl himself. The Seidl Society Archives at the Brooklyn Historical Society contain a Brighton Beach speech, in Seidl's hand, preserving his painstakingly awkward English. It begins:

> Ladies and Few Gentlemen!
> Now we are again on work, to play good music for good men and women. Those who are good, they like the music and go to the places, where the

good music can be heard. Those, who like only the airs as "Jonny get your gun" find places on this shore very many. We will play only good music; we know, the people need it, and this is the cause, that the noble ladies of the Seidl Society don't spare the large expenses and the terrible difficult and heavy work to give the good people, what he needs, and what he must have. It is not only right, to give the poor free music at the different parks, but the Bands must play good music. The people not understand it first, but later he will whistle it with more dash and vigor, as the rich, who sits in his box and—chatter, because—he does not understand it. But the low kind of music demoralizes the people. One of the many good works of the Seidl Society is to give good music for the less rich, for the poor, and in the same time enjoys and educates himself. This is a grand and glorious mission! And a point to which of must direct the eyes of the whole world, is, that this society works not for money, as the so-called managers of nearly all the musical organizations do, but the noble ladies of this society brings many thousands and thousands dollars together, to enable themselves to give good music for 25 cents to the poor and music needing people. This only women can do. The men must stand still and be astonished before such a grand work![42]

. . .

"What she does she does with all her might," the *Eagle* wrote of Laura Langford. "She is not easily daunted by difficulties and ordinary obstacles have no terrors for her."[43] Reports of Langford's activities, and the letters she wrote and received, document a tenacious and combative business personality. Whether acknowledging applause and bouquets onstage, or sharing her aspirations and misgivings, she did not shrink from the public gaze.

Merely typical was an entanglement with Lillian Nordica. The Met's reigning Wagner soprano, Nordica was a singer closely linked to Seidl; he coached her assiduously in the big Wagner roles. Nordica was scheduled to appear at a Seidl Society concert in December 1894. Informed that a Metropolitan Opera engagement the same day would take precedence, Langford wrote not to Maurice Grau, who managed the Met, but to Nordica herself. She also released the letter to the press:

Dear Mme. Nordica—
It seems impossible to believe that you will consent to break a contract with the Seidl Society, made before your opera engagement, and until you tell me yourself I will not withdraw the announcement. . . . Your failure to sing will place the society in an awkward position before the public, and naturally, as its chief officer, I want to have a clear understanding with you before action is taken in the matter. If you will send reply by bearer of this note you will oblige yours sincerely

Laura Carter Langford

In reply, Nordica made it known through a representative that a delayed Atlantic crossing had forced a rescheduling at the Met. Seidl now commented to the *Daily Eagle:* "Certainly it looks queer. . . . Mme. Nordica was bound by contract to sing with us." The Seidl Society was reported to be seeking "legal counsel." Nordica felt forced to speak out directly; she told the *Eagle* she was a victim of "gross injustice"—the late arrival of a steamer constituted "force majeur." Whereupon Langford told the *Eagle:* "Mme. Nordica's letter . . . is well timed as an advertisement for her opera appearances here." Next Seidl pointed that out that he, too, had obligations to Grau: "My case is precisely like that of Mme. Nordica, only I keep my word. Mme. Nordica agreed to sing at the Seidl concert before she made her opera engagement." In a similar situation, he had foregone a conducting invitation at the Met in favor of leading a previously scheduled benefit concert for a Hungarian charity. Nordica was replaced on the Seidl Society program; a program note stated: "Owing to the violation of contract on the part of the soloist who was advertised to sing this evening, the Seidl Society has been compelled to change somewhat its original Wagner program."[44]

Earlier the same year, Langford took no prisoners dealing with a cancellation by a lesser-known singer, Maria Basta Tavary—represented, however, by a leading agent: Henry Wolfsohn. Langford told the press: "She . . . sent word she would not sing, and her agent has given no satisfactory reason. The excuse given was that Mme. Tavary was very busy pushing her own work and could not give up the time. Mr. Wolfsohn has disappointed us before but will not have a chance to do so again."[45] Equally public was a prolonged spat with the Brooklyn Institute, which violated an understanding that the Seidl Society would exclusively present Paderewski in Brooklyn in November 1895. Paderewski's appearance with the Seidl orchestra at the Academy of Music nonetheless represented a Seidl Society coup; normally, the society frugally eschewed celebrity instrumentalists. Its grandest expectations were reserved for fully staged Wagner performances—an aspiration never satisfied, but frequently discussed. When a planned Academy of Music production of *Siegfried* fell through in 1892, the society published a "Card to the Public" signed by Langford:

> The Seidl Society, with deep regret announces its inability to give German Opera in Brooklyn this season. . . .
>
> The scenery belonging to the Metropolitan Opera House, having been promised, the Society felt full security in making public its plans for this bril-

liant conclusion of its season of 1891–92. The following telegram will verify the position of the Society in proceeding with its arrangements:

> Metropolitan Opera House, April 5th
> "You can have the scenery if you will tell me what you can use."
>
> In addition to this telegram Mr. Edmund C. Stanton [the company manager, long a colleague of Anton Seidl] had previously given a verbal promise that "it was all right."
>
> Days later the following telegram came: "I have just received this notice, 'the Directors don't care to loan the scenery as it would have to be cut.'"
>
> It is but just to Mr. Stanton to say that he did all in his power to obtain the use of the scenery for the Seidl Society, especially for Mr. Seidl's sake; and it is due to Mr. Seidl also to say that he did all in his power from first to last to complete the arrangements and enable the Society to maintain its assumed obligation to the public.
>
> The Society therefore relies upon the generosity of its patrons and friends to believe that it has not failed because of lack of effort and honest dealing on its part to give the opera.[46]

If in matters of public tact Langford went her own way, her dealings with Seidl were a model of harmonious efficiency. Beyond a doubt, many in the Seidl Society were enamored of Wagner and Seidl both; one newspaper account observed "hundreds of adoring eyes from hundreds of pretty faces" following Herr Seidl's afternoon constitutional fronting the hotel veranda. Langford's correspondence with Seidl discloses no evidence of such infatuation; rather, it evokes a relationship remarkable for its equality. She wrote "Dear Mr. Seidl" and "Sincerely"; he called her "Mrs. Langford." The transportation of music and musicians, the arrangements for meals and hotel rooms, the payment of salary and back salary were her daily concerns. If Seidl needed an extra rehearsal, he asked understanding that Langford might say no. If he needed a soloist, he might invite her input. Sometimes he asked her to choose a soloist herself. Mrs. Seidl, writing to "Mrs. Langford," called her "my best friend. . . . you have my love for ever." Lilli Lehmann, an imperious artist, was at the same time a no-nonsense activist who might rummage through the Met's property room or rearrange scenery. Writing to Langford, she was utterly familiar; she signed herself "Lilli."[47]

Mutual appreciation girded Seidl's relationship to Langford. At one 1894 dinner, he quipped that Grau and Henry Abbey, at the Met, could be taught a "lesson" by the Seidl Society in how to give sixteen performances for seventy thousand dollars. When the society gave him a rocking chair for a present, he wrote to Langford: "As much pleasure this chair has given me, I don't favor the idea, that my friends trouble themselves, to reward my artistic doings which come from the bottom of my heart." A revealing episode: in 1896, Seidl's Brighton Beach orchestra hired its first female member—the harpist Inez Carusi ("a handsome Italian-American, with the temperament of a woman and the touch of a man"). Some musicians objected that she was not a member of the union—which, being female, she could not be. She complained that she was paid less than her male predecessor—whereupon Seidl's long-time orchestra manager, Samuel (or Siegmund or Sigismund) Bernstein, reportedly threatened to fire her. Langford took Carusi's side—publicly. She told the press she had placed the matter in Seidl's hands: "I trust him." Carusi stayed.[48]

A single crisis interrupted the equanimity of the Langford/Seidl relationship. The Met's Wagner-dominated "German seasons" of 1884 to 1891 were ended by a boxholders' rebellion in favor of more glamorous French and Italian fare. No longer engaged by the Met, Seidl took over the New York Philharmonic. But the Germans would not be put down: opera in German returned to the house in 1895. For whatever reasons, the Met dates offered to Seidl conflicted with scheduled Seidl Society commitments in Brooklyn—which Seidl elected to abandon. "It would be a strange thing if a body of women, who have kept Mr. Seidl in bread and butter for several years should go on doing it after he had repudiated his contract," mused the *Daily Eagle*. "If they were men there would be but one answer to the question." Other articles inferred that Seidl had used the society while pursuing his main interests elsewhere. Seidl himself said: "I will not answer any question. But I will say that I do not ask any women for my bread."[49]

In an agonizing move, the Seidl Society changed its name to the Brooklyn Symphony Society and hired Seidl's onetime New York rival, Theodore Thomas, to perform in Brooklyn with his Chicago Orchestra. But New York had outgrown Thomas's staid manner; his concerts—in March 1896—failed to ignite. Weeks later, the "Seidl Society" was back, and so was Seidl; he called himself a "victim of circumstances." "I suppose you know that we have gone back to our old Seidolatry," said the *Musical Courier*. "There was this winter an effort to convert [Brooklyn] from false gods to a worship of music as divorced from any personality whatever. The attempt has failed." The pertinent correspondence discloses a behind-the-scenes story at variance with such gloating reports. The society itself had supported Seidl's return to the Met. "The position in which the Seidl Society is placed by reason of your inability to direct its concerts this winter is such that the public must have an explanation," Langford wrote to Seidl. "I cannot consent to bear this responsibility." Seidl explained to Langford that he had necessarily agreed to Brooklyn dates before getting his New York dates because Grau had been abroad and the Met schedule was late to congeal; "I wish I had never spoken to Grau about opera dates," he told her. As for not asking "any woman for bread," he explained to Langford that a reporter had read to him the *Eagle*'s characterization of "a body of women, who have kept Mr. Seidl in bread and butter." "Then I said, to him, I never asked anybody for bread and butter; and then left him alone. Now I see in the evening paper of the Eagle this misrepresented in a very impertinent manner. . . . I think, you will hardly believe, that I can use such language toward women or the Seidl Society."[50]

The resumption of Seidl Society concerts on May 1, 1896, was sealed by the participation of Lillian Nordica, likewise returned to Langford's good graces. She sang the Liebestod and an aria from Goldmark's *The Queen of Sheba*. The other numbers were Beethoven's *Leonore* Overture No. 3, the *Siegfried Idyll,* and—a Langford favorite—Liszt's *Les préludes*. The audience's "smolding affection leaped into flame again when the object of it appeared in his jovian impassiveness and suffered himself to be decorated," reported the *Eagle*. The *Musical Courier*'s version of the same event acquired a different tone and must be quoted at length:

> Ever eat crow? Like it? Come over here and learn how to cook it, and maybe you will find it not displeasing. Take a crow that has ripened in the ice box, and stuff it with ingyuns, serve it with sauce piquante, have proper drinks and side dishes, the prejudice against this useful bird will be at least partially dispelled. The great lesson in how to eat crow was given at the Academy of Music on Friday night. If you have seen our papers you will know that on that evening, Mr. Seidl played there for the Seidl Society, to raise money for a continuation of Seidl Society concerts by the Seidl Orchestra at Brighton Beach. You will also remember that a little while ago there wasn't any Seidl Society. It committed suicidl in a huff, and its ashes were reincarnated as the Brooklyn Symphony Society. . . .
>
> Mr. Seidl was applauded with rapture when he appeared on the stage a quarter of an hour late and lightly flushed, but firm and outwardly calm. They wouldn't even let him play until he had allowed the multitude to encore his charming bow two or three times, and it was well that he struck into the third Leonora overture with some precipitation, or the reception might have advanced to hysterics. After the Liszt Preludes an usher ran up with a big laurel wreath.
>
> At the conclusion of the Siegfried Idyl [*sic*] there was another rush and

> another big wreath, only this time it had roses on it. Nordica, too, who was freighted in a similar manner, spared one of her bouquets to Mr. Seidl, and put it on his desk, so that after he got into this carriage the director must have felt more like a greenhouse than a crow. And every time he came on or went out there was a hurrah, and it is all over, and the crow has been digested.[51]

To the *Eagle,* the Seidl Society would have been tougher with Seidl's dereliction "if they were men." To the *Musical Courier,* unctuously satisfied to see Langford "eat crow," the gushing Seidlites were prone to "hysterics," "rapture," and "Seidolatry." They adored bouquets and decorations, suffragettes and orphans. Earlier, in 1889, the *Courier* opined that it seemed "rather ridiculous" to serve "a Beethoven symphony after dinner." The "bands of matrons" required "special cars" and "Seidl club rooms." Their "struggles to found a Seidl cult were not calculated to attract real lovers of music." And yet the same women were in 1895 equally castigated, in the same publication, for being insufficiently feminine: "There are a few of us who do not admire the earnest, manly women of the Seidl Society." As of 1896, the *Musical Courier* further complained: "The press"—comprised of men—"has not been treated with the courtesy that insures attention, the whole scheme has been retained and carried on for the effort at personal aggrandizement of a few enterprising people." A "narrow-minded policy"—that is, women only—"dictated the display of the names of a few women who sought social supremacy as the total object of their efforts." They were humorlessly smitten and pretentious; they were boastful and combative. They were too feminine; they were too masculine.[52]

Langford, to be sure, was no humorist or ironist. Her disastrous first marriage, her post–Civil War impoverishment, her biographical fabrications contributed to a quest both purposeful and dire. If Seidl, by comparison, did not lack humor or ease, if he was far less a victim of hardship and prejudice, his was equally a driven mission. Off the podium, he was private, taciturn, retiring. The critic Henry Finck, who knew him well, considered Seidl "too modest"; he "lacked the quality of Yankee 'push' so necessary in this country." Langford pushed. Another of Seidl's handwritten speeches, for an 1894 Seidl Society banquet, assembles these factors as follows:

> Ladies and Gentlemen!
>
> All I feel, can be said with few words, that is to assure <u>you</u>, the <u>Seidl Society</u> and <u>Mrs. Langford</u>, the indefatigable president of this noble Society, of my deep and heartfelt thanks for your enthusiasm to musical art. . . . I

> am proud, that you have selected me to operate with you in this inspiring and dignifying work. The only strange feeling that I have is that anyone can have the courage to belittle and hate our efforts to do the best for art! The result of such unjust and unartistic enmity will be always favorable to us and our affairs, and we can say surely after a five years battle: We are all well in spite of ill will. That means again hard work, enthusiasm, and endurance to continue our successes. I hope, we are all united to carry out our plans. Our Concerts are excellent weapons to spread the education and love for music. . . .
>
> Nobody shall hope, that I will loose my patience and leave for another battlefield. . . . I am in the same way worth of notice here as Bergmann, Anshuetz, Maretzek, Gilmore, Dr. Damrosch and Thomas;* they all born in Europe and came here to fight and stand for Music and Art, why I should let irritate me in my work. Luckiness and smartness is a very important thing in Amerika, and happy is the man, who has it, but I will not cease to believe, that a honest man, who knows his art excellently, and stands for the ideal in art, shall have the victory of his ideal in the future.[53]

• • •

The central purpose of Seidl's 1894 banquet speech, however, was not to deflect criticism and hostility; he preached an irrepressible ultimate goal: a Brooklyn Bayreuth. Alluding to Langford's abortive earlier efforts to stage Wagner, he took the view that mounting "12 or 16 German Opera Programs is not an establishment! . . . You will have perhaps three or four new Singers—nothing more." Rather, the society should present an entire season of staged opera, alternating monthly between two weeks of German opera and two weeks of French. This, Seidl said, would signify "stability."

And there was Seidl Society talk, as well, of building a Brooklyn opera house for Wagner. It was rumored that Wagner's widow, Cosima, might visit Brooklyn, or that her son, Siegfried, would come to study conducting with Seidl, or that Seidl would himself relocate from Manhattan to Brooklyn. Seidl on one occasion proposed that his New York Philharmonic perform regularly under the auspices of the Seidl Society; "you will then be the Queen of the musical world in Brooklyn," he wrote to Langford.[54] Given the society's momentum, these expectations could not be written off as preposterous. If Bayreuth—the Bavarian hamlet in which Wagner had settled, built a theater, and begun a festival—was the rarified European epicenter of Wagnerism, Brooklyn

*The conductors Carl Bergmann, Karl Anschütz, Max Maretzek, Patrick Gilmore, Leopold and Walter Damrosch, and Theodore Thomas.

could become a New World Wagner haven. Juxtaposed with the commercial bustle and immigrant turmoil of Manhattan, it was a city of churches—of aspirant steeples and bucolic parks. And it escaped the Manhattan cliques and rivalries in which Seidl was embroiled. With the termination of the Met's German seasons in 1891, Seidl found himself leading Wagner in Italian at the Met, alongside Luigi Mancinelli and Auguste Vianesi. His New York Philharmonic was a part-time band offering fewer programs than Walter Damrosch's New York Symphony. Finally, in November 1895 Seidl again led German opera in German at the Met, but the house was now in effect split between two companies—one German, one Italian/French, each with its own chorus.

In May 1896, the Seidl Society incorporated, with a capital stock of twenty thousand dollars and an additional official purpose: to "acquire land for . . . a people's music hall." Several architects were reported to have already submitted designs; there was talk of starting construction the following fall. The society would continue to present its summer and winter seasons, would continue its philanthropic work, but there would be no more purely social meetings or functions.[55] Executive power was vested in a board of directors, with Langford as president. Stock in the corporation was only available to women, with an emphasis on women who worked. The corporation was investigating whether to limit the number of shares obtainable by any one person.

The ensuing Brighton Beach season was—as Langford told the press in late August—the biggest ever: nine weeks and five days. A new elevated line running directly from the Brooklyn Bridge every twenty minutes opened late in the summer and was expected to boost future attendance. The 1896 repertoire mirrored the impressively mixed constituency—of veterans and novices, wives and "overawed and somewhat sheepish" husbands—the society had amassed.[56] Wagner, as ever, led the list: 196 performances in the course of 134 concerts. The symphonies—a formidable list—were Beethoven's third, sixth, and seventh, Schubert's C major, and Schumann's fourth. The single most-performed selection was a medley from Bizet's *Carmen.* The fourth and fifth most-performed composers—after Wagner, Liszt, and Saint-Seans—were Gillet and Moszkowski: froth.

Two calamities doomed everything. The first, on October 12, 1896, was a "monster wave" that split the iron pier at Brighton Beach and left the Music Hall a rubble. Tearful women rushed to the site even before the damage had subsided. Never again would the Brighton Beach Hotel host symphonic concerts. The following summer, Seidl, long absent

THE SEIDL SOCIETY'S BICYCLE REST.

The ample accommodations at Brighton Beach Music Hall for bicycles is being appreciated by wheelmen. The Rest is situated near the Music Hall, and is a safe and convenient place for leaving wheels day and evening. Those desiring to leave their bicycles over night are assured that they will be stored in safety and delivered at any time after nine o'clock in the morning.

The Rest can be reached from the Cycle Path, and is situated on the lawn at the end of the Music Hall.

TIRES INFLATED FREE OF CHARGE.

THE CONCERTS

will begin at 3.10 in the afternoons and 8.10 in the evenings, so as to enable all to reach the Hall from the train before the music begins.

10

Seidl Society Concerts

BRIGHTON BEACH MUSIC HALL.

PROGRAMME.

Wednesday Afternoon, July 8th.

AT 8.10 O'CLOCK.

1. Overture, "La Dame Blanche," . . . *Boieldieux*
2. Unfinished Symphony, . . . *Schubert*
   (*a*) Allegro non troppo. (*b*) Andante con moto.
3. Siegfried Forging the Sword, . . . *Wagner*
4. (*a*) Traumerei, . . . *Schumann*
   (*b*) Dream After the Ball, . . . *Czibulka*
5. Cinderella, a Fairy Tale, . . . *Bendel*
6. Night in Lisbon, . . . *Saint-Saëns*
7. Ballet Music, "Sylvia," . . . *Delibes*
   (*a*) The Huntresses. (*b*) Slow Waltz. (*c*) Pizzicati. (*d*) Bacchanale.

Wednesday Evening, July 8th.

AT 8.10 O'CLOCK.

GRAND WAGNER FESTIVAL, I.

Soloists: Madame DE VERE-SAPIO, Miss GERTRUDE STEIN, Mr. H. EVAN WILLIAMS, Mr. EMIL FISCHER, Mr. ROYAL STONE SMITH.

1. Overture, "Tannhäuser,"
2. (*a*) Am stillen Herd, from "Die Meistersinger."
   (*b*) Spring Song, from "Die Walkuere."
   Mr. WILLIAMS.
3. Grand Bacchanale, from "Tannhäuser,"
   (Parisian Version of the Venusberg.)
4. Elizabeth's Aria, from "Tannhäuser."
   Madame DE VERE-SAPIO.
5. Siegfried Forging the Sword, from "Siegfried."
6. Quintet, from "Die Meistersinger."
   Madame DE VERE-SAPIO, Miss GERTRUDE STEIN, Mr. WILLIAMS, Mr. FISCHER, Mr. SMITH.
7. Wotan's Farewell and Magic Fire Scene, from "Die Walkuere."
   Wotan: Mr. EMIL FISCHER.

The Wissner Piano used Exclusively.

The Mason & Hamlin-Liszt Organ used Exclusively at these Concerts.

The above Music is for sale by Edward Schuberth & Co., 23 Union Square, New York

11

FIGURE 10B. From the 1896 Brighton Beach program books. Courtesy Brooklyn Historical Society.

from Europe, returned to Bayreuth to lead *Parsifal.* In 1897–98, Seidl Society concerts resumed at the Academy of Music. A new and better Brighton Beach music pavilion was under discussion. A permanent Seidl Society chorus of two hundred voices was announced, as was a new emphasis on American repertoire. Even the *Musical Courier* called the society's plans "nothing if not prodigious." Then, on December 8, 1897, Anton Seidl died at the age of forty-seven. The funeral, three days later at the Metropolitan Opera House, was a singular occasion.* Langford's house was one of four sites where tickets had been distributed. Seidl's passing was reported and pondered in the New York press for nearly a week. Lillian Nordica wrote: "When a man of such high purpose comes into the world he impresses an influence extending so far beyond his time that it is not given to us to estimate it." Though Seidl had never renounced his Catholic faith, he was cremated, according to his wishes. (One press report, headlined "Church Will Not Bury Anton Seidl," called him "an advanced thinker.") An organist at Fresh Pond Cemetery played Siegfried's Funeral Music and Elsa's Prayer. A floral tribute from the Seidl Society was embellished with the words "Seidl Society" and "Les Préludes."[57]

Months later, on May 2, the Seidl Society held a memorial concert. Lyman Abbott delivered the eulogy. Emil Fischer, a much-loved bass in his final American performance, sang Wotan's Farwell. The program also included the Dream Music from Humperdinck's *Hansel und Gretel,* Liszt's *Les préludes* and *Concerto pathétique* (arranged for piano and orchestra), and, to close, Siegfried's Funeral Music, for which the audience was asked to stand. An additional selection, by Seidl himself, was the children's chorus "Good Night," which he had affectionately composed for the Seidl Society young people's concerts; the poem, by Edna Dean Proctor, read in part:

> Good-night! Good-night! The morn will light
> The east before the dawn,
> And stars arise to gem the skies
> When these have westward gone.
> Good-night! And sweet be thy repose
> Through all their shining way,
> Till darkness goes, and bird and rose,
> With rapture greet the day,—
> Good-night![58]

*Cf. page 89.

Langford rose to explain that, as Fischer was sailing for Europe that very day, Wotan's Farewell would be repositioned near the beginning of the evening. A newspaper account reported: "The audience manifested its pleasure on seeing the woman who has done so much for the advancement of music in Brooklyn, for generous rounds of applause greeted the brave little woman."[59] This short speech effectively ended Laura Langford's public career. A final clipping in the Seidl Society scrapbooks announces the possibility of an October concert at Plymouth Church with string orchestra and the organist William Carl; no such concert took place. A Seidl monument at Brighton Beach was advocated by the *Eagle;* none was erected. The Seidl Society ceased to exist.

• • •

It is probable that Laura Holloway first encountered members of the United Society of Believers in Christ's Second Appearing—the Protestant sect known as the Shakers—in 1873, a few years after moving to Brooklyn from New York City. The occasion was a New York meeting at which Elder Frederick Evans excoriated "the rottenness of manmade creeds and hypocritical professions."[60]

The Shakers' own homemade creed was that God could be found within the individual, rather than through clergy or rituals. The Shaker aesthetic was understated, plain. But Shaker worship featured shaking, trembling, singing, dancing, and shouting—a robust communal purgation. Shaker celibacy—only through conversion or adoption could the community be enlarged—was doubtless a factor in purgative Shaker rites. Celibacy also favored equality of the sexes, as did the Shaker ban on marriage; Shaker women did not submit to the authority of husbands. In communal Shaker families, men and women did all things separately. They used different staircases. They sat on opposite sides of a room. Religious authority, too, was shared. Beginning in the eighteenth century with Mother Ann Lee, the supreme Shaker leader was typically female. God was understood to partake of both male and female traits.

Laura Holloway, in 1873, proposed to Elder Frederick that his North Family—at Mt. Lebanon, in eastern New York State—host a summer holiday for indigent boys. The Mt. Lebanon Central Ministry was lifting restrictions on contacts with non-Shakers. The Shaker regime would be physically invigorating and morally empowering. But Evans said no: "My object, like your own, would be to befriend the better class," he wrote Holloway; "I can do nothing with the lowest." A month later, Holloway sent a youngster named John to live with the North Family.

Elder Frederick deemed the boy "a desperate case," but called Holloway "a queen of Righteousness."[61]

In fact, the Shakers esteemed Holloway as a clairvoyant. And they looked to her to promote their mission. Shakers were sympathetically portrayed in the *Daily Eagle;* one article asserted that Shaker women lived long and serene lives. After her admission to the Theosophical Society in 1884, Holloway became a conduit to the North Family for New Thought, Christian Science, and the "mind cure." Though her theosophical beliefs—in reincarnation, in esoteric knowledge conveyed by spiritual masters—did not align with Shaker gospel, North Family members welcomed mediums and participated in séances. Holloway represented both a challenge and an opportunity. And the Shakers' relative empowerment of women doubtless appealed to her.

The Seidl Society years interrupted Laura Langford's overtures to the North Family. But in 1901, a time of personal crisis, she again inquired about placing children at Mt. Lebanon. Eldress Anna White replied: "We take children but not all kinds, they need sorting. We have taken Asylum children, but the Asylum trait was upon all of them. Most of them were from the slums, and the change was too much for them, and too much for us with their slang . . . , jeer and scoffings." Langford now revealed that her nineteen-year-old nephew, Charles Erasmus Terry, had lost his widowed mother. The North Family accepted him in 1902, but Charles—whom Langford described as "feeble minded"—prove unruly. He returned to Brooklyn and probably lived with Langford for the rest of his life.[62]

When in July 1902 Edward Langford died, Langford's philanthropic energies revived—with the Shakers. In 1903, she expressed interest in purchasing Shaker property for a school for girls. Eldress Anna White offered to rent a large vacant house. "The plan meets the approval of nearly all," she wrote. "Shaker villages are quiet places and too rampageous youngsters would not be acceptable, but of course you will select a good class of children." In 1904 this became "St. Ann's Inn" or "Mountain Home" or "Ana Lee Cottage": Mt. Lebanon's first experiment with hosting outsiders. Twenty-two students, aged three to twelve, enrolled. Eldress White wrote to Langford: "We look to you as a leader in the forth-coming cycle to open anew the spiritual avenues and help build up this cause which is to redeem the world." But Langford, hatching fresh plans for "a model Kindergarten" and a coeducational school, was moving too fast. White explained: "There are two distinct elements existing in this little village of ours diametrically opposite, the one rigid conservatism, the other extreme radicalism, both dangerous when unbalanced by the other. . . . In view of this, it is my judgment, dear Laura . . . not to project beyond what we can perform what will be acceptable."[63]

What Langford had achieved in Brooklyn, supported by Seidl and by her husband's railroad interests, proved untenable in cloistered Mt. Lebanon. Langford eagerly insisted that her efforts would help the Shakers to evolve and survive. While White regarded Langford as an instrument of divine providence, she labored—unsuccessfully—to hold Langford in check. Mountain Home was closed in summer 1905. Shaker opinion remained divided about "Sister Laura"—was she a miracle-worker or an interloper? The Shakers attempted to reopen the home in 1906 under their own strict control—but Langford was not controllable. To Shaker chagrin, she publicized Mountain Home as a fresh-air sanctuary for homeless city children. She continued to press for a school for girls. The Shakers were relieved to see their summer visitors depart.

A business venture gone awry sank Langford's relationship with the Shakers. She hoped to buy Shaker land to create a sanitarium for neurasthenics. Elder Daniel Offord supported a "celebate [*sic*] sanitarium" and in 1906 sold Langford Mt. Lebanon's large Upper Canaan farm for eight thousand dollars, to be paid in installments without interest. "We make this proposition because we are heart and soul in the object and purpose it will be devoted to," Offord testified. But Langford discovered that the buildings she now owned were uninhabitable, and that to fix the largest—the planned sanitarium—would cost as much as building anew. The farm was littered with debris: beer and whiskey bottles, cans and broken crockery. The Shakers evidently idealized the property and remembered it as it had been years before. Worse, the sewers were clogged and the water supply—a spring—was contested. By early 1911, Langford could not sustain her payments. She threatened to sue. She demanded that the Shakers buy back the farm—which they could not afford to do. She fell ill. In December 1910, Eldress Anna died. "If you have any communications from her, will you not let us hear from you?" wrote Elder Daniel—who himself expired in February 1911.[64]

Langford's ties to the Shakers ultimately languished. Her dream of Shaker regeneration had led to her own isolation and impoverishment. By the 1920s, she was living reclusively with her brother Vaulx and nephew Charlie on the Upper Canaan land she had hoped would heal souls. The farm's assessed value had shrunk to seventy-five hundred dollars. She mortgaged it three times and was reduced to begging friends for gifts or loans. She died in obscurity in 1930.

. . .

While the fervor of Anton Seidl's female constituency was exceptional, American opera and concert audiences of the late Gilded Age were preponderantly female. Overwhelmingly, it was women, as well, who read music, taught it, and performed it—playing the piano or singing—at home. Classical music constituted a women's world, and music itself was genteel and "feminine," in contradistinction to a masculine world of business and money, governments and armies.

But it does not follow that America's fin-de-siècle musical life was cloistered, superficial, or bland. Henry Krehbiel's Seidl Society lectures bristled with technical and historical detail. His *How to Listen to Music: Hints and Suggestions to Untaught Lovers of the Art* extolled "the capacity properly to listen to music" as a "rare accomplishment."* If the stereotype of the parlor soprano, chirping sentimental songs under the loving gaze of a mother or potential spouse, is not fictitious,† neither was the Seidl Society regimen of instructional books and lectures, fortifying a bracing engagement of mind and heart. The refinements thus acquired meshed seamlessly with the society's formidable philanthropic activities and enthralled spiritual flights.

As early as 1855, the formidable Moravian-born impresario Max Maretzek marveled that "the artistic thought of the United States is at the present moment engaged in developing itself through the female half of the population. . . . The ladies in this country are the real amateurs and patrons of our own Art. . . . Indeed, beyond the principal cities, it is the ladies alone that patronize and love the Arts. These, alone, know anything about them." When decades later Seidl at Brighton Beach exclaimed "Hats off before these noble women!" this was no pro forma salute, but a precise observation: that "only women," functioning not as businessmen but as missionaries, could so morally energize the "grand and glorious mission" of edifying a mass audience, of giving "good music for 25 cents to the poor and music needing people." Theodore Thomas credited Midwestern advances in musical understanding "almost wholly" to women: "They have more time to study and perfect themselves in the arts."[65] To be sure, women did not lead orchestras in

*See pages 102–5.

†See, for example, Ann Douglas, *The Feminization of American Culture* (1977).

turn-of-the century America. Boston's Amy Beach was the rare exception who proved the rule: no women composers. But America's touring instrumentalists included such prominent artists as the violinist Maud Powell and the pianist Fannie Bloomfield Zeisler—both soloists at the Seidl Society's Academy of Music concerts. And eminent sopranos were not all of the diva variety. Clara Louise Kellogg headed a vigorous touring company whose accomplishments included America's first English-language *Flying Dutchman* (with Kellogg as Senta). Lilli Lehmann, at the Met, was a redoubtable backstage force; at Lüchow's or Lienau's, she fraternized easily with her boisterous male colleagues.

Mainly, however, it was behind the scenes that powerful women notably shaped American musical life. Of America's first orchestras, Chicago's, founded in 1891, was managed by Anna Millar from 1895 to 1899. She was earlier the architect of a prescient subscription plan, securing commitments on a pledge-now/pay-later basis. As the orchestra's chief executive, she planned its first two East Coast tours, the second of which she stocked with celebrated soloists whom she knew would be important for ticket sales and reviews. It was Millar, too, who went to Europe and booked Josef Hofmann. Her tenure was cut short by a scandal: she was discovered to have purchased lavish advertising space in the *Musical Courier* in return for good tour reviews. Her board, taken by surprise, refused to pay until legal action was threatened. She became a casualty of her own enterprise.[66] Meanwhile, her conductor, Theodore Thomas, was buoyed by Rose Fay Thomas—his dynamic second wife and aide de camp, whose activities included chairing a three-day national convention of women's music clubs at the 1893 World's Columbian Exposition.

The Chicago Orchestra catalyzed the Cincinnati Symphony, initiated in 1895 by the local Ladies Music Club. The orchestra's fifteen-member board was exclusively female, its president being Helen Herron Taft, wife of the future president. Taft later wrote that administering an orchestra she had found "at last, a practical method for expressing and making use of my love and knowledge of music." Her successor, in 1900, was Bettie Fleischmann Holmes, heiress to the Fleischmann Yeast fortune. When Holmes's Cincinnati Symphony hosted Richard Strauss, one newspaper account observed: "The occasion was notable not so much as a brilliant gathering of the four hundred, representative of the wealth and culture of Cincinnati, but rather for the significance of the underlying meaning, the epitomizing in a most graceful but unmistakable manner [of] the fact that women, while preserving all the charm that is the birthright of their sex, may exert a powerful influence for good, may mold society as it were, establish standards of right thinking and living by elevating the public tone."[67]

Though the Philadelphia Orchestra, founded in 1904, was run by men, its women's auxiliary committee proved an indispensable force in fund-raising and ticket sales. Committee president Frances Anne Wister found that the orchestra required "constant begging on the part of everybody," given "the attitude of business men who felt that after a few years the orchestra should be making a return on the investment, or at least be self-supporting. Their opinion was that an institution that was a constant expense did not deserve the support of the community."[68]

In New York, Andrew Carnegie was the president of the New York Symphony as of 1890; his Carnegie Music Hall opened a year later. Carnegie was no informed devotee of concerts and opera, and his business sense told him that orchestras and concert halls should turn a profit. His wife, an avid amateur singer, exerted a crucial countervailing influence. But the woman who most impacted on symphonic New York was Mary Sheldon, who resolved to create an orchestra comparable to Boston's. As leader of a group of philanthropic "guarantors," she shaped and oversaw the transformation of the New York Philharmonic from an anachronistic musicians' cooperative to a cultural bulwark backed by great wealth. Like Taft in Cincinnati, she was married to an important man—a Republican Party operative who helped to put Theodore Roosevelt and William Howard Taft in the White House—and knew the ways of power. It was Sheldon who went to Munich to seek advice from Richard Strauss and Felix Mottl, who engaged Gustav Mahler as her conductor, who raised large sums of money in support of expanding the Philharmonic season.

In Cleveland in 1901, Adella Prentiss, an accomplished pianist whose family friends included the Rockefellers, began a concert series that for two decades brought leading orchestras to town. Victor Herbert, conductor of the Pittsburgh Symphony, said that Adella Prentiss Hughes—her husband of 1903, Felix Hughes, was a professional singer—knew "more about the business of music than anyone," and that he "would rather have her for . . . manager than any man in the world."[69] In 1918, Hughes decided she had found, in Nikolai Sokoloff, the conductor for a Cleveland Orchestra—which she duly founded.

In Boston, Henry Higginson was the Boston Symphony—but his friend Isabella Stewart Gardner was a musical factor to be reckoned with. Like other local arts patrons of high prestige, Gardner hosted private concerts—including recitals by such luminaries as Busoni and Paderewski. Her Fenway Court had a music room so capacious that it was inaugurated by fifty members of the Boston Symphony. Here, Gardner occasionally presented distinguished public concerts with printed tickets.

In opera, Jeannette Thurber was a singular force whose American Opera Company, founded in 1885, was among the most visionary of all attempts to institutionalize opera in English in the United States. Just as Thurber's National Conservatory aspired to create a native symphonic canon, tutored by Dvořák,* the American Opera Company aspired to create conditions conducive to a native repertoire of operas by and for Americans. Thurber's touring company of three hundred members idealistically eschewed glamour. The singers were mainly American-born. The sets and costumes were lavish, the chorus and ballet ample. Theodore Thomas conducted his world-class orchestra in the pit. The enterprise ran aground after two overextended seasons.

Girding all this activity, one way or another, were women's music clubs of every description. While self-improvement was typically the starting point for such endeavors, in countless communities concerts by local artists, and by touring artists and ensembles, would not have existed without the support of club women. According to the National Federation of Music Clubs, outside of large cities three-quarters of the nation's public concerts were managed by women's music clubs as of 1927. One such, in Columbus, Ohio, reached a remarkable pinnacle of activity and influence under the leadership of Elly May Smith from 1903 to 1916. The programs she established included community music schools in settlement houses, a Saturday music club, a student club, an opera club, a club choir, and an Altruistic Department presenting concerts in city, county, and state institutions.[70]

Many of the women so engaged were subject to skepticism or ridicule. Millar was dismissed for bribing the press. Sheldon was denounced for bullying Mahler. Gardner ignited rumor and innuendo. Thurber was resented as a naïf. The conductor Erich Leinsdorf encountered Adella Prentiss Hughes in 1942 as a seventy-three-year-old Cleveland Orchestra board member. "She acted as if she *were* the Cleveland Orchestra," he recalled. "There were some who not only disliked Mrs. Hughes with great passion but who would almost automatically vote against anything and anyone she promoted. She was, like many dom-

*See pages 89–100.

ineering women, truly formidable, full of vitality, peremptorily decisive, musically knowledgeable—which made her part of a small board minority—and so direct as to be considered by softer and less-outspoken people rather tactless."[71]

Laura Langford, in this company, may be regarded as representative—or as singular. The Seidl Society concerts uniquely proselytized the Music of the Future at minimal prices. The *Parsifal* Entertainment uniquely conflated high purpose, high culture, and high society. Unique, as well, were the Brighton Beach lectures with orchestral accompaniment. There was something of Henry Higginson in Langford's bold self-reliance, and also of Jane Addams—who gravitated to tales of great men, who when not battling depression yearned for a career of self-sacrifice, who was observed to be "keen, alert, and alive in every fiber."[72] Music club, philharmonic society, and shrine; settlement house and self-improvement agency, the Seidl Society was the Boston Symphony Orchestra and Hull House combined.

. . .

As Wagnerism in the United States was fundamentally a woman's movement, Wagner furnishes a final inescapable context for understanding Laura Langford. American audiences for Beethoven, too, were more female than male. But no Beethoven symphony could have forced women atop their chairs to scream their delight "for what seemed hours," as when Anton Seidl conducted *Tristan* at the Met.

The list of eminent American Wagnerites includes Edith Wharton, who found "everything . . . insipid—even Nietzsche!" compared to Wagner's "incomparable" autobiography; she attended the *Ring* in Berlin with Bernard Berenson in 1913. Isabella Stewart Gardner was an inveterate Bayreuth pilgrim whose friends included such Wagner specialists as the soprano Amalia Materna and the conductor Karl Muck. Another inimitable fin-de-siècle *bohemienne,* Mabel Dodge Luhan, went to Bayreuth with her mother and girlfriends. The girls sat holding hands in the darkness. "We . . . were keyed up to the moment. One got the sense of being enveloped and lifted higher into areas of intense feeling. . . . When people listened to [Wagner] they were only listening to their own impatient souls, weary at last of the restraint that had held them." M. Carey Thomas—the founding dean and, in 1894, second president of Bryn Mawr College—throttled her heterosexuality in favor of passionate alliances with women. Beneath her professional aplomb seethed a private Wagnerian identity. Upon hearing Seidl conduct *Tristan* in 1891, she wrote to her intimate friend Mary Garrett: "During the bridal night of Tristam & Iseult as she lies in his arms while this glorious chant rises & falls one thinks passion has said its last word, but when the dying Tristam hears of Iseult's approach & tears open his wound in the wildest excitement it rises higher & over his dead body in the death song of Iseult so high that one fairly breaks down under its weight of splendour. I never in a public place came so near to losing my self control." Later the same year, when Garrett attended *Parsifal,* Thomas wrote: "I think I should be capable of any thing mad and impulsive after a week of Tristam—& there wd be the rest of one's life unlit with Wagner to repent in."*[73]

But it is Willa Cather who most memorably recorded the impact of the Wagner maelstrom on lives fractured and uncomprehended, blurred by a haze of "neurasthenia," estranged from a man's world of commerce. In Cather's 1904 short story "A Wagner Matinee," Aunt Georgiana, who once taught music in Boston, returns to that city to collect a small inheritance. As a girl she had eloped to Nebraska, there to settle a rugged homestead. Her Boston nephew Clark—who narrates Cather's tale—takes her to a Wagner concert at which excerpts from *The Flying Dutchman, Tannhäuser, Tristan, Die Meistersinger,* and *The Ring of the Nibelung* jar awake dormant feeling:

> Soon after the tenor began the "Prize Song" [from *Die Meistersinger*], I heard a quick drawn breath and turned to my aunt. Her eyes were closed, but the tears were glistening on her cheeks, and I think, in a moment more, they were in my eyes as well. It never really died, then—the soul that can suffer so excruciatingly and so interminably; it withers to the outward eye only; like that strange moss which can lie on a dusty shelf has a century and yet, if placed in water, grows green again. . . .
>
> The second half of the programme consisted of four numbers from the *Ring,* and closed with Siegfried's funeral march. My aunt wept quietly, but almost continuously, as a shallow vessel overflows in a rain-storm.

The central character of Cather's 1916 novel *The Song of the Lark* is partly modeled on Olive Fremstad, the Met's leading Wagner soprano

*Carroll Smith-Rosenberg, in a landmark 1975 essay, argued that, in a society whose men and women inhabited distinct, emotionally segregated spheres, women did not necessarily become an oppressed subcategory of male society. Rather, a "female world of love and ritual" nourished a fulfilling life of feeling. Whether or not these women had genital contact, "the supposedly repressive and restrictive Victorian sexual ethos may have been more flexible and responsive to the needs of particular individuals than those of the mid-twentieth century."

from 1903 to 1914 and an artist of fabled dramatic genius. Fremstad's great roles included Kundry, in *Parsifal*—who oscillates between extremes of submission and domination; who mutely serves Parsifal and the Grail Knights yet, commanded by the eunuch Klingsor, seduces and destroys. Writing of Fremstad and Kundry both, Cather observed for *McClure's* Magazine in 1913:

> [Kundry] is a summary of the history of womankind. [Wagner] sees in her an instrument of temptation, of salvation, and of service; but always an instrument, a thing driven and employed. . . . She can not possibly be at peace with herself. Mme. Fremstad preserves the integrity of the character throughout all its changes. In the last act, when Kundry washes Parsifal's feet and dries them with her hair, she is the same driven creature, dragging he long past behind her, an instrument made for purposes eternally contradictory. She had served the grail directly and Klingsor fiercely, but underneath there was a weariness of seduction and comforting—the desire not to be. Mme. Fremstad's Kundry is no exalted penitent, who has visions and ecstasies. Renunciation is not fraught with deep joys for her; it is merely—necessary, and better than some things she has known; above all, better than struggle. Who can say what memories of Klingsor's garden are left on the renunciatory hands that wash Parsifal's feet?

In the late Gilded Age, the perfect wife was an "instrument of temptation, of salvation, and of service," "made for purposes eternally contradictory." In the bedroom, she was a breeder. In times of trouble, she was a pillar. In times more ordinary, she was submissive, a helpmate. At all times, she was a paragon of rectitude. Wagner's women iconically embody all of this and more. They sacrifice themselves to redeem men. They bear heroic offspring. Unsuitably wed, they become scourges. Above all, they are oppressed. Kundry, Cather's "history of womankind," inhabits the climactic pathology of the Wagner heroine in all her strength and weakness, utility and victimization.

Cather knew Fremstad. And Laura Langford knew Lilli Lehmann, who doubtless endowed Kundry, at the *Parsifal* Entertainment, with the high temper and authority she brought to all she did. Seidl was known to esteem *Parsifal* as Wagner's paramount achievement. That *Parsifal* was paramount for Langford, as well, is obvious from the extravagant trappings with which she presented it. Its appeal to her was manifest and manifold. Wagner's sources here include Greeks and Buddhists; no less than theosophy, *Parsifal* embodies an eclectic spiritual quest. Langford's own quest would lead her, Parsifal-like, in the direction of ideals of abstinence—with Mt. Lebanon's Shakers standing in for

Wagner's celibate knights. The drama's core message—of redemption forged through pity and compassion—preaches sacrifice in the service of others. Kundry, its lonely, quintessential woman, embodies such sacrifice and a complexity of consequences.

In Langford's personal saga of sacrifice and service, no motif emerges more poignantly than her contingent relationship to men. Her first husband drove her to disgrace and dissimulation. Seidl enabled her brief glory moment. With the death of Colonel Langford, she drifted into obscurity. Like Cather's Kundry, she was, finally, an instrument, a thing driven and employed. Her quest for a lasting peace was incessant but futile. Empowered, enslaved, she was a woman without a place. In limbo between fin-de-siècle stirrings and the New Woman to come, hers was a notable yet surrogate life.

FIGURE 11. Charles Ives, graduation photograph, Yale University, 1898. MSS 14, photo 57; the Charles Ives Papers in the Irving S. Gilmore Music Library of Yale University.

CHAPTER 4

Charles Ives

Gentility and Rebellion

Charles and Harmony—A life saga—The business of life insurance—Transcendentalism in music—The symphonic ideal—Stream of consciousness—Ives's "nervous complex"—The residual Progressive

Hartford's Reverend Joseph Twichell was gregarious, ebullient, and robustly handsome. The congregants at his fashionable Asylum Hill church included Charles Dudley Warner, Harriet Beecher Stowe, and Mark Twain. Twain was also a close personal friend. Six years after arriving at Asylum Hill—"the Church of the Holy Speculators," Twain called it—Twichell helped to marry Sam and Livy Clemens. He undertook with Clemens a quixotic 1874 walk to Boston (they hitched a ride to the nearest railroad line twenty-eight miles later) and in 1878 cheerfully accompanied him to Europe to participate in the innocent and mock innocent adventures of *A Tramp Abroad*. In 1909 he married Clara Clemens to Ossip Gabrilowitsch. In 1910 he gave the benediction at Mark Twain's funeral.

Twichell espoused a nondogmatic "muscular Christianity" predisposed toward social service. His years of Civil War duty, as chaplain to a hard cursing Irish regiment, had contributed to his tolerance and breadth. His literary circle included John Greenleaf Whittier. His Hartford home was a haven of equanimity.

Of the nine Twichell children, the third daughter, born in 1876, was named Harmony—which everyone found apt. Her features were soft, her eyes luminous. Thanks to financial support from a family friend, she graduated from Miss Porter's School at Farmington. Pursuing a career opportunity for turn-of-the-century women that combined charity and a modicum of independence, she proceeded to nursing school in Hartford. Her graduation speech, in 1900, was titled "The Nurse's Gain."

> The fullest development individually comes from altruistic effort, and fullest development means in the end the greatest usefulness and happiness. . . .
>
> We find how people live, of whose lives we were before in perfect ignorance. Almost unconsciously we are introduced to some of the great sociological questions so widely discussed.
>
> The people of the slums become our acquaintances. We come near the grim affairs of living, poverty and pain—and what food for reflection is offered! See what an immense gain in the *furnishing of our minds!* We come into a sort of humble fellowship with some of the noblest women that ever lived. Florence Nightingale and Sister Dora and Alice Fisher.[1]

Harmony worked as a nurse in the slums of Chicago and Manhattan. She broke off an engagement to a minister whose family was close to hers. She was approaching spinsterhood.

Some years before, in 1896, Harmony had been introduced by her brother Dave to a Yale friend, a shy small-town boy who liked sports and pounded the piano at parties. Dave's friend now reappeared in Harmony's life. On July 30, 1905, Charles Ives, already thirty years old and well embarked on a career selling life insurance, took Harmony Twichell to hear Dvořák's *New World* Symphony in Hartford. Though in later life they would call this night their "Vita Nuova," outwardly little happened. The following August, Ives was at New York's Lake Saranac resort with the Twichells, feeling burned out. In December 1906 he suffered a "heart attack." That summer, Harmony was working at the Henry Street Settlement—and accompanying Charlie to plays and concerts (including some "*Parsifal* music"[2]). Meanwhile, he set some of her poems. At the piano, he shared with her his newly composed *The Unanswered Question* and *Central Park in the Dark,* music unlike any she (or anyone else) had heard. Then he was sick again. Not until October 1907 did he finally announce his intentions, sealed with a kiss. Harmony's brother Joe later remembered "with a lump in my throat" the "meal . . . after you two had returned from an afternoon's walk out around the West Hartford reservoir, . . . both of you surrounded by an impenetrable halo of complete absorption in each other."[3] Reverend Twichell married them on June 9, 1908.

The frequent letters Harmony and Charlie exchanged bring to life these three years of hesitation. The duration of their courtship was not just a product of Victorian reticence. Powerful retarding forces—practical, emotional, psychological—were at play: Ives's uncertain health; the uncertainty of his business prospects. Not least significant was the tug of allegiance to his late father, the bandmaster George Edward Ives, for the son a talisman of legendary proportions whose posthumous presence he daily experienced. The pent-up force unleashed by that first October kiss produced a quivering note from Harmony three days later: "I never wrote a love letter & don't know how. If I don't write this today you won't get mail until Monday and I can't wait that long to have you see in my writing what you've seen these perfect days in my face—that I love & love you & love you and no numbers of times of saying it can ever tell it. But believe it and that I am yours always & utterly—Every bit of me." And another two days after that: "My dearest anything—Everything—I haven't any thoughts except that I love you and I've been thinking of all the 'grandest passions' in history and I know neither Francesca nor Beatrice nor anyone was ever more possessed than I am." And another later the same day: "In church I thought all of a sudden of your Father—so intensely that the tears came into my eyes and I thought how much I love him—actually as if I'd known him—I almost felt him." And another the next day: "I was quite wrong when I said that it was a year ago that I knew I loved you It's been all the time just the same but I never said it right out to myself until a year ago & gloried & rejoiced in it—I believe it's really been since way long before the creation don't you?" Ives, for his part, confided that a year before, bidding Harmony good-bye, he already "felt as if I'd lost and left behind all that meant any thing real to me."[4]

The visible example of Sam and Livy Clemens—Ives had encountered them at the Twichell home; and he had been ceremoniously presented to "Uncle Mark" as Harmony's intended—could not have been lost on either Harmony or Charlie.* Like Livy's, Harmony's moral fortitude would anchor her spousal relationship; like Livy, she would leaven her husband's cranky dissidence and lovingly buoy his artistic probity. "I want to do the big things for you and all the little everyday things too," Harmony wrote on November 7, 1907. Ives wrote to Harmony two weeks later: "Your letters are beautiful and have such a wonderful effect—so lasting and so strong. . . . If you would just send me a line so I could have one to help me start the day then know all day that I'll find one waiting for me when I come home. It gives me courage and more ability all day long. Letters are weak substitutes for you—best beloved—but they're absolutely essential for me now."

*Harmony was in later life president of the Mark Twain Society.

Suffusing Harmony's letters is an aura of high religiosity. She calls Charlie "blessed one" and writes: "We must be careful about our spiritual side. That is all a great part of our love—the foundation almost, a greater part than perhaps you know—Sundays are a necessity—at the same time they will be days that we can always be together every minute through the day."[5]

If Harmony was the clergyman's daughter, and Charlie the son of a secular musician, the moral ethos remained formidably sewn into the fabric of his life and family experience. There were no reverends among the Iveses, but there were George White and Sarah Ives, Charlie's grandparents. Sarah led the rescue of a fugitive slave caught in New Fairfield (a famous family story). She helped to found a "colored school" in Virginia and passionately read Emerson. Charlie's uncle J. Moss Ives knew Emerson and brought him to Danbury; he also wrote a book, *The Ark and the Dove,* about the contribution of Maryland's early Catholics to American religious freedom. And, in the 1870s, there was the "Great Awakening." Methodist camp meetings were a vivid feature of Charlie's Danbury boyhood; he remembered "how the great waves of sound used to come through the trees—when things like Beulah Land, Woodworth, Nearer My God To Thee, The Shining Shore, Nettleton, The Sweet Bye and Bye and the like were sung by thousands of 'let out' souls. The music notes and words on paper were about as much like what they 'were' (at those moments) as the monogram on the man's necktie may be like his face. . . . There was power and exaltation in these great conclaves of sound from humanity."[6]

Finally: at the age of fourteen, Charles Ives, himself brought up in Danbury's Congregational Church, was the youngest salaried church organist in Connecticut. As an equally precocious concert organist, he acquired secular showpieces and others—Bach fugues; Wagner's *Tannhäuser* Overture in his own transcription—quasi-religious in tone. In 1898–99, as organist at New York's Central Presbyterian Church, he composed a seven-movement cantata, *The Celestial Country.* He knew the world of hortatory sermons and songs as familiarly as would his bride. And, no less than for Harmony, the language of religion would for Ives inform life's epiphanies. Recalling his father's band marching down Main Street, he recorded:

> Later in life, the same boy hears the Sabbath morning bell ringing out from the white steeple at the "Center," and as it draws him to it . . . a Gospel hymn of simple devotion comes out to him—"There's a wideness in God's mercy"—an instant suggestion of that Memorial Day morning comes—but the moment

> is of deeper import . . . a profound sense of a spiritual truth. . . . And as the hymn voices die away, there dies at his feet—not the world, but the figure of the Saviour—he sees an unfathomable courage—an immortality for the lowest—the vastness in humility, the kindness of the human heart, man's noblest strength—and he knows that God is nothing—nothing—but love![7]

Alongside Harmony, Ives was not a conventional believer—"many of the sincerest followers of Christ never heard of him," he grumbled—yet partnered her own formulation of the divinity in love. "I dare to love you so fully, so utterly because it is all just God & religion," she wrote to Charlie half a year after their wedding. And months later: "You are the revelation of God to me [and what] it can do and will do is to make our lives good & helpful." Their love would bring "happiness into other lives besides our own."[8]

> I know the joy & beauty of it can be communicated to others and that is what I long to do with it—to give out of my abundance that the world may be a little happier & better & I know I can be more to people than I ever dreamed I could—I haven't any feeling of wanting to shut this divine thing up into my own heart & life—I want every least person I come in contact with to feel this warmth & sweetness & I think they must—with no effort on my part. That is one of the blessed things about it. And my darling, all this because God has given me you to love.[9]

In New York, Charles and Harmony belonged to the First Presbyterian Church on Fifth Avenue. Family prayers were a daily ritual when Harmony's father visited their country home in Redding, Connecticut. Charlie respected religion without regard to creed or sect. He believed in life after death and expected to reunite with his father. He once wrote that "most of the forward movements of life in general and of pioneers in most of the great activities, have been [the work of] essentially religious-minded men."[10]

No less than Beethoven, Ives was religious by temperament. No less than John Sullivan Dwight or Henry Krehbiel, he received Beethoven as a godhead. Unlike Dwight or Krehbiel, he aspired to something higher and purer still. "Music may be yet unborn. Perhaps no music has ever been written or heard. Perhaps the birth of art will take place at the moment in which the last man who is willing to make a living out of art is gone and gone forever. In the history of this youthful world, the best product that human beings can boast of is probably Beethoven; but, maybe, even his art is as nothing in comparison with the future product of some coal-miner's soul in the forty-first century."[11]

Ives's mature output traverses many a high road. With its slow, tolling pulse and eternal pedal point in the organ, his choral setting of Psalm 90 (composed in 1894, revised in 1923–24) attains a rare breadth of sentiment; raw patches of dissonance ("we are consumed by thine anger") dissipate to disclose a plateau of healing consonance ("and let the beauty of the Lord our God be upon us"). *From Hanover Square North, at the End of a Tragic Day, the Voice of the People Again Arose* (1915) is inspired by a singular incident witnessed by Ives: the day after the sinking of the *Lusitania,* commuters at New York's Hanover Square elevated train station spontaneously took up the gospel funeral hymn "In the Sweet Bye and Bye," being played by an organ grinder. In Ives's setting, a fog of urban cacophony is penetrated and surmounted by the hymn tune, which arises from subliminal fragments to a pealing, cathartic paean. The ecstatic upward trajectory of *The Housatonic at Stockbridge* (1914 [for orchestra], 1921 [as a song]) is, again, inspired by personal experience. A month after their wedding, Harmony and Charles took a stroll along the Housatonic River; a hymn, "Dorrnance," floated over the water. Ives's musical recollection of this event, an incorporeal sonic landscape of trembling, oscillating strings, parallels the iconic God-in-nature metaphysics of a Frederic Church or Henry David Thoreau. The quivering ether, a transmutation of mist and water, feeds upon itself in a rush toward the ocean—or toward the heavens and hereafter. Ives's "Thoreau" (1915), from the *Concord* Sonata, discovers a calmer divinity in nature, a rippling serenity. No less than Thoreau, the "religious" Ives aspired to the condition where art, philosophy, and daily life are one and the same; in his valedictory Fourth Symphony (1909–1916) the quotidian and sublime are equally God-infused.

Notwithstanding a lifelong list of infirmities—weaknesses of the body and psyche his marriage and music were partly intended to assuage—Ives was fated to live seventy-nine years. By the time he died in 1954, the Great Depression and two world wars had darkened the human prospect. Other such men, steeped in the nineteenth-century ethos of uplift, succumbed to disillusionment. In Ives's case, the opposite occurred. Ignoring his waning energies, and the mounting sins of unregenerate humankind, he concocted chimerical, millennial enterprises: a Twentieth Amendment to implement direct democracy so as to "reduce to a minimum or possibly to eliminate . . . the effect of too much politics in our representative democracy";[12] a *Universe* Symphony for two large orchestras. Though he did not shut his eyes to the world, his railings against Hitler, and against the craven susceptibility of his supporters, left Ives exhausted. He clung to notions of human perfectibility.

He had long abandoned both composition and insurance. Rather than relinquish his ideals, he withdrew from a century not his own.

. . .

A favorite image of Ives the iconoclastic visionary is of Ives shouting "Sissy!" and "Listen like a man!" at effete concertgoers. But the parlor-bound culture bearers he excoriated were as much a memory as a contemporary reality. New York in the 1910s—when Ives was at his creative peak—was already home to composers like Leo Ornstein and Edgard Varèse, critics like Carl Van Vechten and Paul Rosenfeld. Elsewhere in America, Frank Lloyd Wright, John Marin, Alfred Stieglitz, Isadora Duncan, Carl Sandburg, and Ezra Pound signified the new. With his businessman's lifestyle, Ives stood well apart from these potent figures. His reverence for Beethoven did not extend to Tchaikovsky (too intent on "getting an audience"), Wagner (lacking "wholesomeness" and "manliness"), Debussy ("voluptuous," "slimy,"), or Ravel and Stravinsky ("morbidly fascinating," "false beauty").[13] He disliked the company of bohemians. His disdain for the Connecticut parlor of his youth—for "pansies," "lily-pads," "old ladies," "pussy-boys"—was aggravated by awareness of his complicity; he feared his sentimentality. The aestheticist tendencies he denounced as "effeminate" actually threatened the genteel tradition.

While no portrait of Ives—of any man—is finally "true" or "truer," the twentieth-century image of the dissident Ives, pushing relentlessly into the future, is a distinct twentieth-century product. The American fin de siècle that produced Charles Ives, and to which he so complexly and eccentrically adhered, was on balance neither dissident nor complacent. That it was imperfectly known to the dissident modernists who first discovered Ives is understandable: they needed to reject their parents—and their parents' moral compass—to find themselves. With that moment now expired, Ives seems—the central theme of this portrait—less a proto-modernist than an anomaly within the sanguine genteel tradition that discomfited or ensnared him.

In outline, Ives's life story bristles with the power of legend—and like other legends, may be differently interpreted and applied. Danbury, where Ives was born in 1874, was alive with music. The Opera House, built in 1871, hosted minstrel shows, operettas, and such occasional stellar attractions as the Theodore Thomas Orchestra and the Fisk Jubilee Singers. In 1882, the annual Fireman's Parade featured no fewer than thirty-one bands and drum corps. Seven years later, the Choral Society engaged, as director, New York's Harry Rowe Shelley—who would shortly become one of Dvořák's students at the National Conservatory. The local musical organizations, invariably run by women, also included the Rossini Musical Soiree, the Mozart Musicale, and the Mendelssohn Musicale. In January 1890 the *New York Herald* reported: "All Danbury loves music. Wherever you may go, no matter with whom you talk, ten chances to one music will become the topic of conversation. . . . There are no less than a dozen regularly organized societies, embracing nearly all of the best vocalists, and about as many orchestras, and bands."[14] Amid this activity, George Ives—music teacher, bandmaster, theater-orchestra leader, director of music at the Methodist Church—both partook and stood apart. With his cornet, he led camptown gospel hymns with a fervor that would push the singing into higher keys. As his son's indefatigable mentor, he was unfettered: a Yankee renegade. At the same moment that Dvořák, in New York, advised that "the musician must prick his ear for music—nothing must be too low or insignificant," George Ives was filling Charlie's ears with Bach and Beethoven, hymns and marches, microtonal and polytonal cacophonies.[15] He passed along his own formal training—from a German-born teacher—in harmony, counterpoint, and orchestration. He made the boy sing "Old Folks at Home" in E-flat while accompanying himself in C. He thrilled to sonic mishaps and collisions: bumptious wrong notes and late entrances in the theater pit; bands crowding and contradicting one another on Main Street.

In September 1893 Ives accompanied his uncle Lyman to Chicago's fabulous White City—the World's Columbian Exposition—and there encountered a plethora of potent musical entertainments. He heard the Thomas Orchestra. He heard Alexander Guilmant, whom he considered the world's preeminent organist, in a program of Buxtehude, Bach, Mendelssohn, Liszt, and Wagner; Guilmant also played his own music and improvised (on one occasion, on Stephen Foster's "Old Folks at Home"). Sousa's band gave free concerts daily and made "After the Ball" (which Ives would appropriate) the theme song of the fair. Scott Joplin proffered a foretaste of ragtime. The Midway featured African music, Native American music, Egyptian music. Though these and other ethnic diversions were popularly ranked according to hierarchical notions of race, the music Ives heard at the fair was not yet categorized and stratified as strictly as in decades to come—as in Danbury, "classical" and "popular" blurred and intermingled.

A year later, Ives was at Yale. He had barely begun when his father died on November 4, 1894—a loss so unmooring that in later years he continued to speak of George Ives as if he were a living companion. Ives's principal teacher now became Yale's Horatio Parker, who had himself studied with Josef Rheinberger in Munich. He had also taught at Dvořák's National Conservatory in New York. Ives later recalled: "I had and have great respect and admiration for Parker and most of his music. (It was seldom trivial—his choral works have a dignity and depth that many of [his] contemporaries, especially in the [field of] religious and choral composition did not have. Parker had ideals that carried him higher than the popular) but he was governed too much by the German rule, and in some ways was somewhat hard-boiled." Ives also wrote: "Parker was a composer and widely known, and Father was not a composer and little known—but from every other standpoint I should say that Father was by far the greater man." After a few weeks at Yale, Ives stopped sharing with Parker compositional experiments in which a pandemonium of fugues, hymns, and football cheers textured the sounds he felt born to transmute. For Parker, Ives composed *Lieder* and *chansons,* and also a forty-five-minute First Symphony. Parker made him end the first movement in the same key with which it began, and also tamed the finale. Recalling such Yale assignments, Ives would snort: "The better and more exactly you imitate the Joneses, the surer you are to get a degree."[16]

After graduating in 1898, Ives moved to New York City, where he was helped by relatives to a job with the Mutual Insurance Company. He befriended a young clerk named Julian Myrick. They quickly prospered as a life insurance team, founding Ives & Myrick in 1909. Meanwhile Ives had in 1902 given up his Sunday organ duties in order to reserve more time for composition. Prolific in many genres, he created music evoking dueling ragtime players in Central Park, or the consequences of a baseball hit foul, or a spitting Halloween bonfire, all of it seemingly unperformable and—to musicians of consequence—incomprehensible. In 1912 he and Harmony bought a farm in Redding, Connecticut, as a summer residence. In 1915 they adopted a daughter, Edie. In 1918 Ives suffered another "heart attack." Slowed down after decades of ceaseless activity, he began putting his music in order. He privately printed *114 Songs* in 1922. Four years later, he tearfully confided to Harmony that he could no longer compose—"nothing sounded right." He quit the insurance business in 1930.

Ives's decline coincided with Ives's ascent. For decades Americans had labored to fashion the indigenous "American school" Dvořák had prophesied, only to find themselves encumbered and reencumbered by Old World practices. Nothing as formidably self-made as a musical

Whitman or Melville had appeared. It now transpired that an autonomous American genius had long composed in necessary obscurity, undistracted by precedent or fashion. The abject failure of his rare efforts to secure recognition—as when Walter Damrosch in 1910 abandoned a reading of the First Symphony; or when in 1914 Anton Seidl's onetime concertmaster Franz Milcke, "after a lot of big talk," declared the First Violin Sonata "awful," "not music," "horrible sounds"[17]—more vindicated than diluted his aspirations. Anchored by his wife, secure in his alternative business vocation, counseled by the ghost of his father, fortified by the faith-melodies of his childhood, buoyed by the transcendental ether of nineteenth-century New England, he more than persevered.

Gradually, the interwar avant-garde caught up with what Charles Ives had produced in fin-de-siècle times. In 1931, Nicolas Slonimsky conducted *Three Places in New England* in the United States, Havana, and Paris. The following year, Aaron Copland presented seven Ives songs at his Yaddo festival. The composer and radio conductor Bernard Herrmann made a cause of the fugue from the Fourth Symphony; writing in *Trend* Magazine in 1932, he called Ives's Fourth "the great American symphony that our critics and conductors have cried out for, and yet the symphony has remained unperformed except for an excerpt."[18] In 1939 John Kirkpatrick gave the first performance of the *Concord* Sonata for a tiny audience at New York's Town Hall. He was brought back for seven encores. Lawrence Gilman wrote in the *Herald-Tribune:*

> Music by an unexampled creative artist of our day, probably the most original and extraordinary of American composers, yielded the outstanding experience. . . .
>
> The music in question was written by Charles E. Ives, a New Englander, now dwelling in New York, whose name means nothing whatever to most music-lovers and musicians—although that fact is almost certainly of small interest to the individual in question. For Mr. Ives is one of those exceptional artists whose indifference to reclame is as genuine as it is fantastic and unbelievable. . . .
>
> [Ives's] sonata is exceptionally great music—it is, indeed, the greatest music composed by an American, and the most deeply and essentially American in impulse and implication. It is wide-ranging and capacious. It has passion, tenderness, humour, simplicity, homeliness. It has imaginative and spiritual vastness. It has wisdom and beauty and profundity, and a sense of the encompassing terror and splendor of human life and human destiny—a sense of those mysteries that are both human and divine.[19]

In 1947 Ives was awarded the Pulitzer Prize for his Third Symphony, premiered by the composer Lou Harrison the year before. Ives's building reputation was predicated on the newness of his music, not its oldness. Critics inferred the influence of Stravinsky's *The Rite of Spring* and Schoenberg's *Pierrot lunaire.* One 1931 *New York Times* review chided: "There is no doubt that he knows his Schoenberg, yet gives the impression that he has not always assimilated the lessons of the Viennese master as well as he might have."[20] Ives responded to such feedback with savage ridicule. He had always kept his distance from the music of his own time. He did not know—would never know—his Stravinsky and Schoenberg.

Ives died of a stroke in 1954 in the company of his wife and daughter. According to Kirkpatrick: "Edith told afterwards how the three of them held hands quietly—that it was a time of the kind of luminous serenity that animates his greatest music; he seemed as if transfigured. It was an intimate communion of unspoken awareness she could never have imagined, a serenity resolving all the tensions of his life that somehow persisted intact after he had quietly stopped breathing."[21]

• • •

Ives's twin professions in life insurance and music inhabited separate worlds; at Ives & Myrick, that he composed music was unknown or barely known. But for Ives himself business and music were linked to an exceptional degree—to one another, to the personality and temperament of Ives the man, to common roots in pre–World War I New England. Ives's business ideals mirrored his artistic vocation, his lodestars being uplift and democracy.

To be sure, business was in part compensatory. Ives acknowledged having been "ashamed" of liking music as a child—while other boys drove grocery cars or played ball, he played the piano; it seemed to him an "emasculated art." Business was also financially compensatory. "Father felt that a man could keep his music-interest stronger, cleaner, bigger, and freer, if he didn't try to make a living of it. . . . If he has a nice wife and some nice children, how can he let the children starve on his dissonances—answer that, Eddy! So he has to weaken (and as a man he should weaken for his children), but his music (some of it) more than weakens—it goes 'ta ta' for money—bad for him, bad for music, but good for his boys!!" And Ives added:

> My business experience revealed life to me in many aspects that I might otherwise have missed. In it one sees tragedy, nobility, meanness, high aims, low aims, brave hopes, faint hopes, great ideals, no ideals, and one is able to watch these work inevitable destiny. And it has seemed to me that the finer sides of these traits were not only in the majority but in the ascendancy. . . .

> It is my impression that there is more open-mindedness and willingness to examine carefully the premises underlying a new or unfamiliar thing, in the world of business than in the world of music.
>
> It is not even uncommon in business intercourse to sense a reflection of a philosophy . . . akin to a strong sense of beauty in art. To assume that business is a material process, and only that, is to undervalue the average mind and heart. To an insurance man there *is* an "average man" and he is humanity.
>
> I have experienced a great fullness of life in business. The fabric of existence weaves itself whole. You cannot set an art off in the corner and hope for it to have vitality, reality and substance. There can be nothing *exclusive* about a substantial art. It comes directly out of the heart of experience of life and thinking about life and living life. My work in music helped my business and work in business helped my music.[22]

It is not irrelevant that life insurance itself was in the throes of democratic reform around the time that Ives took it up. In the early 1900s, when profits soared at Mutual Life, fraud and nepotism were rife. Lavish salaries and parties provoked outrage and, in 1905, Congress's tough Armstrong investigation. New laws were written. Public confidence was restored. Life insurance boomed, with Ives & Myrick—"The LARGEST AGENCY without exclusive territory IN THE COUNTRY"—in the lead. Ives's own earnings were exceptional; he retired a wealthy man.[23]

At the office, Myrick headed day-to-day affairs. Ives, in the background, strategized the pitch; in effect, he justified selling life insurance both for his sales team and for his own prickly conscience. "Ives made three points," an Ives & Myrick supervisor recalled many years later:

> First, the information that I imparted to clients was to be always accurate; second, that it was my responsibility to decide what would be best for each individual; third, that there was no service that I could render to my fellow man that was more important than the business of life insurance, because it instilled in the soul and mind of my fellow man the responsibility of meeting his obligations. Charlie was a humanitarian from the bottom of his heart to his head, and I came away from the first meeting feeling that he was a great philosopher and moralist.[24]

One of Ives's ads for Ives &Myrick began:

> "I appeal from your customs: I must be myself"—says Emerson in his "Self-Reliance."
>
> There is a tendency, today, to minimize the individual and to exaggerate the machinelike custom of business and of life.
>
> Some men fit quite easily into a mechanistic system, while others feel that their individuality will be or is being gradually standardized out of them.
>
> Work in the life insurance field certainly doesn't cramp individuality,

> ingenuity, or initiative. Men of character, who are capable of sustained hard work, who like to overcome obstacles, who are interested in human nature, may well consider the profession of life insurance.[25]

Ives trained the instructors who trained the sales staff; he stressed altruism. His pamphlet *The Amount to Carry—Measuring the Prospect* was a salesman's bible; "life insurance is doing its part in the progress of the greater life values," it preached. Underlying Ives's insurance philosophy was a political philosophy—that the average man is honest and intelligent; that accurate and honorable information would impel results profitable to company and client alike. "Sell to the masses!" he shouted. "Get into the lives of the people." Henry Bellamann, who championed Ives before achieving fame himself as the author of the novel *Kings Row,* summarized: "Mr. Ives' business success was founded on the same sort of daring experiment, together with an interest and confidence in human nature, that characterizes his music. . . . It brought him in close relation with thousands of men of all kinds and conditions. This association of over thirty years . . . gave him a high respect for . . . the average man's mind and character. This confidence . . . seemed too visionary and idealistic to many."[26]

At Yale, Ives had been nicknamed "Dasher": always in a hurry. Ives the businessman was intense, restless, creative, private, odd. He was wiry and fit: as of his 1909 agency physical, 5'9¾" and 152 pounds. He was athletic; he pitched for the agency baseball squad. Myrick was gregarious, a dandy. Ives was reclusive, original. His signature feature was not yet the grizzled beard he would grow in retirement, but a narrow brimmed hat perched high atop his brow. According to his nephew Brewster: "Uncle Charlie could be spotted a mile away, and . . . there wasn't a single man in Wall Street who didn't know him. They could see him coming because of that crazy hat he'd wear, and they all were fascinated with him, because he was a real old-fashioned Connecticut Yankee with a sense of humor and eccentric ways."[27] According to an Ives & Myrick supervisor, "Somehow [Ives] taught me without saying everything explicitly. He had a magnetic personality—you could see the radiation from his eyes." According to an Ives & Myrick secretary, "He never asked me to take a letter or do anything for him without being humble almost to a degree that's hard to describe. I never met anyone since like him. He'd almost be ashamed to ask you to do something for him." According to another secretary, "He was loved by everybody and kind of feared, too, because he was so superior to everybody, and because he was a very independent person. He didn't care what anybody said. He had his own opinion, and that was it." His kindness was universally observed. On only one occasion was Ives memorably irate. William Verplanck, an Ives & Myrick associate manager, had called his secretary "Mussolini." She tearfully reported this slur to Ives. The next day, Ives was heard shouting at Verplanck: "You treat her like a lady! She's got nothing more to do with you! She's my secretary now!" He grabbed his coat and hat and stormed out of the office.[28]

Connecticut Yankees are thrifty, pragmatic. They are businessmen, not artists. They are tinkerers: like Ives, when he experimented with quartertones or rival bands. They savor the moral satisfaction of donating the profits of worldly ambition. Ives's charities were legion. He anonymously supplied fully one-third the support of Henry Cowell's *New Music Quarterly* for three decades. When he won the Pulitzer Prize for his Third Symphony, he gave half the award to Lou Harrison, who had conducted the premiere—and who was recuperating from a breakdown; he also assigned a portion of the royalties to Harrison. For years he refused to take any income tax deductions for charitable contributions—and only changed his mind when he realized that doing so would enable him to give away more money. "He was so intensely generous that it's sometimes hard to believe," Brewster testified. "He naturally wanted to help anyone who seemed handicapped in any way, and he was never interested in acquiring worldly possessions of his own. I think that he regarded money as something that should be distributed on as thorough a basis as possible, and yet he rebelled at the idea of a welfare state."[29]

A pertinent Ives motif was his recurrent interest in American race relations—as observed by colleagues and acquaintances during and after his Ives & Myrick years. George Hofmann, an Ives & Myrick supervisor, recalled in 1969:

> If Charlie knew about the disturbed situation between the races in this country now, it would make him very unhappy. Our company never took colored applicants, but I employed a colored gentleman for accounting and he was also an attorney. He was the first colored man the Mutual Life ever insured. I wrote him for fifty thousand dollars, and the application came to the attention of our vice-president for underwriting. He called me down and said "Don't you know the Book of Rules?" But I got that application through, and this opened the way for other colored applicants. When Ives heard about this, he gave me a little tap on the shoulder. "Good work."[30]

Ives's abolitionist grandparents exerted a legacy. During the Civil War George Edward Ives had befriended a black boy, Anderson Brooks, whose mother did washing for his band; George taught the boy to read and write. After the war, George's mother—as Charles Ives would proudly recall—took in Anderson Brooks and raised him. Charles Ives played spirituals at the piano; he found them kindred to the white gospel hymns he absorbed as a child: kindred to himself. The "Black March" he composed in 1911, and which became the first of his *Three Places in New England,* memorialized Colonel Robert Gould Shaw's legendary black regiment as depicted by Augustus Saint-Gaudens's Boston Common bas-relief, with its imagery of proud black faces and striding black bodies. Ives's singular ghost-dirge—music barely tangible, exempt from precedent and contemporary practice—is suffused with weary echoes of Civil War songs, work songs, plantation songs, church songs, minstrel songs: a dream distillation of "black" particles and cadences. Its hypnotic tread evokes a stoic fortitude. Its textural mirage conveys an act of etherealization, of religious sublimation. Ives penned an accompanying poem that, if far less original in syntax and metaphor, gauges the higher message his processional pursues:

> Moving,—Marching—Faces of Souls!
> Marked with generations of pain,
> Part-freers of a Destiny,
> Slowly, restlessly—swaying us on with you
> Towards other Freedom. . . .
>
> You images of a Divine Law
> Carved in the shadow of a saddened heart—
> Never light abandoned—
> Of an age and of a nation.*
>
> Above and beyond that compelling mass
> Rises the drum-beat of the common-heart
> In the silence of a strange and
> Sounding afterglow
> Moving—Marching—Faces of Souls!†

*A draft makes clear that Ives here means something like "not light-hearted and frivolous," according to stereotype. (I am indebted to the music historian Wayne Shirley for this information.)

†During World War II, Ives attempted to interest the conductors Artur Rodzinski and Serge Koussevitzky in his music. He described the "Black March" as "in a way emblematic of the fight against slavery." And he linked his Second Symphony with the "fret and storm and stress for liberty" of the Civil War. Where the marches and dances of the symphony's finale abate for a plaintive horn theme evoking "Old Black Joe," Ives found inspiration in Stephen Foster's "sadness for the Slaves." (See Tom Owens [ed.], *Selected Correspondence of Charles Ives* (2007), pp. 294–295.)

. . .

Like Ives's version of life insurance, Ives's version of Transcendentalism comprises an eloquent act of self-disclosure. Ideals of uplift again mate with earthiness and egalitarianism.

In "Emerson," from his *Essays Before a Sonata,* Ives writes: "We see him standing on a summit, at the door of the infinite, where many man do not dare to climb. Peering into the mysteries of life, contemplating the eternities, hurling back whatever he discovers there. Now thunderbolts for us to grasp, if we can, and translate. Now placing gently, even tenderly, in our hands, things that we may see without effort. . . . If we won't see them, so much the worse for us!"[31]

Published in 1920, the *Essays Before a Sonata* constitute an eighty-page preface to Ives's Piano Sonata No. 2: "Concord, Mass., 1845"—itself a group of four pieces, Ives explains, "called a sonata for want of a more exact name. . . . The whole [comprising "Emerson" (1911), "Hawthorne" (1911), "The Alcotts" (1914), and "Thoreau" (1915)] is an attempt to present [one person's] impression of the spirit of transcendentalism that is associated in the minds of many with Concord, Mass., of over half century ago." Ives writes: "A working woman after coming from one of [Emerson's] lectures said: 'I love to go to hear Emerson, not because I understand him, but because he looks as though he thought everybody was as good as he was.'"[32] While fabulously popular, Emerson's lectures, with their high-pitched, idiosyncratic rhetoric, could also be fabulously elusive. This combination of elevated climes and lowly realities is Emersonian and (especially) Ivesian. "Like all courageous souls," Ives writes, "the higher Emerson soars, the more lowly he becomes." He adds:

> To think hard and deeply and to say what is thought, regardless of consequences, may produce a first impression, either of great translucence, or of great muddiness, but in the latter there may be hidden possibilities. Some accuse Brahms' orchestration of being muddy. This may be a good name for a first impression of it. But if it should seem less so, he might not be saying what he thought. The mud may be a form of sincerity. . . . A clearer scoring might have lowered the thought. Carlyle told Emerson that some of his paragraphs didn't cohere. Emerson wrote by sentence or phrases, rather than by logical sequence.[33]

Emerson himself says: "I embrace the common. I explore and sit at the feet of the familiar, the low." In his journal he writes:

> The language of the street is always strong. . . . I confess to some pleasure from the stinging rhetoric of a rattling oath in the mouth of truckmen and teamsters. How laconic and brisk it is by the side of a page of the North American Review. Cut these words and they would bleed; they are vascular and alive; they walk and run. Moreover, they who speak them have this elegancy, that they do not trip in their speech. It is a shower of bullets, whilst Cambridge men and Yale men correct themselves and begin again at every half sentence.[34]

Emerson's poem "Music" reads:

> 'Tis not in the high stars alone,
> nor in the cup of budding flowers,
> Nor in the redbreast's mellow tone,
> Nor in the bow that smiles in showers,
> But in the mud and scum of things
> There alway, alway something sings.

The resulting breadth is ecumenical, universal. It girds character. It limns an immanent divinity.

Ives contrasts didactic puritan orthodoxies—a lower pre-Transcendental realm—with Emerson's vagueness, which is also a vastness. Emerson "wrings the neck of any law." His "messages are all vital, as much, by reason of his indefiniteness, as in spite of it." This is because "orderly reason does not always have to be a visible part of all great things." "Initial coherence to-day may be dullness to-morrow probably because formal or outward unity depends so much on repetition, sequences, antitheses, paragraphs with inductions and summaries." An Emerson narrative is nonlinear, nonformulaic, allusive. "Thus is Emerson always beating down through the crust towards the first fire of life, of death and of eternity. Read where you will, each sentence seems not to point to the next but to the undercurrent of all."[35]

All these observations fit Ives's music generally, and his dense, vaulting "Emerson" movement specifically. There is no key signature. There is no sonata form. There are few barlines. The trajectory is torrential: an onslaught of questing dissonant ascents in the treble, amplified—rather than anchored—by plunging octaves in the bass. The quieter sections are roughly homespun: parlor piano strains nervously alive to philosophic impulse. It is merely predictable that Ives left different versions of "Emerson," that this is music with no fixed or final form, that it seemed to him "unfinished" every time he assayed it. In letters, he called "Emerson" an "experiment," "not written primarily to be played." In the *Essays,* he writes of "the outward aspect of serenity" of Emerson's "codas," of their "poised strength," of the "'original authentic fire' which Emerson missed in Shelley . . . a kind of furious calm." All this may be heard in the coda to Ives's "Emerson," in which energies well spent yield a higher circle attained. The fading four-note motif dominating this passage—instantly recognizable as the motto theme of Beethoven' Fifth—is poundingly omnipresent in the preceding pages. Emerson's "flashes," writes Ives, "approach as near the Divine as Beethoven in his most inspired moments." For Ives, the Beethoven motto is not, as for others, "fate knocking at the door." Rather, it conveys a sanguine moral imperative: "the soul of humanity knocking at the door of the Divine mysteries, radiant in the faith it *will* be opened—and the human become the Divine!"[36]

Movement two of the *Concord* Sonata is "Hawthorne." For Ives the essayist, Hawthorne's fundamental theme is the influence of sin upon the conscience. Ives's musical portrait, however, fastens on matter more corporeal: the poet of the supernatural. The movement begins with a diaphanous evocation of Berkshire frost, but instantly turns rambunctious. Its phantasmagoric leaps and lunges discover a churchyard haunted by hymns and distant bells (treble clusters depressed by a fourteen-inch wooden block), a circus parade, the locomotive lurch of Hawthorne's demonic "celestial railroad," and—lustily sung or dismembered—"Columbia, the Gem of the Ocean." The crammed textures and bristling dissonances of such characteristic pages seemed modernist to Ives's first adherents and opponents; in retrospect, his musical stream of consciousness, spewing flotsam and jetsam, evokes the turn-of-the century methodology of Gustav Mahler an ocean away.

"The Alcotts," coming next, is the shortest and simplest of the *Concord* movements, a hymn to ordinary things. It "tries to catch something of old man Alcott's—the great talker's—sonorous thought," writes Ives. Ives also writes, of Alcott, that "men accustomed to wander around in the visionary unknown are the quickest and strongest when occasion requires ready action of the lower virtues"—a case in point being Alcott's loyalty to Thomas Wentworth Higginson when the latter stormed the Boston courthouse holding the fugitive slave Anthony Burns. Writing of the Alcott house, Ives finds "a kind of homely but beautiful witness to Concord's common virtue," a "spiritual sturdiness underlying its quaint picturesqueness," overtones that "tell us that there must have been something aesthetic fibered in the Puritan severity." And he mentions Scotch airs and family hymns sung within, and the parlor piano "on which Beth . . . played at the Fifth Symphony." In "The Alcotts," the four-note Beethoven motto surmounts quaint domestic trappings—and scales C major heights as sonorous and sublime as Bronson Alcott's thoughts. Ives in later years sometimes expressed impatience with the tunefulness, plainness, and consonance of this great cameo. His own performance, recorded on an upright piano in 1943, is unsentimental, excitable, and quick; but the climax—romantically rapturous and broad—tells all.*[37]

Versus the hortatory transcendental ecstasies of "Emerson," "Thoreau," completing the sonata, is a contemplative nature ecstasy. Of a boat trip to Fair Haven Pond, Thoreau writes: "The falling dews seemed to strain and purify the air and I was soothed with an infinite stillness. . . . Vast hollows of silence stretched away in every side, and my being expanded in proportion, and filled them. Then first could I appreciate sound, and find it musical."[38] In *Walden,* Thoreau writes: "I wish to hear the silence of the night. . . . The silence rings; it is musical and thrills me." And he reports the "faint," "sweet" melodies of distant bells: "At a sufficient distance over the woods, this sound acquires a certain vibratory hum, as if the pine needles in the horizon were the strings of a harp which it swept. All sound heard at the great possible distance produces one and the same effect: a vibration of the universal lyre."

God-in-nature here translates into a transcendental ether, physically and metaphysically aquiver. In "The Housatonic at Stockbridge," from *Three Places in New England,* trembling strings recorded the "thrilling music" of Thoreau's silence, a half-heard, half-seen aureole crowning mist, water, and floating leaves. In "Thoreau," Ives's soft keyboard clusters and arpeggios, rendered with "both pedals . . . used almost constantly," distill music from Walden mists. Ives's "Thoreau" essay offers a corresponding programmatic vignette. It is Indian summer. The poet sits in his sun-drenched doorway, "rapt in reverie." "His meditations are interrupted only by the faint sound of the Concord bell," windswept over the water. As night falls, he plays his flute. Ives's bells are tolling octaves in the bass. The flute—and Ives supplies an optional flute part—plays the sonata's "human faith melody," a sublimation of the omnipresent Beethoven theme, here realized in its fullest, most perfect form. A final whispered five-octave ascent, a final bell echo, a

*According to Charles Ruggles, "Ives was a grand pianist. I never heard a better pianist in my life than he was." Vivian Perlis (ed.), *Charles Ives Remembered: An Oral History* (1974), p. 173.

final ghost image of the four-note Beethoven rhythm, and the music vaporizes.[39]

With its "higher" and "more lowly" strains sustained in equipoise, the *Concord* Sonata embodies an Ivesian ideal: inclusive uplift. Its raptures and grit, its hymns and bands, are evanescent and earthy, sublime and egalitarian. Ives the composer is here an apotheosis of the life insurance salesman: meliorist, democratic, embracing the "average" and quotidian even while striving toward philosophic climes. Self-evidently, he was born into a musical world incomparably less stratified than the one in which he died four decades later—in which "operas" could be intimate, informal, and sung in English; in which "concerts" could intermingle parlor songs with overtures. Fin-de-siècle bands (and Ives's father was a bandmaster) were potently promiscuous: Sousa's programs ranged from polkas to the *Parsifal* Prelude. So, too, were fin-de-siècle organists (and Ives was an organist): Dudley Buck's compositions ranged from cantatas and psalms to variations on "Home Sweet Home" (performed by Ives in 1890).

In a later period, such unprejudiced passion for the vernacular would have seemed intellectually suspect. And yet Ives was a product of a strenuous (and strenuously conservative) undergraduate education; he relished the life of the mind. The *Essays Before a Sonata* mention Plato, Virgil, Ariosto, Petrarch, Shelley, Goethe, Dante, Pope, Voltaire, Rousseau, Hegel, Ricardo, John Stuart Mill, Schelling, Montaigne, Spenser, Nietzsche, Tolstoy, Ruskin, Carlyle. Of American names, there is no mention of such prophets of the future as Carl Van Vechten or Paul Rosenfeld. As for American musicians: the *Essays* predictably omit the avant-garde madman Leo Ornstein, and also Boston's Charles Martin Loeffler, as of 1920 arguably America's most prestigious composer—a Francophile aesthete whose decadent tendencies could only have irritated Ives. In passing, Ives praises Mark Twain, chastises Henry James, and chides Mark Van Doren. Daniel Gregory Mason's *Contemporary Composers* (1918) earns a more-than-passing reference for its "wholesome influence"; explaining his needling omission of Ravel, Stravinsky, Scriabin, Reger, Schoenberg, and Ornstein, Mason writes:

> The reader will look in vain for these names, in recent years on everyone's lips, the table of contents of this book on "Contemporary Composers."* In the work of most of them there is, indeed, much of charm or interest, of vividness, perhaps of permanent power. . . . They all represent in one way

*The Table of Contents lists Richard Strauss, Elgar, Debussy, and D'Indy.

> or another that trivializing of the great art, the degradation of it to sensationalism, luxury, or merely illustration. . . . No sincere lover of music can regard with anything but the gravest apprehensions such tendencies toward decadence.[40]

Mason was a precise contemporary of Ives, born eleven months earlier; Ives would have appreciated his distinguished Yankee lineage (his grandfather, Lowell Mason, having been the famous hymn composer).

The American poets mentioned in the *Essays* include Bayard Taylor, Sidney Lanier, John Greenleaf Whittier, and Oliver Wendell Holmes—of whom Whittier and Holmes were set by Ives. Though Ives's sentimental poetic taste is sometimes considered incongruous, an Ives setting of more cutting-edge verse would have been more truly confounding. One of his most ecstatic songs, "The Housatonic at Stockbridge" (using the same material as the symphonic tone-picture), transcendentally inflames polite drawing room verses by Robert Underwood Johnson—who in a 1916 *New York Times* article deplored the excesses of Edgar Lee Masters and other "ultra-moderns."[41] A singular exception to Ives's eschewal of important contemporary poets is his 1915 setting of Louis Untermeyer's "Swimmers." Untermeyer subsequently visited Ives, in 1943 or 1944, and later reminisced:

> Ives admired Emerson, Thoreau, and that whole New England school of writers to such a degree that he shut out the earlier and later school of New England writers. . . . I wonder why he didn't compose songs to more contemporary poetry. There was good poetry being written all around him at this time. He loved the past more. . . . He didn't want to say outright that the New England poets of the past did a damned sight better than these people of the present. But I think if he had read Frost, he wouldn't have liked him very much. He needed the thing that Emerson gave him, the thing which was both beautiful to listen to, beautiful to think about, and a kind of moral lesson. He liked tremendously the fact that there was a moral import to it. With the poetry of his day that had ceased. You didn't do a maxim or say, "Thanks for the heavenly message brought by thee, Child of the wandering sea," as Oliver Wendell Holmes wrote in "The Chambered Nautilus."[42]

In fact, the rebel in Ives paradoxically fed on the idealism of the genteel tradition. He is actually kindred to such bellwethers of New England gentility as Harvard's Charles Eliot Norton, for whom culture was an inspirational bulwark of democratic society. Norton's ethos of sociability, extolling "open-mindedness, independence of judgment, generosity, elevation of purpose," does not depict Ives:[43] his vision of intellectual composure, shading into snobbery, is as placid as Ives is restlessly combative. And Ives was not the social activist that Norton was, running a night school for the poor, or supporting multiple family housing for Irish immigrants. But Norton's sanguine application of culture to citizen-building, an antidote to encroaching vulgarity and materialism, is Ivesian. So, too, were the larger purposes of the turn-of-the-century Boston Symphony, with its twenty-five-cent rush tickets. Boston's Symphony Hall, its external severity framing interior sublimities, extrapolates both the man and the musician in Ives. "In the stern outward life of the old settlers, pioneers and Puritans, there was a life generally of inward beauty, but with a rather harsh exterior," Ives writes, describing the "Thanksgiving" movement of his *Holidays* Symphony. "And the Puritan 'no-compromise' with mellow colors and bodily ease gives a natural reason for trying tonal and uneven off-counterpoints and combinations which would be and sound of sterner things. . . . This music must, before all else, be something in art removed from physical comfort."[44]

The conductor Theodore Thomas—another Gilded Age icon, another embodiment of harsh beauty—likewise bears comparison with Ives. Thomas personified tradition: his repertoire stopped with Bruckner, Sibelius, and Richard Strauss. He had no use for gospel hymns or ragtime. If he had ever examined a typical Ives score, he would have found no music in it. But he would have identified with Ives's moral fervor, with his pugnacity and self-reliance. Like Ives, Thomas was religious by temperament, an optimist and a democrat. He was athletic. He looked like a banker. Ives demanded music of "wholesomeness, manliness, humility, and deep spiritual, possibly religious feeling."[45] So did Thomas. Ives rejected music dominated by "manner"; Thomas, too , spurned aestheticism. For Thomas, Beethoven was paramount: a moral paragon; he outgrew an earlier enthusiasm for Wagner. For Ives, Beethoven was paramount: "in the history of this youthful world the best product that human-beings can boast of." George Ives had worshipped Wagner. As a young organist, Charlie played transcriptions of Wagner favorites. His teenage organ Postlude in F borrows from Wagner's *Siegfried Idyll.* In 1894 he attended *Götterdämmerung* at the Metropolitan Opera House.* In his twenties, he was "deeply stirred" by the Prize Song from *Die Meistersinger.* No less than for Theodore Thomas, Wagner for Ives

*This was not a Metropolitan Opera production, but a presentation by Walter Damrosch's company "much below the level of the good old days" (the *New York Times,* reviewing the performance of March 29, 1894); Ives attended on March 31.

signified redemptive music. But, no less than Thomas, Ives ultimately rejected Wagner as a false prophet: "The bravery was make-believe, the love was make-believe, the passion, the virtues, all make believe." Wagner was "cloying," "slimy." In the history of Western music, he illuminated a "weakening of moral strength and vitality." By 1932, when Ives visited Berlin, Wagner could not be discussed in his presence.[46]

Beethoven, by comparison, was ethical. He tore up his *Eroica* Symphony inscription to Napoleon when Napoleon named himself emperor. He celebrated the freedom fighters Egmont and Florestan. In Beethoven, writes Ives in *Essays before a Sonata,* "the moral and the intellectual" are one. "It is told, and the story is so well known that we hesitate to repeat it here, that [Beethoven and Goethe] were standing in the street one day when the Emperor drove by—Goethe, like the rest of the crowd, bowed and uncovered—but Beethoven stood bolt upright, and refused even to salute, saying: 'Let him bow to us, for ours is a nobler empire.' Goethe's *mind* knew this was true, but his moral courage was not instinctive."[47]

Like Ives, like Emerson, Beethoven embodies ideals of uplift and equality—and yet will not pander. His language grows arcane. Ives knows this paradox and solves it: Beethoven writes symphonies "to the people," not "for the people"; he composes "for the human-soul," not for the "human-ear."[48] In fact, with their Beethoven encomiums, the *Concord* Sonata and *Essays Before a Sonata* mutually testify that Ives saw himself striding alongside Emerson and Beethoven in a common high endeavor—that the human, morally empowered, might become divine.

• • •

According to John Sullivan Dwight, the instrumental music of the master composers was "sacred," the most "religious" ever conceived. He dismissed church music in favor of absolute symphonies, with Beethoven the pinnacle practitioner and Beethoven adagios "almost the very essence of prayer."[49]

For decades after, the nine Beethoven symphonies constituted a canonical text, narrating an exemplary creative odyssey. The four numbered symphonies of Charles Ives, too, make up an evolutionary sequence shadowed by Beethoven's example, and embedded in hallowed Germanic practice. The Beethoven narrative is commonly read as progressive, with "late Beethoven"—the Ninth Symphony, and kindred late piano sonatas and string quartets—foretasting a challenging future. So, too, with Ives. But the Beethoven trajectory can be differently read: as a retreat into subjective depths of experience and expression by a composer—deaf and eccentric—increasingly cut off from the world. And so it is, as well, with Ives.

In later life, when he no longer composed, Ives felt the need to respond to claims that his music "could not be played," "could not be sung," "made no sense." He himself, he stated, could sing all but a few of his songs. "There is nothing that I have ever written for a piano that I haven't been able to play."[50] Unlike such idiosyncratic Americans as Henry Cowell and John Cage, Ives was trained to compose within the mainstream. His entire musical education, beginning with his father and culminating with Horatio Parker, was fundamentally Germanic. Among his surviving student exercises at Yale, two German *Lieder* stand apart as achievements not merely auspicious, but altogether astonishing: they are among the best American songs ever composed.

Parker had his students set poems already famously set. Ives's version of "Feldeinsamkeit"—perhaps the most sublime of all Brahms's songs—became the topic of a well-worn anecdote. It was under classroom scrutiny when George Chadwick—New England's saltiest "official" composer—happened to turn up, reeking of beer. Parker was objecting to the mobile harmonic raptures of Ives's ersatz *Lied*. Chadwick winked at Parker and quipped: "That's as good a song as you could write."[51] It remains that and more. Ives hews to the Romantic and yet goes his own way; his "Feldeinsamkeit" sounds like no one else's. He follows Brahms's repetition of "nach oben" at the end of line two; after that, the pattern of text repetition, including a final reprise of the entire first stanza, is original. Brahms's accompaniment pulsates. Ives's ripples—and the tingle of dissonant particles, beginning with the D-natural disturbance of the A-flat major/E-flat major harmonies of measure two, forecasts the quivering metaphysical nature-music of Ives's maturity.

As remarkable is Ives's "Ich grolle nicht"—a setting Chadwick might not have winked at. It cannot be accidental that Ives's alterations of the original poetic form, beginning with the repetition of "Ewig verlor'nes Lieb," duplicate Schumann's familiar setting. Schumann's reading of this lover's lament ("I bear no grudge, though my heart breaks") is impulsive. The response of the twenty-four-year-old Ives, by comparison, is ripe: subdued, philosophic. The lover's disappointment takes the form of a slow burn: a poised cadential phrase slipping into the chromatically intensified harmonies of suppressed heartbreak. When, finally, he permits himself to glimpse "the serpent gnawing at [the] heart" of his beloved, a nightmare of crashing dissonance erupts—and is as quickly subdued. Ives liked these songs well enough to include them among the 114 he published in 1922, with the inimitable note:

> The writer has been severely criticized for attempting to put music to texts of songs, which are masterpieces of great composers. The song above ["Ich grolle nicht"], and some of the others, were written primarily as studies. It should be unnecessary to say that they were not composed in the spirit of competition; neither Schumann, Brahms or Franz will be the one to suffer by a comparison; another unnecessary statement. Moreover, they would probably be the last to claim a monopoly of anything—especially the right of man to the pleasure of trying to express in music whatever he wants to. These songs are inserted not so much in spite of this criticism as because of it.

But it was "symphony" that fundamentally beckoned. In the United States, the genre remained nascent. Three mid-nineteenth-century originals—Anthony Philip Heinrich, William Henry Fry, and Louis Moreau Gottschalk—had concocted "symphonies" bearing no relationship to the Beethoven template. Heinrich's bear names like *The History of Kentucky, The Tower of Babel,* and *Manitou Mysteries;* the scores deploy up to forty-four individual parts, often moving at implausible speeds. Fry's punctiliously programmatic *Santa Claus* Symphony, controversially purveyed by Louis Jullien's virtuoso orchestra beginning in 1853, includes a snowstorm and "Episode of a perishing Traveler" (a lachrymose star turn for Jullien's double bass soloist Giovanni Bottesini); Santa Claus is a high bassoon with sleigh bells. Gottschalk's two-movement "Romantic symphony" *Night in the Tropics,* composed in 1859 for a monster orchestra including the latest valved brass and Afro-Cuban drums and maracas, links a languorous sunset with a roof-rattling *fiesta criolla*—a superlatively cinematic effort, but a symphony in name only. New York's George Bristow, by comparison, composed actual symphonies on the German model between 1848 and 1872—but these works, along with Heinrich's, Fry's, and (alas) Gottschalk's, were dormant by the time Ives arrived at Yale.

In Ives's New England, the first symphonist of note was John Knowles Paine. To George Chadwick, upon hearing Theodore Thomas conduct the wildly applauded 1876 premiere of Paine's First, Paine "proved we could have a great musician, and that he could get a hearing"; at the premiere of Paine's Second Symphony, in 1880, John Sullivan Dwight was observed "frantically opening and shutting his umbrella as an expression of uncontrollable emotion." These big works, both over half an hour long, make no attempt to sound indigenous: No. 1, in C minor, keys on Beethoven's Fifth; No. 2, "Im Frühling," appropriates Schumann without apology. Of Paine's New England progeny, Horatio Parker was fundamentally a church composer; he wrote no symphonies. Though Chadwick's best métier was froth, he produced three Germanic symphonies, of which Nos. 2 (1886) and 3 (1894) are distinguished by the breeziness of their elegantly turned scherzos; the weightier movements bog down. Amy Beach's *Gaelic* Symphony (1896) is an exercise in *Sturm und Drang* constrained by the genteel. New York, meanwhile, in 1892 heard an authentic Romantic symphony by an American: George Templeton Strong's sixty-minute *Sintram,* inspired by Dürer. But it was the Bohemian Antonín Dvořák who in 1893 singularly produced a symphony both durable and distinguishably "From the New World." With Dvořák's triumphant example in play, Henry Krehbiel, long a frustrated champion of the American symphonic enterprise, lost patience; he called for American composers to find common cause with Dvořák and *consciously* appropriate African-American folksong, Native American dance, and other vernacular ingredients.

Ives had no need for such advice. Presumably, he was ignorant of Gottschalk, Fry, and Heinrich—the latter two being free spirits in some ways kindred to his own truculent muse. But he had heard his father's call. He produced his First Symphony, fully forty-five minutes long, over the course of his four Yale years and submitted it in partial fulfillment of his graduation requirements. Though its standard four movements, its sonata and scherzo forms, satisfied Parker's most basic requirements, this remains a stubbornly odd work, quirky in its virtues and shortcomings both. The first and longest movement—nearly nineteen minutes with the exposition repeat—is the best; it shows what Charlie can and cannot do. A clarinet sings a catchy D minor waltz that instantly meanders. The violins improvise a response, decorated by flutes in corny thirds: a salon whiff. A series of detours is punctuated by acrid harmonies, spiky arpeggios, or a timpani roll. We know from Ives that Parker objected to so much instability; he insisted that the movement end in D minor. And so it does: with a vengeance: *agitato,* triple-*forte,* reinforced by stentorian brass, the waltz's dotted rhythms suddenly declaim a march. The prolixity of the resulting sonata form, if obviously uncalculated, is not unconscious; though he had yet to hear much symphonic music, Ives could have more tamely obeyed the rules had he wished.* Instead, to the degree his classroom obligations permitted, he is willfully experimental.

Movement two of Ives's First is impressively elevated. As in move-

*The same is notably true of Schubert's first sonata forms.

ment one, the tunes are superb. Their swift filigree, in an Adagio molto, is decidedly odd. Movement three is a rollicking Scherzo with canonic textures and a proper Trio. The high jinks of movement four are preposterously prolonged; at the close Ives tosses in themes from the first two movements (but not the third). The discernible influence of Dvořák's *New World* Symphony on Ives's First is unsurprising. Parker had taught alongside Dvořák in New York. The *New World* was instantly popular, instantly influential in the United States. In Boston, Beach's *Gaelic* Symphony was a response in the same key (E minor), quoting folk tunes, leaning toward the pentatonic, featuring an English horn in the slow movement.* Ives's slow movement features a memorably plaintive English horn tune resembling in part Dvořák's already famous English horn melody, with its folkish pentatonic inflections. At the same time, no less than Heinrich or Fry, Ives is already authentically eccentric. What is more, his energies and informalities already seem authentically "American." As often as not, the symphony's courtesies are cockeyed or cheeky. The propensity toward abruption, the alternation of "high" and "low" forecast Ives's future.

In 1900—two years after finishing the First Symphony—Ives embarked on a Symphony No. 2. He completed it two years later. If this, too, is "early Ives," it far surpasses any previous American symphony and remains a pinnacle American symphonic achievement. In *Essays Before a Sonata,* Ives would pertinently write:

> The man "born down to Babbitt's Corners" may find a deep appeal in the simple but acute Gospel hymns of the New England "camp meeting" of a generation or so ago. He finds in them . . . a vigor, a depth of feeling, a natural-soil rhythm, a sincerity—emphatic but inartistic—which . . . carries him nearer the "Christ of the people" than does the Te Deum of the greatest cathedral. . . . If the Yankee can reflect the fervency with which "his gospels" were sung—the fervency of "Aunt Sarah," who scrubbed her life away for her brother's ten orphans, the fervency with which this woman, after a fourteen-hour work day on the farm, would hitch up and drive five miles through the mud and rain to "prayer meetin'," her one articulate outlet for the fullness of her unselfish soul—if he can reflect the fervency of such a spirit, he may find there a local color that will do all the world good. If his music but catch that spirit by being a part of itself, it will come somewhere near his idea—and it will be American, too—perhaps nearer so than of the devotee of Indian or negro melody.[52]

*Dvořák quotes no folk tunes in the *New World* Symphony. But his themes, pentatonically inflected, gesture unmistakably toward "Negro melodies" and Native American imagery.

Such "devotees" being, of course, Dvořák and his acolytes. Ives insisted that to capture and convey a native spirit it was not enough that, say, Henry Gilbert compose a *Dance in Place Congo* (1908). "A composer born in America, but who has not been interested in the 'cause of the Freedmen,' may be so interested in 'negro melodies' that he writes a symphony over them. He is conscious . . . that he wishes it to be 'American music.' . . . [But] if this composer isn't as deeply interested in the 'cause' as Wendell Phillips was, when he fought his way through that anti-abolitionist crowd at Faneuil Hall, his music is liable to be less American than he wishes."[53]

Following Dvořák, admiring his roots in Slavic song and dance, Henry Krehbiel had pointed American composers to American folk and indigenous music. But in fact Dvořák equally adored composed Stephen Foster tunes like "Old Folks at Home." Ives, too, deeply served an unprejudiced breadth of musical speech. As a Danbury Yankee, he shared personal experience not with slaves and Navajos, or even (excepting some handed-down fiddle tunes) with the folk musicians of North America. Rather, via the parlor and salon, he identified with hymns and minstrel tunes; via the organ loft, he identified with Bach; via his father and Parker, he identified with Beethoven and Brahms. That all of these influences intermingle in the Second Symphony, that all are equally audible and equally privileged, creates a musical kaleidoscope more multifarious than any by Mahler. What is more, Ives, in cosmopolitan Manhattan, has quite suddenly, even unaccountably, mastered the symphonic template—the Second Symphony's sonata forms are fluent; its five-movement structure is original and sound. What Ives here achieves, in effect, is a polarization of high and low: his egalitarian ethos, and the ethos of uplift, are equally served.

The symphony begins with a contrapuntal Andante moderato—"sacred" music ennobling vernacular strains.* Movement two is a bright Allegro sonata form whose tunes include "Bringing in the Sheaves." Movement three is an Adagio centerpiece fixing on the hymn "Beulah Land."† Movement four, Largo maestoso, is both an intense recollection of movement one and the setup for a joke: a riotous dancing finale

*Peter Burkholder has traced the "original" tunes in this work to songs mainly by Stephen Foster. Burkholder, *All Made of Tunes: Charles Ives and the Uses of Musical Borrowing* (1955).

†A seeming citation of "America the Beautiful" was for Ives "O Mother Dear, Jerusalem." See Peter Burkholder, *All Made of Tunes,* p. 114.

refracting "Turkey in the Straw" and "Camptown Races" en route to a culminating reprise of the symphony's pervasive motto: "Columbia, the Gem of the Ocean."

Chadwick, in his Second and Third Symphonies, tweaks Germanic formalities. His *Jubilee,* a close cousin to Dvořák's *Carnival* Overture, impulsively samples "Camptown Races." His *Melpomene* Overture nearly quotes Wagner's *Tristan* Prelude. These gentle gestures, in their different ways, explore an emerging dialectic with Europe—a testing of the umbilical cord. Ives, in his Symphony No. 2, is already father to the parent: whatever he appropriates, he makes his own. In movement two, a passage from Brahms's Third Symphony provokes a polytonal disruption. A subsequent allusion to Brahms's First is italicized by a snare drum. *Tristan* twice thickens the religious Largo. At the close of movement four, a striding bass line uses Bach as a straight man for slapstick. In each case, Ives maximizes the incongruity of his borrowings. At the same time, these variegated thematic ingredients—high and low, European and American—are plastically treated: they migrate, transmute, intermingle.

Echoing modernist conventional wisdom, Leonard Bernstein called the composer of Ives's Second an "authentic primitive"—an observation itself primitive.[54] Ives's mediation of New World and Old, simple and complex, is knowing, not naïve.* In American classical music, the tensions afflicting a cultural colony of course produced ambivalence toward the parent culture. Beginning with Paine, the symphonies directly preceding Ives are to varying degrees imitative, deferent, or tentative. Ives alone brusquely levels the playing field. His paradoxical methodology is to burrow deep within the genteel tradition—its Germanic templates, beloved of the sanctimonious John Sullivan Dwight; its hymns and parlor songs, remembered from his Danbury home. A fin-de-siècle masterpiece, the Second Symphony is the handwork of a cocky subversive, a master practitioner of the inside job.

. . .

There may be an analogy, Ives writes, "between both the state and power of artistic perceptions and the law of perpetual change, that ever-flowing stream partly biological, partly cosmic, ever going on in ourselves, in nature, in all life."[55]

*Ives's way of ending a piece—*The Housatonic at Stockbridge* is an unforgettable example—is never naïve.

It was William James who coined the term *stream of consciousness* in his massive and influential *Principles of Psychology* of 1890. James's "stream of thought, of consciousness, or of subjective life" encompassed every mental stratum—whether subconscious, unconscious, or wholly overt. His fascination with the evolutionary flow of mental attention was pervasive. It fed an American preoccupation as manifest in spiritualism, séances, and mind cures as in weighty cultural and intellectual discourse. Theosophists explored subcurrents of thought and feeling, and conducted research in psychic communication. Wagnerites attended to the interior convolutions of a Tristan or Isolde, or the ultimate exaltation of a Brünnhilde or Parsifal.

With its roots in Eastern mysticism and German Romanticism, Transcendentalism was a potent precursor to these fin-de-siècle currents. And the "ever-flowing stream" Ives ponders in his *Essays* of course connects to such nature portraits as the symphonic "Housatonic at Stockbridge" or the pianistic "Thoreau," both aquiver with elemental living matter. Such "formless," fractured narratives as "Emerson" and "Hawthorne," freely associating the "muddy" and sublime, are brave experiments in musical stream of consciousness—experiments that climax in what Ives considered his highest utterance, culminating his symphonic output: the *Largo* finale of the Fourth Symphony that he finished in 1916.[56]

Ives cautioned against the dangers of a "superimposed idiomatic [musical] education" that may not fit a composer's "constitution."[57] He also wrote: "Unity is too generally conceived of . . . as analogous to form; and form as analogous to custom; and custom to habit. . . . Perhaps all unity in art, at its inception, is half-natural and half-artificial, but time . . . inclines to make us feel that it is all natural."[58] If the sonata forms of Ives's First and Second symphonies signify "artifice," the Fourth Symphony is "all natural"; it abandons "superimposed" idioms. At the same time, the example of Beethoven—revered by the Transcendentalists—remains pertinent. "Late Beethoven" and "late Ives" are cognates. In Beethoven's Ninth Symphony, a universal message of uplift becomes explicit: all men are to become brothers. In Ives's Fourth, as well, a sung text—"Watchman tell us of the night"—interpolates the sacred. The Ninth Symphony begins, famously, in a cosmic void: an "ever-flowing stream" of preconscious thought. In the finale, stream of consciousness takes the form of fragmentary, evolutionary remembrances of the three preceding movements. This intense *Innigkeit* is as surely correlative with Beethoven's deafness and eccentricity as Ives's is with growing seclusion:* "As I look back, I seem to have worked with more natural freedom when I knew the music was not going to be inflicted on others. And this is probably one of the reasons that, not until I got to work on the Fourth Symphony, did I feel justified in writing quite as I wanted to, when the subject matter was religious."[59] As in late Ives, the narratives of the late Beethoven piano sonatas disregard practicalities of public performance; can the abnormally dense, precipitously rapid fugue of the *Hammerklavier* Sonata really be heard as written?

Also pertinent to late Beethoven and late Ives is stream of consciousness as explored in fin-de-siècle Germany and Austria. Ives wrote of Beethoven as a beginning: a step toward a liberated music of the future. Here is Ferruccio Busoni, in his *Sketch of a New Aesthetic of Music:* "[Beethoven] ascended one short step on the way leading music back to its loftier self. . . . He did not quite reach absolute music, but in certain moments he divined it, as in the introduction to the fugue of the *Hammerklavier* Sonata. Indeed, all composers have drawn nearest the true nature of music . . . where they felt at liberty to disregard symmetrical proportions, and unconsciously drew free breath."[60] Busoni's idealized "Ur-Musik" is an unfettered stream. Composers, he complains, "have retained Form as a symbol, and made it into a fetish, a religion. . . . Is it not singular, to demand of a composer originality in all things, and to forbid it as regards form? No wonder that, once he becomes original, he is accused of 'formlessness.' "

This was written by an Italian in Berlin in 1911. In Vienna, Freud and Klimt, Mahler and Schoenberg were charting a darker, more menacing unconscious. Like Freud, like Mahler, Klimt favors a psychological realism stressing desire and anxiety, neurosis and transcendence. His mural "Philosophy" (1900) shows a tangle of naked bodies floating aimlessly: an aqueous cosmos inhabited by torpid humanity. As in other Klimt paintings, the liquefied medium suggests a stratum of primal subjectivity, an unconscious world of instinct dissipating every "I," a fatalistic vision of transient humanity more Eastern than Western. Klimt's imagery of particles adrift is made palpable by the gently irregu-

*Ives's response to Toscanini—a "stopwatch," a "clicking machine," a "little metronome"—is that of a Germanic true believer in the interior life of music. See his letter to Nicolas Slonimsky, ca. June 18, 1936, in Tom Owens (ed.), *Selected Correspondence of Charles Ives* (2007), p. 125.

lar harp tones punctuating the *Adagietto* of Mahler's Fifth Symphony. In Mahler's Ninth, harp tones articulate the slow motion of both outer movements. Near the close, the harp's naked oscillating thirds occupy a musical space as groundless as Klimt's visual field where he shows bodies drifting in and out of the frame. Ives, too, is obsessed with water. The transcendental nature portraits "The Housatonic at Stockbridge" and "Thoreau" are of course also river and pond portraits: elemental musical watercolors. In his Fourth Symphony, the finale's gathering current constitutes Ives's most heroic Ur-Musik: an ocean. Mahler's Ninth—his final completed symphony, posthumously premiered in 1912—is a psychic autobiography infested with Old World demons, defiantly swimming against the tide toward apotheosis. Ives knows nothing of floating nudes and deviant sexuality; a New World meliorist (who was also a New World prude), he simply rides an upward wave.*

An early program note for the Fourth Symphony, written by Henry Bellamann in consultation with Ives, summarizes: "The aesthetic program of the work is . . . the searching questions of What? and Why? which the spirit of man asks of life. This is particularly the sense of the Prelude. The three succeeding movements are the diverse answers, in which existence replies." Movement two, "Comedy," is "not a scherzo." Rather, like the "Hawthorne" movement of the *Concord* Sonata, it takes inspiration from Hawthorne's "Celestial Railroad," a riff on Bunyan's *The Pilgrim's Progress* ending with "an interruption of reality": a raucous Fourth of July in Concord. Movement three, a fugue, "is an expression of the reaction of life into formalism and ritualism." The finale, Bellamann writes, "is an apotheosis of the preceding content, in terms having something to do with the reality of existence and its religious experience."[61]

In Beethoven's late string quartets, guttural shouts are juxtaposed with a "Hymn of Thanksgiving" and other *innig* exaltations. Ives's symphony, too, maximizes high and low, religious and secular. It is at once more overt and more interior than the Second Symphony's "inside job." Like the Symphony No. 3 ("The Camp Meeting," 1904), it abandons sonata form; more than the Third Symphony, it dispenses with "bound-

*Pursuing the fin-de-siècle Mahler-Ives equation: The aesthetic signature of Mahler the composer is an unprecedented mixture of high art and quotidian dross: he juxtaposes the influences of Beethoven and Wagner with that of barracks marches, barrel organs, or klezmer bands. The iconic creators Mahler and Ives—the one so Central European, the other so American—are at the same time outsiders. They seize local dialects of speech and song, and rescue them from cliché. Haunted by the pastimes of childhood, they are chronically nostalgic.

aries." The corporeal or narrative musical streams of the *Concord* Sonata are made cosmic. Ives's culminating transcendental statement, the Fourth Symphony's finale fathoms the "ever-flowing stream," biological and metaphysical, of Ives's ontology. Its Ur-Musik bristles or trembles with particles of active elemental matter, stabilized (like the coda to "Emerson" or long stretches of "Thoreau") by the sonorous Ur-rhythm of an infinite tread in the bass. Its intimations of "Nearer My God to Thee" are omnipresent.*

In *Essays Before a Sonata,* Ives likens God to "being true to ourselves." In an ecstatic epiphany, he alternatively declares God "nothing but love." Peering into the future, he writes: "We would . . . believe that music is beyond any analogy to word language and that the time is coming, but not in our lifetime, when it will develop possibilities unconceivable now,—a language, so transcendent, that its heights and depths will be common to all mankind."[62] But in 1920, when these words were published, Ives was practically done composing.† Three decades of silence would ensue.

• • •

Neurasthenia, the *New York Times* reported in 1907, had become "our national malady": "Not without reason has nervous prostration been called the 'National disease.' Wherever Americans work and worry, and

*Elliott Carter, a quintessential twentieth-century modernist, was an ambivalent and inconstant Ives admirer. Carter of course appreciated the newness of Ives; he questioned Ives's technical capacity. But, having known and drawn inspiration from Ives as a young man, Carter sympathetically understood Ives's Transcendentalism; both overtly and subliminally, his own music, while not "religious," conveys a bracing density of elemental activity. In his 1944 essay "Ives Today" (*Modern Music,* vol. 21, May–June 1944, pp. 199–202), Carter pertinently writes: "Ives is always in quest of the transcendental. On the surface of his work, the infinite complexity of nature, the rapidly changing moods of forest and plain, the web of counterbalancing forces appear confused and dissociated. But Ives' involved texture, while mirroring this superficial confusion, at the same time attempts to show the larger harmony of rhythm behind the natural process. Faith in the purpose and goodness of nature rather than concern over its savage conflicts and hostility determines his choice of moods. In his essays he says that Debussy, in works like *La Mer,* appears interested only in the physical aspects and never sees beyond them."

†But Gayle Sherwood Magee cautions: "Despite later claims to the contrary, Ives was in all respects a practicing composer during the decade after his breakdown in 1918 and despite later descriptions, Ives appears to have been healthy enough during this period to produce a significant amount of music, both in completions of earlier works and entirely new ones. If he returned to a work that he had written ten years earlier and changed it, it was the work of an active composer engaging in the creative process. " Magee, *Charles Ives Reconsidered* (2008), p. 175.

especially in New York, where the pressure is at its worst, thousands of men, women, and children throw down their tools or leave their desks prostrated, to go to hospitals and sanitariums."

The physician George Beard in 1881 identified as "neurasthenia" a prevalent condition whose variegated symptoms included depression, despondency, palpitations, tachycardia (an abnormally rapid heartbeat), chronic eye strain, hypersensitive hearing, trembling hands or fingers, and cold or sweaty feet. By 1896 neurasthenia was "almost a household word." Neurasthenics were advised to avoid excitement. Bed rest was typically prescribed for women, moderate exercise for men. Mountain or rural resorts, or a trip abroad, were considered useful. The origins of the disease were as vague as its eclectic symptomatology. An exhaustion of "nerve energy," produced by "overwork" and "mental strain," was commonly postulated. Less directly, neurasthenia was believed to have something to do with "overcivilization": changes rapidly wrought by urbanization, industrialization, immigration.[63]

Paradoxically, the stresses of overcivilization also promoted a different diagnosis with a different cure. A species of turn-of-the-century anomie was linked to passivity and inhibition, to material comforts and Victorian codes. Its victims craved intense experience. This might take the form of bracing alternatives to traditional religions: mind cures and spiritualism; theosophy and Wagnerism. A fin-de-siècle craft revival correlated with Tolstoy's vision of the simple life and Ruskin's critique of capitalist labor. Martial celebrants of the strenuous life followed the urgings of Theodore Roosevelt. Fin-de-siècle Medievalists agreed with James Russell Lowell:

> Fagot and stake were desperately sincere;
> Our cooler martyrdoms are done in types
> . . . .
> This is no age to get cathedrals built.

The primal, the robust, the rustic were privileged over the diffuse Nietzschean "weightlessness" of the modern urban regime, with its technologically honed amenities and luxuries.[64]

This double condition—requiring rest; demanding stimulation—resonates with the complexities of Charles Ives's mental and physical health, including the "heart attacks" of 1906, 1918, and 1929. He was rejected for civilian ambulance service in World War I because of unspecified physical problems. He was diabetic (and was treated with insulin beginning around 1930). He was prone to extreme nervous excitation. His recurrent cardiac symptoms were classically "neurasthenic." His Aunt Amelia, in 1907, expressed her concern: "It is not strange that men in business circles break down—for many of them are working to the very *limit*—in ordinary times and then when additional strain comes . . . , there is no reserve strength to meet the emergency." Harmony Ives, as a trained nurse, had habitually treated neurasthenics—including her brother David, who later as a physician attended patients at the Saranac Lake Sanitarium. Saranac, Elk Lake, Keene Valley, and the Berkshires were all retreats for the Iveses preceding the purchase of their Connecticut country property in Redding. When in 1908 Aunt Amelia worried that Ives "was on the verge of a nervous collapse," Harmony opined that he was "bankrupt of nervous energy"—the neurasthenic diagnosis.[65]

Ives himself reported in 1929 that he suffered from a form of depression his doctor called "a kind of nx"—suggesting "neurasthenia." The same year he reported "a general running down . . . a kind of depression that I can't account for." Ives's transcendental ecstasies were a form of cure additional to the sanitarium route. His "eccentricities" shouted his preference for moral certainties and rustic simplicities over the sensory overload and hyper-refinements of city life. For his 1913 song "The New River," he wrote this poem:

Down the river comes a noise!
It is not the voice of rolling waters
It's only the sounds of man,
Dancing halls and tambourine,
Phonographs and gasoline.
Human beings gone machine.

What might be termed Ives's "nervous complex" was fraught with tensions and contradictions large and small: the implausibly long days he kept as a businessman/composer; the respectability he courted and flouted as a businessman/eccentric; his athleticism and infirmities; his gentleness and irascibility. His first cardiac incidents roughly coincided with vocational upheaval: no sooner did the church organist become an insurance salesman than the Armstrong investigation rocked the life insurance trade; one of Armstrong's victims, in 1906, was Ives's cousin Robert Granniss, who had helped to bring Charlie to Mutual Insurance. Ives's 1918 heart episode coincided with World War I. These intense instabilities—of vocation, health, temperament, and circumstance—in some ways energized the artist in Ives. They were also debilitating. That he stopped composing in the 1920s parallels the fate of two other late-Romantic symphonists who outlived their fin-de-siècle moment. After 1929, Sibelius worked fruitlessly on his Eighth Symphony before finally expiring in 1957. Elgar's output petered out after his valedictory Cello Concerto of 1919—fifteen years before his death. But for Harmony, the nurse, Ives the beleaguered composer was not aesthetically challenged. "It wasn't lack of audience & appreciation that made Mr. Ives stop composing," she wrote to Nicolas Slonimsky in 1936. "It just happened—the War & the complete breakdown in health. He had worked tremendously hard in his quarry all those years & exhausted the vein I suppose. I am always hoping he may open up a new vein & he may—His ideas are by no means exhausted, but there are the physical disabilities to be contended with. He is such a wonderful person—and he has such strength of character and will & sense. In all family troubles & decisions & problems he is the one they all come to." Her diagnosis was cumulative neurasthenic collapse.

. . .

Ives's nervous complex informs his music in ways obvious and not. To be sure, his predisposition to extreme dissonance partly registers an exaggerated masculinity. Also, he characteristically uses dissonance not to register pain or violence, in the fashion of other composers, but to suggest bristling transcendental energies.* Nevertheless, an element of irritation, rising to rage, is unmistakable, the Second String Quartet (1911–1913) being the most livid example. He began the work, he later recalled, "after one of those Kneisel Quartet concerts . . . half mad, half in fun, and half to try out, practice, and have some fun with making those men fiddlers get up and do something like men." The result is a scenario in which the players "converse, discuss, argue . . . fight, shake hands, shut up—then walk up the mountainside to view the firmament." The second movement ("Arguments"), especially, is packed with unpleasant music. Snatches of Tchaikovsky's Sixth and Beethoven's Ninth are shouted down by "Columbia, the Gem of the Ocean" and "Marching through Georgia." In Ives's manuscript a Romantic violin cadenza reads "Alla Rubato Elman" and "Andante emasculata"; a raucous chordal response reads "Cut it Out! Rollo!"†[66] Ives is here a fettered composer—stranded by an uncomprehending concert environment, beleaguered by interior

*His evanescent "shadow" dissonances are of this kind.

†Mischa Elman (1891–1967) was a famous Russian-born violinist.

demons of nervous frustration. The intensity of his ongoing quest for the high ground he so potently attains calibrates psychological and physical discomforts as well as a religious resilience.

Henry Krehbiel, in *How to Listen to Music,* defined "Romantic composers" as "those who have sought their ideals in other [i.e., extra-musical] regions and striven to give expression to them irrespective of the restrictions and limitations of form and conventions of law—composers with whom, in brief, content outweighs manner."[67] Ives, quintessentially, is the Romantic possessed and driven by forces greater than himself. In contradistinction to more self-controlled contemporaries, he does not deploy a system like Schoenberg's twelve tones; he does not define an aesthetic, like Stravinsky theorizing that music can only be about itself; he does not strategize to target a "new audience," like Copland redefining himself as a populist. If he bears little salient relationship to these seminal composers, Ives is in fact less influenced by the music of others than any other important composer one can think of. His aversion to auditioning contemporary music is subject to some exaggeration. His correspondence discloses familiarity with Scriabin as of 1924. Around the same time, Elliott Carter sometimes accompanied him to hear the Boston Symphony at Carnegie Hall; back at the house, Ives would rail against the Ravel and Stravinsky he had encountered. But according to Nicolas Slonimsky, Ives knew no Schoenberg. Ives told Slonimsky that he knew "very little" of the new music Paul Rosenfeld—a central advocate of modernism—reviewed. Ives's reminiscences record that, as early as 1910 or 1911, he found that

> listening to music (especially if in the programs there were things with which I was not familiar) tended to throw me out of my stride. I'll admit it may have been a kind of weakness on my part, but I found that listening to concert music seemed to confuse me in my own work, maybe not to a great extent, but enough to throw me off somewhat from what I had in mind or purposed. Hearing the old pieces that I'd been familiar with all my life (for instance, the Beethoven and Brahms symphonies, Bach, or even the *William Tell Overture,* etc.) did not, as I remember, seem to have this effect. I remember hearing something of Max Reger . . . and when I got back to what I'd been working on, I was conscious of a kind of interference or lapse.[68]

Writ large, what Ives realized was the necessity to escape European schooling. No less than Frederic Church, who heretically elected not to study painting in Paris, or Herman Melville, who sampled the South Seas rather than the Old World, or Walt Whitman, who stayed a vagabond, Ives is the type of American artist for whom greater refinement or worldliness would have negated a defining originality. He rejected the anchoring influence that his own musical generation would have exerted and instead rendered himself susceptible to a potpourri of unstable notions and memories of which his nervous complex was part cause, part product.

Once Ives ceased composing and working, this instability, being unchanneled, mounted afresh. His palsy prevented him from writing or shaving; grizzled, nursed, he grew a beard and relied on Harmony to write letters for him. His vision and hearing deteriorated. He was unable to play the piano for months at a time. He experienced "short of breath days" during which he could only talk when flat on his back.[69] Carter, visiting him in Redding, observed Ives playing "Emerson": "A vein on the side of his neck began to bulge as if it were going to burst with the tremendous energy and excitement he was putting into the performance. Apparently accustomed to this, he stopped playing, pinched the vein as if to stop the flow of blood and went to lie down on a sofa to recover, his wife bringing him a glass of milk."[70]

Lehman Engel, visiting Ives around 1937, was "terrified" to see Ives throw himself on a couch, panting for air, in the midst of a diatribe against the music establishment. "Mrs. Ives never looked up from her knitting, never looked concerned, never frowned. She'd made some remark, such as, 'Well, Charlie, if you're going to carry on that way, you know this is going to happen.' And she'd say to me, 'Don't worry.' And he'd catch his breath and be up and going about the same thing again." Ives asked Engel to publish a symphony by a friend:

> I said, "Mr. Ives, I think it's wonderful that you want to do this for your friend, but I think it's misguided. This is going to be very expensive, and I'm sure it would be better if you could make him a gift of money that he could use in his way. To my utter amazement, instead of rising to white fury, which I would have thought he would have done, he burst into tears, and it was very hard for him to get in control again. And finally when he did, wiping his eyes, with the backs of his hands, he said, "It's so terrible that God should create a man who's as good as he is, who works so hard at his music, and that he can't get anything performed or published."[71]

The alternating blasts of energy and enforced repose continued, a mirror of larger instabilities.

• • •

In 1896, when Charles Ives was working on his iconoclastic First Symphony at Yale, another iconoclast, William Jennings Bryan, nearly became president of the United States. No less than Ives, Bryan is a restless fin-de-siècle phenomenon, nostalgic and yet a harbinger. The populist in Bryan was rural and religious. The Progressive in Bryan cued on his backwoods independence; anticipating the New Deal, he crusaded for economic egalitarianism. He took no interest in new thinking in the arts, religion, or philosophy; in his own field—politics—he was mercurial. The whole of Bryan was consumed by moral certitude; his sense of justice and mercy was evangelical.

Ives's world of ideas intersects Bryan's world. His thinking was populist, Progressive, morally charged, antimodern, inflamed within the confines of his special calling.

In 1920, Ives undertook a singular political initiative: a Twentieth Amendment to the Constitution of the United States. This began as a six-page article submitted to eight New York City newspapers. That they ignored it is understandable. In pursuit of direct democracy, Ives wanted the general public annually to submit proposals to Congress, which would select no more than twenty for further consideration. All citizens would be called upon to respond in turn. The outcome would be ten referendum questions, put to public vote. A majority vote would promulgate a new law. Ives argued: "If one will admit that God made man's brain as well as his stomach, one must then admit that the brain (that is the majority-brain!) if it has the normal amount of wholesome food—truth, in its outward ministrations, specific knowledge, facts, premises, etc., which universal education is fast bringing—will digest and will function, as normally as the stomach, when it has the right kind of food. If one won't admit that, he comes pretty near admitting that God is incapable."[72]

Ives next submitted his amendment to the *Atlantic Monthly* and to various politicians. When this, too, led nowhere, he printed five thousand copies of a broadside that shouted:

> The following contains an attempt to suggest a "20th AMENDMENT" to the Federal Constitution—AN ATTEMPT clumsy and far from adequate, we admit . . . but as its general purpose is TO REDUCE to a minimum, or possibly to eliminate, something which all our great political leaders talk about but never eliminate, to wit: THE EFFECTS OF TOO MUCH POLITICS IN OUR representative DEMOCRACY. . . . A dispassionate examination of social phenomena in this and other civilizations indicates that the intuitive reasoning of the masses is more scientifically true and so OF GREATER VALUE TO the wholesome PROGRESS of social evolution THAN the PERSONAL ADMONITIONS of the intellectual only.[73]

Ives tried to distribute his harangue at the Republican and Democratic National Conventions. He wound up with a mountain of unused pamphlets. It bears stressing that he remained serious about this brainstorm, that he never abandoned hope that others would take notice of it.

Though Bryan was one of the politicians who ignored Ives's solicitations, the political side of the composer—utopian, harebrained, and anticosmopolitan; full of ranting "common sense," of faith in God and common folk—is nothing if not Bryanesque. To be sure, Ives was not the type to press a Scopes trial. His compassion for blacks was not part of Bryan's Christian compassion. And the artist in Ives was of course subtler and more subversive than Bryan the renegade politician. But it remains unquestionable that, taken as a social and political thinker, Ives proudly and truculently inhabited pre–World War I America. Like Ives the symphonist, preaching uplift, Ives the pamphleteer was an eccentric embodiment of fin-de-siècle circumstances and mores. That he remained so dictated the seclusion to which he was increasingly condemned.

The Progressive movement Ives's amendment caricatures was born in Christian condemnation of slavery and alcohol, corruption and privilege. Jane Addams's crusade against the slum writ large Harmony Ives's stint at the Henry Street Settlement. Teddy Roosevelt's rhetoric of masculinity and nonconformity echoed on in decades of bellicose Ivesian rhetoric. Woodrow Wilson's dream of reforming the world became a stubborn Ivesian dream. Having in 1912 disgustedly rejected the candidacies of Roosevelt, Wilson, and William Howard Taft as insufficiently lofty, Ives became a Wilson man five years after, galvanized by the president's global zeal. No less than for Wilson, World War I represented for Ives an opportunity to vindicate mankind's majority goodness. Months after Wilson proclaimed his Fourteen Points—including a "general association of nations"—in January 1918, Ives began conceiving a People's World Union, calling for universal disarmament, free trade, and an international police force and court of arbitration. It would ensure that "every honest man and every honest country has a fair chance to work out their own problems in their own way and live their own natural life—a life that God Almighty will be proud of."[74] The United States failed to join the League of Nations founded abroad in 1920, but Ives persevered. He called nationalism "medieval—the only thing it does today is make war."[75] As with his Twentieth Amendment, he petitioned newspapers to no avail.

Wilson was shattered by Congress's refusal to countenance American membership in a world assemblage; he succumbed to a stroke and died three years after leaving office in 1921. For Ives, World War I (which he blamed on international moneyed interests) and the collapse of

Progressive idealism (rupturing the Bryan synthesis of evangelical and egalitarian zeal) produced a cranky resilience conditioned by estrangement and denial. The Jazz Age, the cardboard Harding presidency were not for him. Neither, in music, was the up-and-coming Francophile Aaron Copland. Shutting his eyes, closing his ears, he sporadically sketched a *Universe* Symphony for "two huge orchestras" on dual mountaintops "to paint . . . the mysterious beginning of all things, . . . the evolution of all life."[76] In 1932, he began dictating a series of "thoughts and reminiscences," published by John Kirkpatrick in 1973 as *Memos*. The informal idiom of these late writings is cranky and impatient. Ives's alienation from the twentieth century takes such interesting forms as:

> Emasculating America for money! Is the Anglo-Saxon going "Pussy"?—the nice Lizzies—the do-it-proper boys of today—the cushions of complacency—the champions of bodily ease—the play-it-pretty minds—the cautious old gals running the broadcasting companies—those great national brain-softeners, the movies—the mind-dulling tabloids with their headlines of half-truths and heroic pictures of the most popular detectives—the lady-birds—the femaled male crooners—the easy-ear concert-hall parlor entertainments with not even one "god-damn" in them—they are all getting theirs, and America is not! Is she gradually losing her manhood? The puritans may have been everything that the lollers called them, but they weren't soft. They may have been cold, narrow, hard-minded rock-eaters outwardly, but they weren't effeminates. . . .
>
> Even today probably about 83% of the so-called best musical programs—that is, of the large city symphony orchestras, of educational institutions, and of the opera—lean more to the molly-coddle than the rough way up the mountain. And 98¼% of all radio music is worse than molly-coddle—it's the one-syllable gossip for the soft-ears-and-stomach, easy for their bodies, and is fundamentally art, prostituted for commercialism. . . .
>
> When I think of some music that I liked to hear and play 35 or 40 years ago—if I hear some of it now, I feel like saying, "Rollo, how did you fall for that sop, those 'ta tas' and greasy ringlets?" In this I would include the *Preislied, The Rosary,** a certain amount of Mozart, Mendelssohn, a small amount of early Beethoven, the easy-made Haydn, a large amount of Massenet, Sibelius, Tchaikovsky, etc. (to say nothing of Gounod), most Italian operas (not exactly most of the operas, but most of each opera), some of Chopin (pretty soft, but you don't mind it in him so much, because one just naturally thinks of him with a skirt on, but one which he made himself). Notwithstanding the above slants, which many would say are insults, it seems to me, as it did then and ever, that still today Bach, Beethoven, and Brahms (No) are among the strongest and greatest in all art, and nothing since is stronger or greater than their strongest and greatest—(not quite as

*The Prize Song from Wagner's *Die Meistersinger;* "The Rosary" by Ethelbert Nevin.

> strong and great as Carl Ruggles, because B., B., and B. have too much of the sugar-plum for the soft-ears—but even with that, they have some manhood of their own).[77]

If this rant against mass culture and midcult parallels many a plausible modernist critique,* Ives's Puritan bedrock was anything but modernist. George Tyler, who married Edith Ives in 1939, heard many a harangue against "lily pads" and "soft ears." He also observed his father-in-law responding to airplanes violating the solitude of his Redding farm: he would "rush and wave his cane in the air [and] call out a good many uncomplimentary remarks to the pilot."[78]

Ives's diatribes against "ladies" and "pansies," however notorious, deserve consideration in the context of the genteel parlor, which he abhorred, and of compensatory masculine ideals, which he absorbed. A footnote to one of his *Memos* helpfully adds: "Emasculated is used not as a reflection on the ladies—that is all the ladies—or because Prof. Ladd finds according to his examination of the premises . . . that ladies are inherently incapable of composing music."[79] But if Ives cannot be glibly condemned as a misogynist, his homophobia was real enough. (He was even squeamish about nudity, and once went so far as to assert that "the human anatomy can never be and has never been the inspiration for a great work of art. It's a medium to be used in God's service and not stared at by God's servants."[80]) In 1936 Henry Cowell—who in addition to being one of Ives's staunchest and most influential advocates was a nearly filial presence in the lives of Charles and Harmony—was accused of sodomizing teenage boys. He admitted to years of such behavior and wound up in San Quentin Prison.[81] Harmony wrote to Charles Ruggles's wife, Charlotte: "If true it is the saddest thing in our experience. I had no inkling of this defect, had you? . . . I am dreading this disclosure to Charlie." Cowell himself wrote to the Iveses—and Harmony wrote to Charlotte again: "I told Charlie & he & I feel just as you do. A thing more abhorrent to Charlie's nature couldn't be found. We think these things are too much condoned. He will never willingly see Henry again—he can't. . . . The shock used him up & he hasn't had a long breath since. . . . He said characteristically 'I thought he was a man he's nothing but a g—d— sap!'"[82] Harmony and Charles proceeded to pretend that Henry Cowell no longer existed. When in September 1941

*It also parallels my own rant: *Understanding Toscanini: How He Became an American Culture-God and Helped Create a New Audience for Old Music* (1987).

Cowell wrote to say that he was getting married, reconciliation was swift: the intrusive episode was eagerly swept away.

By now Ives had had to cope with news even more intrusive: of Hitler and of Pearl Harbor. The Third Reich of course impugned his worldview more fundamentally than had the Great War or Wilson's debacle. He responded to America's entry into World War II patriotically—by revising the lyrics of his World War I song "He is There!" and producing "They are There!" And in 1943 he privately recorded it, singing and finger-pounding with a frenzied energy and breathless conviction at once impressive and disconcerting. The tune seizes "Columbia, the Gem of the Ocean," "The Star-Spangled Banner," and other Americana. The words fasten Ives's die-hard Progressive dream:

Then it's build a People's World Nation, Hooray!
Ev'ry honest country free to live its own native life. . . .
Then the people, not just politicians,
Will rule their own lands and lives.
Then you'll hear the whole universe
Shouting the battle cry of Freedom,
Tenting on a new camp ground!

Ives envisioned this anachronistic outburst rallying the troops and inspiring the home front. But his efforts to get it performed led nowhere. Like the Twentieth Amendment, the People's World Union, and the *Universe* Symphony, "They are There!" proved a futile polemic.

The concrete reality of Hitler provoked in Ives a combination of inescapable rage, and of avoidance equally inescapable. More typical than his fist-pounding tirades were instances when he was too overcome to speak; Harmony treated the war as an off-limits topic. Ives himself had for some time distanced himself from world events. He did not read newspapers or listen to the radio. Nicolas Slonimsky discovered that Ives was not aware of Roosevelt's 1936 reelection.

• • •

In old age, Ives remained energetic and emphatic. Louis Untermeyer, who visited in 1943 or 1944, observed in Ives an exceptional dignity and self-assurance: "He knew what he had done. . . . I spoke a little about it, and he sort of waved it away. It was taken for granted that I knew who he was and that he knew, and that was that. I have had that [experience] with a few people only. Robert Frost was one. . . . I felt it immediately with Ives." Lou Harrison visited Ives in 1947: "The first

FIGURE 12. Harmony and Charles Ives, West Redding, Conn., c. 1946. Photographer: Halley Erskine. MSS 14, photo 181; the Charles Ives Papers in the Irving S. Gilmore Music Library of Yale University.

thing I encountered was Mr. Ives waving a cane so vigorously in a whirling fashion that I was quite frightened. He was shouting, 'My old friend! My old friend!' and I had never seen the man before in my life! Then he greeted me, so grandly, so enthusiastically. . . . He literally danced, he got so excited."[83]

The same year, Ives submitted to being photographed by W. Eugene Smith for *Life* Magazine. "In all of my years and experience of making photographs I have never seen anyone more terrified of the camera than Charles Ives," Smith recalled.

> The only comparable reaction I have seen is that of the so-called uncivilized native who feels that the camera takes away something of his soul. It was not that he was not friendly, but he was plainly terrified. . . .

> The house on 74th Street was dimly lit which disturbed me, but I began to made some pictures. Suddenly Ives got terribly upset and threw himself down on the couch. I thought I had killed him. He was panting and palpitating. After a while he sat up and recited a poem for me that he wrote. . . . By now he was sitting in the wicker chair and had put his left arm way out which would have made it look chopped off in a picture. Ives leaned forward and glowered at me but his left hand was still up. So I asked him to bring his arm in next to his body. He said, "No!" very angrily, but then a twinkle came into his eyes and he pulled his arm in and put it on the cane. He leaned forward and I took a terribly long exposure. And that's the best picture—the one everyone knows and uses.[84]

In 1951—three years before Ives's death—Leonard Bernstein led the New York Philharmonic in the premiere of the Second Symphony: a subscription program, nationally broadcast. Compared to the efforts of Cowell, Slonimsky, Harrison, Herrmann, and Kirkpatrick, this was something new: mainstream advocacy. Although Bernstein offered to conduct a special rehearsal for him, Ives, in Connecticut, could not persuade himself to go to Carnegie Hall. He permitted himself to listen to the symphony in a neighbor's kitchen. When the audience began to cheer and applaud, he got up, spat in the fireplace, and left without a word. Harmony (who attended the concert) wrote:

> Dear Mr. Bernstein:
> It was a wonderful and thrilling experience to hear Mr. Ives 2nd Symphony as you conducted it on February 22nd. I have been familiar with it—in snatches—for forty years and more and to hear the whole performed at last was a big event in my life. People did like it, didn't they? . . .
>
> Mr. Ives heard the broadcast tho' he does not hear well over the radio and it took him back so to his father and his youth that he had tears in his eyes.

She added that Ives found the fast movements "too slow."[85]

Howard Taubman interviewed Ives in 1949 for the *New York Times* Magazine. "It's good of you to come and see the old broom," Ives said. Taubman wrote: "As you go down the walk he stands there waving at you. You look back at this proud and humble man knowing that time is working steadily to raise him to his deserved place among the great creative figures of American musical history."[86]

Other late Ives vignettes document a poignant seclusion. His interest in politics waned. He disapproved of FDR and of the welfare state. He visited Danbury and found it too much changed; he moaned aloud, burying his head in his hands. In Redding, he kept up acquaintance with the Ryders next door. On one occasion, when he could not locate Harmony, Luemily Ryder located her for him.

> We went home and when she climbed out of the car he put his arms around her and said, "Harmony, oh Harmony! I couldn't *find* you!" She kept him alive with her training and her concern. . . . She told me one time that he would not go out in the evening. At first he did, but he hated it. And so she decided that she could either go alone or stay home, and she decided to stay home. She sort of retired along with him. . . .
>
> Once in about 1950 or 1951, he came here for dinner. I don't think he had been to anyone else's house for dinner in a good many years. But he liked roast pork, and I had mentioned that we were having it. [Mrs. Ives] said, "Charlie likes roast pork so much." . . . Our daughter called up that night from the hospital where she was training, and he talked to her on the telephone, which was unusual. He hated the telephone. The day he couldn't find Mrs. Ives, she said that "It proved that he could use it if he needed to, and that was quite an accomplishment."[87]

And Ives ached to "see father again."

Writing to Carl and Charlotte Ruggles after Ives's funeral, John Kirkpatrick surmised: "In retrospect . . . it seemed clearer to me than ever before that Charlie was probably here for a purpose, that the complacent patterns had to be upset, and that the specially shaped personality . . . had necessarily to have all kinds of corresponding disadvantages—for instance, the tragic enforced seclusion of one who (I firmly believe) was really temperamentally gregarious—of the dogged continuance of rebellion long after the complacent conventions had been overthrown."[88]

Though Ives is sometimes written about as if an accidental inhabitant of his own time and place—as if the circumstances and mores of the late Gilded Age fractured or disfigured him—he is in fact a complex but intelligible product of America's fin de siècle. Rooted in the past, seeking the future, pursuing strenuous dual lives in business and art, he embodies dissonances—paradoxes and contradictions—that fired his genius even as they strained body and soul. Insisting on the goodness of mankind, he ultimately withdrew from the twentieth century with an eccentric tenacity that calibrated the existential abyss into which he would otherwise have plunged. If his idealism today seems delusional or naïve, if his increasingly willful innocence rendered him defenseless, his stature is not thereby diminished; his own goodness was empowering. In the modernist view of things, the creative artist is frequently a confrontational, even obstreperous personality. Ives's diatribes against "pansies" seem to fit this picture. But his generosities were the more defining.

In 1942, Edith Ives, age twenty-eight, wrote her father a letter for his sixty-eighth birthday.

> You are so very modest and sweet Daddy, that I don't think you realize the full import of the words people use about you, "A great man." . . .
>
> Daddy, I have had a chance to see so many men lately—fine fellows, and no doubt the cream of our generation. But I have never in all my life come across one who could measure up to the fine standard of life and living that you believe in, and that I have always seen you put into action no matter how many counts were against you. What you have done all your life takes a man—the kind of man that God wants all men to be. You have fire and imagination that is truly a divine spark, but to me the great thing about this is that never once have you tried to turn your gift to your own ends. Instead you have continually given to humanity right from your heart, asking nothing in return;—and all too often getting nothing. The thing that makes me happiest about your recognition today is to see the bread you have so generously cast upon most ungrateful waters, finally beginning to return to you. All that great love is flowing back to you at last. Don't refuse it because it comes so late, Daddy. As I once said to you, it is a wonderful thing to know that you have a friend in every part of this world. Someday, I hope, all the nations will catch up to you in that respect! . . .
>
> Just one word more. I want to tell you—as I know mother does too—how very patient, uncomplaining, and courageous I think you have been all through these long years of physical pain. No matter how we try, I don't believe we will ever know the full extent of what you have gone through in this matter, nor how much of the suffering you have kept to yourself. But we have understood enough to see again—in this part of your life—the great, fine man shining through. So don't feel downcast because physical troubles often keep you from doing many things you want to do;—you are always doing bigger and finer and stronger things than you realize,—things that men with perfect health seldom come up to. And don't ever feel you've been a burden to mother or me. You have been our mainstay, our guide and the sun of our world! We've leaned against you and turned to you for everything—and we have never been made to turn away empty-handed.[89]

. . .

Charles Buesing, who joined Ives & Myrick in 1929, decades later remembered Ives as "a very shy, retiring man." He was "very kindly," never harsh or angry. He "would talk to anyone." He "made everyone feel important." The first time Buesing entered Ives's office—which was "out of sight," "around a corner"—he thought Ives was asleep. His eyes were shut, his feet rested on a desk drawer, his desk was a mass of papers. "Come in and sit down," Ives said, his eyes still closed. He asked Buesing about his family, his work, his future plans. He encouraged him to stick with the life insurance business.

One day, an Ives & Myrick salesman named Charlie came to Buesing with tears in his eyes. Charlie had gone months without a sale: he had no income. Ives had just paid him a visit. "Charlie," Ives had said, "will you take out your wallet?" Charlie did. "Now, you open it," said Ives. The wallet was empty. "I thought so," said Ives. "No one can ever make a sale of anything with an empty wallet. Now, I want you to take this as a business loan. I know you'll have so much confidence with what I am going to put in that wallet that you will pay me back, and I don't want an I.O.U. or anything else." And Ives put fifty dollars in Charlie's wallet. As Ives left the office, Charlie said to Buesing, "There is a great man."[90]

Summation

Defining an American Fin de Siècle

Boston decadents—A fin-de-siècle template—Mark Twain and hybridity—"Social control" and "sacralization"—World War I poisons Romantic uplift

In a program note for the Boston Symphony, Philip Hale referenced Henry Krehbiel's view that with the *New World* Symphony Dvořák had successfully embarked on an "American school" of composition based in part on "Negro melodies." Hale continued:

> It was said by some in answer to [Krehbiel's] statements that, while the negro is undoubtedly fond of music, he is not inherently musical, that this has been observed by all careful observers of the negro in Africa, from Bosman to Sir Richard F. Burton[;] that the American negro, peculiarly mimetic, founded his "folk-songs" on sentimental ballads sung by the white women of the plantation, or on camp-meeting tunes; that he brought no primitive melodies with him from Africa, and that the "originality" of his "folk-songs" was misunderstanding or perversion of the tunes he imitated; . . . that it would be absurd to characterize a school of music based on such a foundation as an "American school."

Citing "Bohemians who knew Dvorak," Hale further imputed:

> 1. The "New World" symphony expresses the state of soul of an uncultured Czech in America, the state of a homesick soul remembering his native land and stupefied by the din and hustle of a new life.
>
> 2. The uncultured Czech is a born musician, a master of his trade. He is interested in the only traces of music that he finds in America. Negro airs, not copied, adapted, imitated, tint slightly two or three passages of the symphony without injury to its Czech character. . . .
>
> Yet some will undoubtedly continue to insist that the symphony "From the New World" is based, for the most part, on negro themes, and that the

> future of American music rests on the use of Congo, North American Indian, Creole, Greaser and Cowboy ditties, whinings, yawps, and whoopings.

All this was written in 1910[1]—six years after Dvořák's death and fully seventeen years after Hale's irritable joustings over a New World vision that New York embraced as prescient and Boston denounced as vulgar. Hale remained irritated.

Centrist musical taste in turn-of-the-century Boston stuck with Beethoven and ranked "Anglo-Saxons" over "Slavs." Hale's take on Dvořák's deficient "cultivation" furnishes a needling case in point. But Hale, whose Paris studies (1885–1887) included organ and composition lessons with the same Alexandre Guilmont who would inspire Charles Ives at the World's Columbian Exposition, did not at heart align with a John Sullivan Dwight or Henry Higginson; rather, he was a finicky Francophile. An encounter with Debussy's *Prelude to the Afternoon of a Faun,* at a 1902 Boston Symphony concert, decisively focused his aesthetic predilections. "The music is exquisite for suggestive vagueness, refined sensuousness that is cerebral rather than bodily, delicate shades of color that melt and fade into each other. . . . I know of no such ravishing measures as those that bring the end."

In 1908 Hale traveled to New York for the first American performance of the same composer's *Pelléas et Mélisande,* setting Maeterlinck, and judged it "lonely and incomparable," "wholly original in form and expression," "a strange manifestation of poetic individuality in a grossly material and commercial age." Krehbiel, in the *Tribune,* wrote of the same premiere: "No one should be ashamed to proclaim his pleasure in four hours of uninterrupted, musically inflected speech over a substratum of shifting harmonies, each with its individual tang and instrumental color; but neither should anybody be afraid to say that nine-tenths of the music is a dreary monotony because of the absence of what to him stands for musical thought."[2] In 1912, *Pelléas* came to Boston via the three-year-old Boston Opera Company, which braved local prejudice against opera and theater with high-minded productions of French novelties (and in 1913 visited Paris itself). Richard Strauss's *Salome* was off limits in Boston. Even *Tosca* proved problematic when Vanni Marcoux, as Scarpia, threw himself upon Mary Garden, as Tosca; Mayor John F. Fitzgerald protested: "I think artists who appear at the Opera House can be effective without offending public taste!"[3] But Maeterlinck himself came to town for *Pelléas.* He was loudly accompanied by his "wife" (actually his mistress), Georgette Leblanc, who materialized beneath a brown beaver hat trimmed with parrots' wings and a long veil of golden chiffon. Leblanc was Boston's Mélisande; she also appeared in a spoken version of *Pelléas* with music by Fauré, and in Maeterlinck's *Monna Vanna*.

In fact a Boston subculture of aestheticist Gallic delights was the closest American equivalent to the fin-de-siècle decadents of London, Paris, and Vienna.* Hale's writings document fashionable indulgences on the margins of New England taste. They equally chart New England's limits. In 1895, he was discomfited by the incest of Siegmund and Sieglinde. In 1896, he called Strauss's *Til Eulenspiegel* a "selection . . . that should not have been heard at this concert, neither at any respectable concert," a "musical obscenity of the most unique and remarkable description," "stupidly unsuccessful," "grotesquely uninteresting," miscrafted by "a heavy, dull and witless Teuton." Schoenberg's Five Pieces for Orchestra appealed to Hale's ear for "mood" and "strangely beautiful effects of color"; he also found Schoenberg disturbingly "anarchistic." Stravinsky's *The Rite of Spring,* which only reached Boston in 1924, seemed to Hale "without significance and irritatingly tiresome" as a concert work. But Prokofiev's savage *Scythian* Suite, in 1914, was a favorite of Hale's: "No matter how wild this music is there is admirable method in the madness; there is a refreshing mastery in the development of the composer's purpose. . . . And throughout the Suite there is singular dramatic intensity."[4]

To attempt a summary: Philip Hale cherished the beautiful, whether chaste or sensual. His responsiveness was shaded by aversion to Germanic pretension and by a lingering puritanism. He was no evangelical and gratefully appreciated Debussy's eschewal of preaching and prescription. He relished the beauties of the *Prelude to an Afternoon of a Faun* and *Pelléas* for their own sake; they conveyed no ethics of "truth." Temperamentally and stylistically, he savored the caustic. But at root his heresies were mild.

The Boston composer Hale liked best was Charles Martin Loeffler—who equally illuminates the limits of New England decadence. Though recent scholarship suggests that he was born in Berlin, Loeffler claimed to be Alsatian. He also lived in Hungary and Russia before winding

*New York, meanwhile, had its individual decadents: Edgar Saltus, George Sylvester Viereck, Charles Tomlinson Griffes.

up in Boston in 1882. He was phobic toward things German—he called German composers "big-mouthed" and "conceited"—and partial toward things French. Dapper, trimly aristocratic, he was well read in three languages; his German-accented English was laced with French felicities. Reticence, instability, melancholia, and hypersensitivity supported his exotic persona. During a twenty-year courtship of his future wife, he once wrote: "We love each other without loving and yet we love each other." His compositions, scented by French, Russian, and Slavic aromas, diffidently exercise symbolism and a morbid delicacy. Reviewing Loeffler's *La Mort de Tintagiles* (1897), after a marionette drama by Maeterlinck, Hale usefully observed: "It would be easy to call him a decadent in a loose way, and then go cheerfully to supper."[5]

Loeffler was an associate concertmaster of the Boston Symphony—which gave 117 Loeffler performances during his lifetime. But he was more truly situated at Isabella Stewart Gardner's Fenway Court. A Back Bay queen bee, Gardner was once seen in a carriage with a pair of lion cubs. When she broke her ankle, she had herself conveyed to Symphony Hall in a hammock. Her palazzo-like mansion, its glass-roofed courtyard framed by carved Venetian balconies, housed a fabulous art collection, fabulously orchestrated. It also hosted a coterie of refined young men and formal concerts often featuring Loeffler as performer or composer. Fenway's aura of escapism and irony resonated with the exquisite self-disparagements of Henry Adams and with homoerotic rituals purveyed by the "visionist" bibliophile/photographer Fred Holland Day. But, as with Hale and Loeffler, Gardner's vanguard tastes were modest by fin-de-siècle European standards: in music, they reached no further than Wagner and Fauré. The great talent of the Gardner circle—John Singer Sargent, who played sonatas with Loeffler and painted Gardner in décolleté—mainly lived abroad. The Boston aestheticists represent an ephemeral sublimation of the genteel, an etherealization into realms of discreet amorality and pessimism. When George Santayana framed the genteel tradition as "an old head on young shoulders," he could equally have been describing the cozy self-captivity of Fenway Court.*[6]

In short, neither the urgent energies driving a Henry Higginson nor the subversive panache of an Oscar Wilde or Stéphane Mallarmé were to

*Santayana himself was a Boston phenomenon: a resident outsider, yet unsuited to New York. Concomitantly. Antonín Dvořák, a resident outsider at New York's National Conservatory, could not conceivably have directed Boston's New England Conservatory. In both cases, an acute outside perspective balanced distance with affinity.

be found among Boston's decadents. Absent the fibered influence of genteel imperatives, such once-popular Loeffler compositions as *A Pagan Poem* (1902, rev. 1906) today seem toothless and slack. Reencountered, Philip Hale's pungent pen, equally forgotten, seems hyper-refined and self-indulgent (Ives called him "Aunt Maria" and "a nice old lady"). In fin-se-siècle America, high achievement could be inspired by *resistance* to skepticism, relativism, and other forms of discontent fueled abroad by social and political upheaval. The snobberies of a Hale, the lassitudes of a Loeffler, the rarified eccentricities of a Gardner found no echo in the purposefulness of a Henry Krehbiel or Laura Langford. Even at his most sensual, Loeffler, compared to Ives, is a victim of inbred gentilities.* Henry Higginson, finally, is the ringmaster whose genius was to be "Boston" and yet transcend the sectarian. Loeffler was part of his eclectic musical brain trust. Higginson supervised Gardner's investments and urged her philanthropies.

To be sure, the democratic meliorists of my study did not exercise a monopoly over fin-de-siècle achievement. A short list of significant turn-of-the-century contemporaries who subscribed to neither gentility nor genteel decadence would include such writers as Stephen Crane and Theodore Dreiser, such artists and architects as Thomas Eakins, Winslow Homer, and Louis Sullivan. In the course of the twentieth century, the reputations of these men proved resilient. And yet what more endures than Higginson's Boston Symphony and Symphony Hall, or the symphonies, songs, and sonatas of Ives, or Krehbiel's vision of an American cultural identity rooted in African-American song and dance? Had Anton Seidl not prematurely died, Langford's vision—of a Brooklyn Bayreuth—might also have been enduringly realized. No less than Higginson, Krehbiel, or Ives, she was a prodigious activist.

. . .

The phenomenon of fin-de-siècle musical uplift—the larger American subject matter of this book—may be said to have crested during the two decades beginning with Henry Higginson's sudden creation of the Boston Symphony in 1881. Its Boston manifestations included the incendiary rapture of Beethoven's Fifth as rendered by Arthur Nikisch (1889)

*George Chadwick, by far the saltiest of the Boston composers, sanitizes the quotidian in comparison to Ives. In such works as *Jubilee* (1895), Chadwick's circumscribed naturalism parallels that of William Dean Howells. Ives and Mark Twain equally serve as counterexamples, steeped in unmitigated vernacular song and speech.

and the opening of the church of music Higginson would only call Symphony Hall (1900). In New York, the Met's screaming Wagnerites and Dvořák's *New World* Symphony (1893) were characteristic sensations. Laura Langford's *Parsifal* Entertainment (1890) was a defining Brooklyn moment. Charles Ives's Symphony No. 2 (1900–1902) was another such breakthrough into realms of wholesome ecstatic release. In Chicago, the visionary White City (1893) was preceded by the visionary forty-two-hundred-seat Auditorium Theatre (1889), conceived by Ferdinand Peck as "an enduring temple where the rich and the poor and all classes could meet together upon common ground and be elevated and enlightened by the power of music." Further west, and outside music, there was John Muir, who helped to drive to passage a bill (1899) creating national parks: "mountain temples" where the "overcivilized" could discover "rest, inspiration, and prayers." The millennial paradise of Edward Bellamy's *Looking Backward* (1888) was a pertinent literary sensation. The pertinent oratorical sensations included the Memorial Day address of Oliver Wendell Holmes Jr. ("In our youth our hearts were touched with fire") affirming that "to act with enthusiasm and faith is the condition of acting greatly" (1884), William Jennings Bryan's millennial "cross of gold" speech (1896), and Theodore Roosevelt's "strenuous life" speech espousing "the higher life, the life of aspiration, of toil and risk" (1899). Concurrently, a raft of mass social movements, comprising the progressive "Social Gospel," were infused with the moral fire of muscular Christianity.

At least five traits may be extrapolated from the four fin-de-siècle portraits I have here assembled, using classical music in cross section to glean a larger New World panorama. Fundamentally, I have studied agents of uplift for whom great art seemed—a conviction so self-evident as to barely warrant argument—inherently ennobling. For Henry Higginson no opportunity for catharsis could surpass the slow variations of Beethoven's *Eroica*—a "passage of entire relief and joy" during which "the gates of Heaven open, as we see the angels singing and reaching their hands to us with perfect welcome." For Henry Krehbiel, Beethoven epitomized "soul-fortifying aspiration." For Laura Langford, *Parsifal* was the urgent experience that enlightened and transcended human travail. For Charles Ives, art was about divinity and God was "nothing but love."

A second core trait my subjects share—a second self-evident conviction—was commitment to a democratic ethos. Higginson's Civil War service had intimately acquainted him with a range of men. His twenty-five-cent Boston Symphony tickets broke precedent. That his audience was "not from the Back Bay or from any particular set of people" was a delight necessary to his cause. Even more than Higginson, Langford made her inexpensive ticket prices a missionary thrust. Her Seidl Society was even more classless than Higginson's naked Symphony Hall. She insisted on small donations and targeted working women. Krehbiel mistrusted Brahmin elitism. His affinity for Dvořák, the butcher's son, was as natural to him as his tireless and disinterested inquiries into "music of the soil." Ives, in Redding, identified with the barber and the farmer. No previous American composer had so wedded the quotidian with high art.

For Higginson and for Ives, the purpose of amassing money was to give it away. The generosities of Krehbiel and Langford took other, equally insistent forms. For all four, empathy with the common man dictated empathy for the black man. Higginson attempted a plantation with freedmen. Krehbiel crusaded for African-American music. Langford lavishly hosted black orphans at Brighton Beach. Ives, with a family legacy of abolitionism, composed his dead march in honor of the black Civil War regiment led by Robert Gould Shaw—whom Higginson had memorialized as a fallen comrade.

Thirdly, I portray fighters. Higginson forbade "playing for dances" or unionization; Krehbiel took exception to Hale, Mahler, and Strauss; Langford denounced broken concert commitments; Ives rejected music for "sissies." These were in every case declarations of war, kindred to the bellicose harangues of a Mark Twain or Teddy Roosevelt.

Estrangement from the new century is the fourth trait linking my portraits. Betrayed by Muck, Higginson was betrayed by a world of culture and art that had been his lodestar. Krehbiel died disillusioned by the fate of music and mankind—by Mahler and Strauss, by Einstein's relativity, by the tumult and bustle of automobiles and machines. Langford's late efforts to rekindle the Seidl Society's ideals of service pathetically expired. Ives withdrew into denial, railing against airplanes, disdaining the telephone, radio, and phonograph.

Finally, fifthly, my subjects are fin-de-siècle fulcrum figures. They inhabit a moment in flux: a subtle condition inviting further exploration.

• • •

Consider the case of Mark Twain as an informative representative of America's fin de siècle. To the degree that Twain the sometime cynic or nihilist was no true believer, he imperfectly suits the five-point template at hand. But he craved uplift and sampled it. He earnestly pondered good and evil. His personal morality remained unimpeachable: his marriage was spotless; when business adventures left him bankrupt, he insisted on paying creditors every penny he owed ("a man of unsullied honor," the *Boston Transcript* called him).[7] If he was undeniably less sanguine than he wished to be, he thrilled to Huck's ethical epiphany on the raft with Jim.

Notwithstanding his chronic bouts of despair, Twain's common touch projects—the second component of my template—a democratic ethos. Belligerence—coming third—was of course a Mark Twain trademark: droll, earnestly impassioned, or both. And—the fourth component—Twain's alienation from the twentieth century is copiously documented; he died an agent of Weltschmerz and a prophet of doom. But it is Twain's hybridity—his way of inhabiting past and future, New World and Old, one thing and another—that makes his fin-de-siècle example supremely heuristic. He brandishes tensions and contradictions that remain discreet or concealed in others. He had two names. His smoky writer's domicile was kept apart from the opulent parlors of his Hartford mansion. He fantasized a second lifetime piloting the Mississippi, but coveted respectability in the cultural citadels of the northeast. He did not overpolish his lazy drawl, yet regularly contributed to William Dean Howell's *Atlantic*. Become a Victorian paterfamilias, he remained, if not the lubricated buffoon of his San Francisco saloon days, a rude interloper in salons. A connoisseur of dirty jokes, he once lectured in praise of the high antiquity of masturbation; but the novelist in Twain was reticent about sex. A Yankee entrepreneur, he invested in a steam generator and a steam pulley; he patented three inventions; he embarked on two disastrous businesses: a publishing house that sold books door-to-door and an automatic typesetting machine. He was rescued by Standard Oil's Henry Huddleston Rogers ("the best man I have ever known"), who reorganized his finances yet personified the Gilded Age rapacity Twain had helped to make notorious.[8] His writings document preoccupation with the divided self. The prince and the pauper are mistaken for one another. Huck masquerades as a girl. Hank Morgan poses as a medieval magician. The "extraordinary twins" Luigi and Angelo are conjoined siblings with radically different personalities. Reading Robert Louis Stevenson's *Dr. Jekyll and Mr. Hyde* sharpened Twain's experience of "our seeming duality—the presence in us of another person." The strain of Twain's own duality showed in violent fits of temper and troughs of depression.

Twain and Charles Ives share dualities: gentility and rebellion; business and art; philosophic gravitas and vernacular exuberance. Ives married the daughter of one of Twain's best friends. Both settled in Redding, Connecticut. But their most telling affinity, the one they most shared with other fin-de-siècle activists, was the restlessness of Americans jostled and challenged by changing times. Their multiple worlds and unruly energies were equally self-generated and outwardly inflicted. So it was, as well, with Henry Higginson, however much he may have seemed Boston's daunting "foremost citizen"; with Henry Krehbiel, however much he may have seemed the pontifical "dean" of New York's critics; and with Laura Langford, however much Seidl judged her the irrepressible "queen of Brooklyn."

The motif of hybridity plays out on many levels. Higginson was a banker and an orchestra inventor. Krehbiel was German and American, a scholar, a "newspaperman," and—before there was a word for it—a leading exponent of ethnomusicology. Langford was a genteel socialite and a militant impresario. Ives sold insurance and wrote symphonies. As with Twain, who oscillated abroad between deference and smugness, a conflicted relationship to the Old World parent culture is pertinent. Higginson adored venerable European traditions and proudly asserted the supremacy of American freedoms. Krehbiel embodied Germanic art and scholarship yet tenaciously pursued a new world of pragmatic self-instruction and democratized learning. Langford identified with Wagnerites and with Shakers. Ives eschewed study abroad: the German models he pursued were kept at bay.

The New World, too, supplied pertinent roots. A strain of puritan inhibition informs the severities Higginson imposed on Symphony Hall, Krehbiel's discomfort with Wagnerian lusts, Langford's prim portraits of her First Ladies, and Ives's traumatic response to Henry Cowell's homosexuality. Even the forward velocities of these high achievers may be read as backward motion. The culture of Wagnerism was partly a culture of the primal or mythic: of robust premodern times. The same could be said of Krehbiel's investigation of racial roots and of Langford's investigation of theosophy. Langford's fresh-air cures for indigent children revisited living conditions preceding modern cities and machines. The vernacular strategies of aesthetic renewal pioneered by Twain and Ives were at the same time retreats to the comforts of a cozier era.*

*On "anti-modernism and the transformation of American culture" in the late Gilded Age, see Jackson Lears, *No Place of Grace* (1981).

Fin-de-siècle contradictions of conjoined forward and backward motion were personally stressful. Higginson's lineage directed him to Harvard and he remained all his life a "Harvard man"; but he was not suited to Harvard, and during his freshman year was plagued by eye problems of undisclosed origin. Higginson's passion directed him to music; but to forge the alliances that made him a musical power, he had to acquire a more respectable, less enthralling fin-de-siècle vocation. Langford's pugnacity registered the contradictions she negotiated as a woman of power. Krehbiel's lapses into hyperbolic disparagement—of Mahler when he died, of Germany when it made war—document abnormal states of arousal. No less than Twain, Higginson, and Langford, he became a study in beleaguerment; his eulogists alluded to a long period of painful physical decline stoically endured. Ives, finally, is a veritable summa of stress and strain—of intemperance, of neurasthenia, of multiple vocations dictated by necessity and rationalized with exaggerated claims to the beneficence of selling life insurance.

In the final analysis, however, what seems most salient about this turn-of-the-century nexus of contradiction and self-contradiction is less confusion wrought than texture gained. That Twain, Higginson, Krehbiel, Langford, and Ives in every case inhabited multiple worlds and vocations more enhanced than diminished their capacities. The frictionless genteel tradition delineated by Santayana is not their genteel tradition. If for early nineteenth-century Americans Longfellow's sanitized *Song of Hiawatha* seemed a defining New World saga, half a century later Ives's Second furnished a New World symphony layered with eclectic catalytic synergies, the whole of which was infused and bound with a believer's fervor. Fifteen years later, cloistered in his fin-de-siècle moment, Ives issued a triumphal evangelical blast: his valedictory Fourth Symphony.

Mahler's contemporaneous symphonies, with their fraught recesses of darkness, confront an amoral world of culture in upheaval—a world in which progress and revolution seemed inextricable. That America's fin de siècle, in comparison, retained religious and puritanical values of Victorian and pre-Victorian times fortified the inherited Germanic idealism of many an American thinker. Challenged by such imports as *Pelléas et Mélisande* and *Salome,* this wholesome predisposition proved resourceful. After 1900 it blended into the Progressive politics of an Ives, Bryan, or Theodore Roosevelt.

At century's end, "Brahmin," "German-American," "artist," and "woman" were shifting American concepts. And so, finally, was "genteel"—the resilience of which prolonged the conditions for heroic positive endeavor.

. . .

Shunning the term "Gilded Age," Howard Mumford Jones adroitly redubbed the half-century preceding 1915 the "Age of Energy." "We have no good name for the period from the end of the Civil War to the opening of World War I," he wrote in 1970.

> One may refer by energy to the exercise of power, to the actual operation, working or activity of man or thing, or to the product or the effect of such energy. One may mean by it personal vigor of action or utterance, as when one says that Theodore Roosevelt was characterized by energy. One may have in mind the individual power or capacity to produce such and such an effect. . . . Common to all these meanings is the idea of energy as the power by which anything or anybody acts effectively to move or change other things or persons. In this rough general sense it may be said that the Age of Energy was distinguished by producing in two generations . . . some of the most extraordinarily energetic persons in American history.

And he added: "Activism has long been thought to be a characteristic American quality."*[9]

Certainly a brave individualism is one hallmark of the late Gilded Age. The continent remained vast—and so, too, were corporations and monopolies. Politics were not for the faint-hearted. In the absence of adequate personal and institutional precedents, self-invention was both possible and necessary. Jones observes individuals of heroic or unfettered energy proliferating in business, science, and politics. He also takes pains to include writers and painters. In passing, he takes note of Henry Higginson and Charles Ives. They fit his reportrayal. So do Henry Krehbiel and Laura Langford.

Thomas Kessner's *Capital City: New York City and the Men Behind America's Rise to Economic Eminence, 1860–1900* (2003) revisits

*Much more recently, Rebecca Edwards has explored dropping the term "Gilded Age" in favor of a Long Progressive Era beginning in the 1870s. She writes: "The breadth, complexity, and intensity of grassroots movements and ideas that arose before 1900 refutes the standard view that they were simply a prologue, and that the 'real' era of reform began after 1900. In many ways, in fact, the 1880s and early 1890s were decades of great activism and political creativity, while the long decade from 1896 to 1910 was less so." Edwards, "Politics, Social Movements, and the Periodization of U.S. History," in *The Journal of the Gilded Age and Progressive Era*, Oct. 2009 (vol. 8, no. 4), p. 468.

Andrew Carnegie, J.P. Morgan, John D. Rockefeller, and Cornelius Vanderbilt with fresh appreciation for their audacity and resolve. He pertinently cites Henry Adams observing corporations demanding "a new type of man,—a man of ten times the endurance, energy, will and mind of the old type. . . . The new man could be only a child born of contact between the new and old energies."[10] Higginson, Krehbiel, Langford, and Ives, too, are of this type. As I have here argued, taking a barbed Old World term and exploring buoyant New World meanings, they embody "fin-de-siècle" American cultural energies.

The opposite notion of an inhibiting turn-of-the-century American high-cultural milieu, suffocated by gentility, will never die. For one thing, there is more than a little truth to it. For another, it has for some time been ideologically driven. Venerable tools of economic determinism and class analysis understand pioneering late nineteenth-century institutions of culture and education as elitist instruments of "social control."* To be sure, these tools have their uses. But they poorly align with impassioned Wagnerites, or with rival operatic constituencies fighting for control of the Met, or with rush-ticketholders bolting up the staircases of Symphony Hall, or with the seashore trappings and intense reverence of Wagner nights at Coney Island, or with the boisterous vulgate of Ives's Second.

The literature of social control is sizable and tenacious. It promotes an impression insidiously whole and yet implausible. Educated Americans of an earlier era could not have been so much more timid or arrogant than educated American historians of a later period. Not all such studies are abstract or theoretical. Ronald Story's *Harvard and the Boston Upper Class: The Forging of an American Aristocracy 1800–1870* (1980) closely observes certain aspects of Henry Higginson's

*Alan Trachtenburg, in chapter 5 of his highly influential *The Incorporation of America* (1982), discerns Gilded Age museums, libraries, universities, orchestras, and opera companies created partly to co-opt the restless strivings of the less privileged. They promoted a chimerical "vision of a harmonious body politic under the rule of reason, light, and sweet, cheerful emotion," a "normative ideal of culture which served as protection against other realities." They embodied "an anti-democratic bias," "the wish for a conspicuous display of philanthropy on the part of wealthy donors, and for status on the part of the gentry, for whom the custodianship of culture provided desirable opportunities for *noblesse oblige*." They afforded a "feminine" aesthetic experience—"receptive, passive, spectatorial." They furnished "an alternative to class hostilities." They signified a "hierarchy of values corresponding to a social hierarchy of stations or classes." Trachtenburg's case in point is the museum, a palace of "hushed corridors" organized "by the urban elite, dominated by ladies of high society."

Boston. The city's cultural institutions are here analyzed as "agents of class development or class maintenance." In addition to Harvard, the institutions under study include the Athenaeum, the Lowell Institute, and Massachusetts General Hospital. The ruling Brahmins, a network of overlapping clans, are depicted as political conservatives partial to refined demeanor and habits of exclusivity, their relationship to the general public being "almost adversarial." Socioeconomic shocks comprising a midcentury "crisis," however, impelled reform: driven more by "fear," "anger," and "resentment" than by "genuine concern for the poor," the aristocrats opened public doors somewhat wider. The result was a second wave of such institutions, including the Boston Symphony Orchestra. "The civic institutions of this era were products . . . of the same basic objective as their precursors: to provide their patrons with a sense of stability and order and to preserve culture and philanthropy from the excessive incursions of the populace." The larger outcome was to support the evolution of "a distinctive, modern urban upper class." "But what benefits a class may sometimes damage a society. It seems likely, in fact, that the emergence of overweening, elite-dominated institutions seriously exacerbated the regional and class divisions that already attended New England's nineteenth-century development. . . . Thereafter, people would peer at one another across vast gulfs of culture as well as of wealth."[11]

As Story's methodology is "dialectical materialism," a subtheme of his account is the increasing hegemony of business interests within the cultural realm.[12] Certainly Higginson embodies the post–Civil War nexus of business and culture that Story persuasively documents, not neglecting to mention Lee, Higginson and Company. Certain, too, is that John Sullivan Dwight's Harvard Musical Association, with its exclusive membership, fits Story's narrative. And Dwight himself (not mentioned by Story) poisonously personifies snobbish discomfort with socioeconomic strains associated with immigration, urbanization, and industrialization. But Higginson is of course not a Brahmin type as here defined. He dropped out of Harvard. He was schooled less in manners than in music; not in New England, but in Vienna and the Civil War South. His benefactions to Harvard included a clubhouse designed to discourage exclusivity. His radically low Boston Symphony ticket prices made a considered and controversial statement. Story discerns an aristocratic sense of duty increasingly directed toward "one's peers." Higginson's sense of duty was driven by an egalitarian passion for music. No informed portrait of such a man could summarize him as a tyrannical monopolist, a "cultural policeman," or a "cultural capitalist" for whom the Boston Symphony represented a "refuge from the slings and arrows of the troubled world."[13]

The rubric of social control has even been applied to New York City, where the forces dictating cultural fashion and authority were overtly confused and contradictory. The rival musical institutions included the New York Philharmonic, the New York Symphony, the Metropolitan Opera, and the Manhattan Opera (whose self-made impresario, Oscar Hammerstein, harbored an uncontrollable antipathy toward persons of great wealth). The rival conductors included Leopold Damrosch, Theodore Thomas, and Anton Seidl. The rival musical constituencies—each containing subconstituencies—were Anglo, German, Italian. The *Musical Courier* dryly summarized as of 1903: "In New York, where there is no civic pride, . . . the mixture of population prevents a consolidation of any one artistic direction." Kessner, in his study of the city's business magnates, observes: "Rather than work together to advance a big-business hegemony, they kept their exchanges to a minimum at a level that was barely civil. . . . New York's circle of businessmen was too large and too diverse for any one group or interest to dominate." In place of musical consensus were countless acrid New York feuds—of which Henry Krehbiel's potent broadsides against the Met's embattled boxholders and the Philharmonic's embattled guarantors were mere samples. And yet enduring Gilded Age stereotypes prompt a prominent historian of New York to blithely opine that between 1850 and 1896 "cultural institutions," including the Met and the Philharmonic, "derived their programmatic ideas" from the upper classes, and "principally catered to the city's economic elite."[14]

A kindred discourse, invoking derogatory Gilded Age meanings, chronicles the "sacralization" of high culture as a move by self-centered elitists to divorce Shakespeare and Beethoven from the quotidian. Genteel culture bearers are again depicted as upper-class snobs spurning the rabble. In effect, they strive to inculcate a desiccated facsimile of high art worshipped by a rarified, pacified audience preoccupied with status.[15]

That some such sacralization occurred after the Civil War is undeniable—in music, the most obvious example is Wagnerism, and the most obvious artwork, sacralizing grand opera (whether in Brooklyn or Bayreuth), is *Parsifal*. Wagner's explicit preoccupation with the "spiritual" is embedded in his late Romantic Weltanschauung. Its primary agents were not aristocrats intent upon consolidating a monied class; they were musicians, impresarios, and critics. In New York, they included Henry Krehbiel, who also espoused applying "red" and "black" folk song to New World symphonies, and Laura Langford, who treated orphans to ice cream and Seidl concerts. The same spirit impelled Henry Higginson to employ freedmen, and Charles Ives to compassionately sample Stephen Foster's "Old Black Joe" in his Second Symphony. Fin-de-siècle sacralizers could be egalitarians.*

In combination, social control and sacralization have been used to fashion an ugly high-cultural metaphor for Gilded Age social inequality and corporate dominion. Just as George Pullman, eyeing labor unrest and economic instability, created a model workers' town that in fact patronized and suppressed its beneficiaries, captains of culture ostensibly patronized and suppressed susceptible newcomers to the arts. In fact, the impact of late nineteenth-century socioeconomic turmoil on high culture—an obvious ingredient in the turbulent writings, paintings, and symphonies of fin-de-siècle Vienna—has barely been studied by writers familiar with the musical high culture of fin-de-siècle America. The obvious starting point would be Chicago, where the Haymarket Riot impelled Ferdinand Peck to create his forty-two-hundred-seat Auditorium Building as a socially engineered temple for class harmonization. But Peck was a utopian pragmatist, a full-blown social reformer for whom the auditorium would bridge the gap between rich and poor.[16] There were no cultural Pullmans.

• • •

The aesthetic upheaval following World War I was partly conditioned by the Great War itself. No previous military conflict had seemed so impersonal or illogical, so meaningless or absurd. "The plunge of civilization into this abyss of blood and darkness," wrote Henry James, "is a thing that . . . gives away the whole long age during which we have supposed the world to be, with whatever abatement, gradually bettering."[17]

In the wake of the Great War, the concept of civilization as pursuant to truth and beauty was shattered, and so was confidence in music, art, and literature as a civilizing force. With Hitler, who understood the

*It was mainly after World War I that the sacralization dynamic turned snobbish—a major theme of my *Understanding Toscanini: How He Became an American Culture-God and Helped Create a New Audience for Old Music* (1987). See also Joseph Horowitz, "Music and the Gilded Age: Social Control and Sacralization Revisited," *Journal of the Gilded Age and Progressive Era*, vol. 3, no. 3 (July 2004).

importance of public ceremony, culture as a vehicle for Romantic communal catharsis underwent a hideous reprise. In Russia, too, the tyrant was a music lover. Like Hitler, Stalin was a grotesque misembodiment of Romantic greatness: of an ethics of strength, nobility, and visionary achievement. He understood the uses of music for public uplift. His enthusiasms included Mozart, to whose sublime Piano Concerto in A major (K. 488) he was reportedly listening when he died.

Totalitarian war was all-consuming, and dictated a consuming response. For the first time, civilian populations were bombed. Cities of culture were devastated. In combination with the Great War, World War II seemingly sealed the century's identity. In the short run, the impact of total war on culture was literal and visceral: it became the very topic of art. In the long run, the poisoning of Romantic uplift had the more enduring impact. Stravinsky called music "essentially powerless to *express* anything at all." Said Arnold Schoenberg of the listener: "All I know is that he exists, and insofar as he isn't indispensable for acoustic reasons (since music doesn't sound well in an empty hall), he's only a nuisance." The culture of mass catharsis was in abeyance. Schoenberg boasted that his twelve-tone system would ensure the supremacy of German music for a century to come—a dated sectarian forecast. More prophetic were such resistors as Dmitri Shostakovich, who insisted on the resilience of tonality and the futility of Schoenberg's revolution.[18]

Had there been no Great War, some other form of upheaval would have destroyed the relative innocence of Gilded Age traditions. In fact, by the 1910s skepticism and relativism, in various belated manifestations, were eroding the moral consensus and mainstream evangelical temper that America's fin de siècle had retained. One 1913 list of heterodoxies, in the *Nation,* read: "Tango, eugenics, the slit skirt, sex hygiene, Brieux, white slaves, Richard Strauss, John Masefield, the double standard of morality . . . a conglomerate of things important and unimportant, of age-old problems and momentary fads, which nevertheless have this one thing in common, that they do involve an abandonment of the old proprieties and the old reticences."[19]

This was the year that the Armory Show brandished Henri Matisse and Marcel Duchamp—and that Alfred Stieglitz, in response, brandished a comparable show of his own. The Greenwich Village art scene already included the urban realists who would become known as the Ashcan School. The new American poets included Amy Lowell, Ezra Pound, and Carl Sandburg, the new critics Carl Van Vechten. Thorstein Veblen had attained notoriety for skewering "the leisure class" and "conspicuous consumption." *The Brothers Karamazov* had been published in English. Sigmund Freud had influentially visited the United States. Charles Beard was discovering that the Constitution enshrined the financial self-interest of the founding fathers. Leo Ornstein, the wild man of American music, composed a *Danse Sauvage* of pounding tonal clusters. In 1915 H.L. Mencken announced his "low, sniffish opinion of the whole rumble-bumble of Uplift"; it had "failed in all directions."[20]

These dissident developments raised the stakes. But generations of optimistic culture bearers had not yet been condemned to anything like irrelevance. Their idealism remained plausible, intact. Americans had basked in decades of apparent progress. The conviction that an elite of "Anglo-Saxon" nations pursued a coming world order of peace and prosperity was not discardable as mere racial snobbery. Even Darwinian science, implying a mechanistic universe, had acquired a positive Spencerian spin. As for war, it was sporadic: there was no language of extermination, of a war to end all wars.

The Great War, when it came, tested an entire worldview and found it wanting. In the realm of American classical music, the rhetoric of uplift afterward turned hollow—as when interwar music appreciators anointed the conductor Arturo Toscanini (whose New World mission was rarely bigger than himself) "vicar of the immortals" and "priest of enlightenment."[21] Arthur Judson—manager of the New York Philharmonic, the Philadelphia Orchestra, and countless conductors and instrumentalists of high consequence—was the reigning powerbroker, for whom music was frankly a business.[22] The labor of love pursued by a Higginson, Krehbiel, Langford, or Ives betokened a bygone ethical conscience. And yet the high tasks they undertook cannot be dismissed as naïve.

Though not all supreme art is uplifting, or intended to uplift, culture as a moral force is a concept that fills human needs stronger than any dogmas, be they aesthetic, political, or intellectual.

Notes

INTRODUCTION

1. Quotations from Alan Lessoff, "Van Wyck Brooks, Lewis Mumford, and the Gilded Age: Provenance of a Usable Past," a talk delivered March 2, 2005, at the University of Illinois, Chicago.

PROLOGUE

1. Higinbotham quoted in Joseph Horowitz, *Classical Music in America: A History* (2005), p. 167. Depew quoted in Alan Trachtenberg, *The Incorporation of America* (1982), p. 208.

2. Horowitz, p. 167.

3. Debs, Wister, Van Brunt quoted in Trachtenberg, pp. 216, 218.

4. James F. Muirhead, *The Land of Contrasts* (1893), p. 205.

5. "Information Bureau," *The Musical Courier,* June 22, 1922.

6. Joseph Horowitz, *Wagner Nights: An American History* (1994), p. 115.

7. Douglas L. Wilson (ed.), George Santayana, *The Genteel Tradition* (1967), p. 39.

8. Debby Applegate, *The Most Famous Man in America: The Biography of Henry Ward Beecher* (2006), pp. 354, 468, 470.

9. Michael Kazin, *A Godly Hero: The Life of William Jennings Bryan* (2007), pp. 214, 45, 207.

10. Brenda Wineapple, *White Heat: The Friendship of Emily Dickinson and Thomas Wentworth Higginson* (2008), p. 311.

11. Kazin, p. 257.

12. *New York Tribune,* May 21, 1911.

13. Riis and Adams quoted in Page Smith, *The Rise of Industrial America* (1984), p. 366.

14. Jackson Lears, *No Place of Grace: Antimodernism and the Transformation of American Culture* (1981), p. 215.

15. John Higham, *Writing American History* (1970).

16. Henry May, *The End of American Innocence* (1959), p. 247.

17. Jean Strouse, *Morgan: American Financier* (1999), Introduction.

CHAPTER 1

1. Bliss Perry, *Life and Letters of Henry Lee Higginson* (1921), pp. 142–143.
2. Perry, p. 160.
3. Perry, pp. 162, 164.
4. Perry, pp. 176, 179.
5. Perry, pp. 180, 165.
6. Perry, pp. 208, 211.
7. Perry, p. 232.
8. Perry, p. 232.
9. Perry, pp. 229–236.
10. Perry, p. 10.
11. Perry, pp. 39, 57.
12. Perry, pp. 93, 95, 124.
13. Perry, pp. 129, 50.
14. Perry, p. 125.
15. Perry, pp. 37, 108.
16. Perry, pp. 113, 134, 87.
17. Perry, p. 110.
18. Perry, p. 248.
19. Perry, pp. 257–266.
20. Perry, pp. 21, 261.
21. Perry, pp. 271, 267, 341.
22. Perry, pp. 378, 385, 377, 361.
23. Michael Broyles, *Music of the Highest Class: Elitism and Populism in Antebellum Boston* (1992), pp. 244–257. Joseph Horowitz, *Classical Music in America: A History* (2005), pp. 32–33.
24. Horowitz, pp. 26–28.
25. S. Frederick Starr, *Bamboula* (1995), p. 166.
26. Perry, p. 393.
27. *Dwight's Journal of Music,* April 9, 1881. Higginson and *Advertiser* quoted in M.A.D. Howe, *The Boston Symphony Orchestra 1881–1931* (1931), p. 67.
28. Howe, p. 67.
29. Howe, p. 73.
30. Howe, p. 65.
31. Richard P. Stebbins, *The Making of Symphony Hall Boston* (2000), p. 113.
32. Stebbins, pp. 114–116.
33. Stebbins, pp. 44–45.
34. Stebbins, p. 69.

35. Stebbins, pp. 160, 170.
36. Stebbins, pp. 75, 186–189.
37. Stebbins, pp. 101, 98, 99, 79.
38. Stebbins, pp. 91, 184, 95.
39. Stebbins, p. 93.
40. Stebbins, p. 93.
41. Ellen Knight, *Charles Martin Loeffler: A Life Apart* (1993), p. 57.
42. Horowitz, pp. 57, 62.
43. Higginson letters (Harvard Business School Library), see especially April 25, 1893.
44. Horowitz, pp. 75–78.
45. Horowitz, p. 76.
46. Knud Martner (ed.), *Selected Letters of Gustav Mahler* (1979), p. 314.
47. *The Musical Courier,* March 19, 1890.
48. Howe, p. 87.
49. Perry, pp. 350–355.
50. Perry, pp. 354, 356.
51. Perry, pp. 111, 402. Howe in Stebbins, p. 12.
52. Perry, pp. 326, 327, 116.
53. Perry, pp. 315, 439, 405.
54. Perry, pp. 391, 313.
55. Perry, pp. 402, 304.
56. Norton in Rochelle Gurstein, *The Repeal of Reticence* (1996), pp. 19–28. Dwight in Horowitz, p. 22.
57. Bliss, pp. 329, 535.
58. Perry, pp. 391, 524, 92.
59. Stebbins, p. 12.
60. Gayle Turk, "The Case of Dr. Karl Muck: Anti-German Hysteria and Enemy Alien Internment During World War I," Harvard University thesis, 1994 (Boston Symphony Archives), pp. 24–25.
61. Higginson letters, March 20, 1912.
62. Perry, pp. 464, 468, 481.
63. Turk, p. 7.
64. Perry, p. 487.
65. Turk, p. 21.
66. Perry, pp. 496, 491–492.
67. Higginson letters, March 13, 1918.
68. Articles in New York newspapers (e.g., *New York Times,* March 15, 1918).
69. Turk, pp. 58, 59, 60.
70. Tuck, p. 65.
71. Perry, p. 516.
72. Perry, p. 505. Mark A. DeWolfe Howe, "A Great Private Citizen: Henry Lee Higginson," *Atlantic Monthly,* March 1920, p. 33.
73. Telegrams in Boston Symphony Archives.
74. Correspondence in Boston Symphony Archives.
75. Howe, *Boston Symphony Orchestra,* p. 138.

76. Turk, p. 75.
77. Turk, p. 81.
78. Higginson letters.
79. Perry, p. 473.
80. Perry, 516; and Higginson letters, May 14, 1915; May 4, 1915; Jan. 30, 1919.
81. Howe, "A Great Private Citizen," p. 38; Eliot in Perry, p. 323.
82. Perry, p. 507.
83. Perry, p. 402.
84. Howe, "A Great Private Citizen," pp. 17–18.

CHAPTER 2

1. *Chicago Tribune* in Horowitz, p. 225. Leslie in Robert Rydell, *All the World's a Fair* (1984), p. 66; Buell in Robert Winter and Peter Bogdanoff, "From the New World: A Celebrated Composer's American Odyssey," DVD-ROM. www.artsinteractive.org.
2. Krehbiel's reports from the Chicago fair: *New York Tribune,* July 30, Aug. 6 and 13, 1893.
3. Smith in *New York Tribune,* March 21, 1923. For weeping, see Horowitz, p. 186.
4. Michael Beckerman, "Henry Krehbiel, Antonin Dvorak, and the Symphony "From the New World," *MLA Notes* 49 (Dec. 1992), p. 452.
5. *Musical Courier* (presumably, Leonard Liebling), quoted in Henry-Louis de La Grange, *Gustav Mahler, Volume 4: A New Life Cut Short* (1907–1911), p. 569.
6. Henry Krehbiel, *How to Listen to Music* (1896), p. 317. Finck quotes in Mark Grant, *Maestros of the Pen* (1989), p. 82. Josephine Huneker (ed.), *Letters of James Gibbons Huneker* (1927). Aldrich, Gabriel, and Taylor in Krehbiel obituaries, *New York Tribune,* March 12, 1923.
7. Henry Krehbiel, *Chapters of Opera* (1909/1980), pp. 170–171.
8. Krehbiel, *Chapters of Opera,* p. 168.
9. Henry Finck (ed.), *Anton Seidl: A Memorial by His Friends* (1899/1983), pp. 116, 131–139.
10. Joseph Horowitz, *Wagner Nights: An American History* (1994), p. 21.
11. Krehbiel, *Chapters of Opera,* pp. 167, 207.
12. Krehbiel, *How to Listen to Music* (1896), pp. 323, 313.
13. Krehbiel on *Tristan, Die Meistersinger,* and the *Ring* in Krehbiel, *Studies in the Wagnerian Drama* (1891), pp. 40–45, 94–111, 112–119. Also see Horowitz, *Wagner Nights,* pp. 145, 147.
14. Alan Trachtenberg, *The Incorporation of America: Culture and Society in the Gilded Age* (1982), p. 14.
15. Krehbiel, *Chapters of Opera,* p. 167.
16. Krehbiel, *Studies in the Wagnerian Drama,* pp. 68–69.
17. Walter Kaufmann (ed. and trans.), *The Portable Nietzsche* (1954), pp. 666–667.

18. Adams, Ryder, and Ingersoll in Horowitz, *Wagner Nights,* pp. 143, 231, 4. W.E.B. DuBois, "Of the Coming of John" in *The Souls of Black Folk* (1903).

19. Krehbiel, *Chapters of Opera,* pp. 44, 207.

20. Huneker and Krehbiel in Finck (ed.), pp. 116, 131.

21. Otakar Sourek, *Antonin Dvořák: Letters and Reminiscences* (trans. Roberta Samsour) (1954), p. 152.

22. Henry Krehbiel, "Antonin Dvořák," *Century* Magazine, vol. 44 (May–Oct. 1892).

23. *New York Tribune,* Nov. 17, 1893.

24. Krehbiel in *New York Tribune,* Dec. 17, 1893; Henderson in *New York Times,* Dec. 17, 1893.

25. *Musical Courier,* Dec. 20, 1893.

26. Karl Baedeker (ed.), *The United States: A Handbook for Travelers* (Leipzig, 1893), p. 23.

27. Horowitz, *Classical Music in America,* p. 7.

28. Undated *Boston Journal* clipping, Boston Symphony Orchestra Archives. Hale on "excavation" in *Musical Courier,* Jan. 4, 1894.

29. "Negrophile" in *Boston Home Journal,* Feb. 1, 1890. Additional clippings (many unidentified) in Brown Collection, Boston Public Library (music division).

30. *New York Tribune,* Jan. 1, 1894.

31. Krehbiel letter in Beckerman, p. 453. Hale reviews in Jean Ann Boyd: *Philip Hale, American Music Critic,* dissertation, University of Texas (1985).

32. Horowitz, *Wagner Nights,* p. 332.

33. Program notes for the concerts of Dec. 23–24, 1910.

34. Oscar Thompson, "An American School of Criticism: The Legacies Left by William J. Henderson, Richard Aldrich, and Their Colleagues of an Old Guard," *Musical Quarterly,* vol. 23 (Oct. 1937), pp. 28–39.

35. Krehbiel notebooks at Performing Arts branch of New York Public Library, Music Research division. Henderson and Aldrich quoted in Krehbiel obituaries, *New York Tribune,* March 21, 1923.

36. On Dvořák and Creelman: Michael Beckerman, *New Worlds of Dvořák* (2003), chap. 7.

37. Krehbiel, *How to Listen to Music* (1896), pp. 313, 310, 312.

38. Krehbiel, *How to Listen to Music* (1896), pp. 27, 44, 50, 30, 197, 48, 4, 310, 262.

39. Krehbiel, *How to Listen to Music* (1896), p. 45. Olin Downes, "Be Your Own Music Critic," in Robert Simon (ed.), *Be Your Own Music Critic* (1941).

40. Krehbiel, *How to Listen to Music* (1896), pp. 6–7, 4, 300.

41. Henderson quote in Horowitz, *Understanding Toscanini: How He Became an American Culture-God and Helped Create a New Audience for Old Music* (1987), p. 249; Krehbiel, *How to Listen to Music* (1896), p. 6.

42. Krehbiel, *How to Listen to Music* (1896), p. 46.

43. Henry Krehbiel, *More Chapters of Opera* (1919/1980), pp. 5–7.

44. Chauffeur in Stanley Jackson, *Caruso* (1972), p. 106. Krehbiel quotes in Krehbiel, *More Chapters of Opera,* p. v; and Horowitz, *Understanding Toscanini,* p. 40.

45. Krehbiel quoted in Horowitz, *Understanding Toscanini,* p. 50. Knud Martner (ed.), *Selected Letters of Gustav Mahler* (1979), p. 309.

46. Alma Mahler, *Gustav Mahler: Memories and Letters* (London, 1946), p. 160.

47. *New York Tribune,* Dec. 13, 1909.

48. *New York Tribune,* May 21, 1911, and Dec. 18, 1909.

49. *New York Tribune,* May 21, 1911.

50. Zoltan Roman, *Gustav Mahler's American Years 1907–1911: A Documentary History* (1989), p. 487.

51. *New York Tribune,* Nov. 23, 1910.

52. W.J. Henderson, *What Is Good Music?* (1898), pp. 117–118. Finck in Mark Grant, *Maestros of the Pen* (1989), p. 197.

53. Dwight and Thomas in Horowitz, *Classical Music in America,* pp. 26, 36, 174.

54. Krehbiel, *More Chapters of Opera,* p. 382.

55. Henry Krehbiel, *Review of the New York Musical Season 1885–1886* (1886), p. 116.

56. Krehbiel, *How to Listen to Music* (1924), p. 70.

57. Huneker and *Pierrot* in Horowitz, *Understanding Toscanini,* p. 248. Krehbiel on Schoenberg in Barbara Mueser, *The Criticism of New Music in New York 1919–1929,* dissertation, City University of New York (1975), p. 65. "The Curse" in *New York Tribune,* Feb. 11, 1923.

58. *New York Tribune,* March 21, 1923.

59. Horowitz, *Wagner Nights,* p. 286.

60. Paul H. Shurtz, *W.J. Henderson: His Views on the New York Musical World 1887–1937,* dissertation, University of Colorado at Boulder (1980).

CHAPTER 3

1. The Seidl Society Archive at the Brooklyn Historical Society comprises a multitude of programs, clippings, and letters.

2. Cf. clippings, Seidl Society Archive. Diane Sasson's remarkable exploration of Langford's personal history may be found in two articles: "The Self-Inventions of Laura Carter Holloway," *Tennessee Historical Quarterly* vol. 67 (2008), pp. 178–207; and "'Dear Friend and Sister' Laura Holloway-Langford and the Shakers," *American Communal Societies Quarterly* vol. 1 (2007), pp. 170–190. The *Ladies Home Journal* (Sept. 1888) citation may be found in the first of Sasson's articles. The author is grateful to Diane Sasson for her generous assistance.

3. Sasson, "Self-Inventions," pp. 178–180.

4. Laura Langford, "A Reminiscence," *Brooklyn Eagle,* July 31, 1875, cited in Sasson, "The Self-Inventions," p. 181.

5. Sasson, "Self-Inventions," p. 193.

6. All quotes cited by Sasson, "Self-Inventions," p. 181.

7. Chapters on Beethoven and Mendelssohn, Laura Langford, *The Mothers of Great Men and Women* (1883).

8. All quotes from Hayes chapter, Laura Langford, *The Ladies of the White House* (1881).

9. Langford, *The Ladies of the White House* (1881), preface and p. 566.

10. www.firstladies.org/biographies/firstladies.aspx?biography+20.

11. Sasson, "Self-Inventions," pp. 182–183.

12. "Pure whiskey" from papers of Andrew Johnson; *Century* Magazine 85 (1912)—both cited in Sasson, "Self-Inventions," pp. 183, 186.

13. Sasson, "Self-Inventions," pp. 188–190.

14. Sasson, "Self-Inventions," p. 187.

15. Sasson, "Self-Inventions," pp. 197–198.

16. Sasson, "Self-Inventions," pp. 199, 201.

17. Wells and "fresh air" in Sasson, "'Dear Friend,' " pp. 171–172. "Old Grudge," parents and son in Sasson, "Self-Inventions," pp. 201, 196.

18. Robert D. Richardson, *William James: In the Maelstrom of American Modernism* (2006), pp. 257–264.

19. Alma Mahler, *Gustav Mahler: Memories and Letters* (1946), p. 134.

20. On the general phenomenon, see Jackson Lears, *No Place of Grace* (1981).

21. "In search of health," undated clipping, Seidl Society Archive. Peter Washington, *Madame Blavatzky's Baboon* (1993), p. 69.

22. Sasson, "'Dear Friend,'" p. 174.

23. Laura Holloway (ed.), *The Woman's Story, as told by twenty American women* (1888), preface, p. 483.

24. On Seidl, see Joseph Horowitz, *Wagner Nights: An American History* (1994). Huneker quote in Henry Finck (ed.), *Anton Seidl: A Memorial by His Friends* (1899/R1983), pp. 114–117.

25. *Musical Courier*, Oct. 28, 1896. Seidl quoted in *Brooklyn Daily Eagle,* June 6, 1889.

26. Bylaws in Seidl Society Archive.

27. Undated clippings, Seidl Society Archive.

28. Mariana Van Rensselaer, "*Parsifal,*" *Harper's* Magazine, March 1883, pp. 540–557. Charles Dudley Warner, *A Roundabout Journey* (1904), p. 313.

29. W.J. Henderson, *Richard Wagner: His Life and His Dramas* (1901), p. 474. *Brooklyn Daily Eagle,* March 20, 1891. Jackson quoted in Seidl Society program book, March 19, 1891. Washington Gladden, *Witnesses of Light* (1903), p. 222.

30. Undated clippings, Seidl Society Archive. Lilli Lehmann, *My Path Through Life* (1914), pp. 279–281.

31. *Brooklyn Daily Eagle,* May 2, 1890.

32. Undated *Mirror* and *Courier* clippings, Seidl Society Archive. *Brooklyn Daily Eagle,* July 28, 1895, and August 27, 1894.

33. Bicycle rest (advertisement) and Eminent Divinities: unidentified clipping, Seidl Society Archive. *Brooklyn Daily Eagle,* Aug. 11 and 12, 1890.

34. Programs in Seidl Society Archive. *Brooklyn Daily Eagle,* March 19, 1893.

35. Unidentified clipping, Seidl Society Archive.

36. Unidentified clippings, summer 1891 and summer 1889, Seidl Society Archive.

37. Unidentified clipping, Seidl Society Archive. "Speaking in all earnestness," *Brooklyn Daily Eagle,* March 6, 1891.

38. "Larger contributions" in *Brooklyn Daily Eagle,* Aug. 5, 1894. Unidentified *New York World* clipping, Seidl Society Archive.

39. Program, 1894 summer season, Seidl Society Archive.

40. *Brooklyn Daily Eagle,* June 21, 1896. "Baseball managers" in undated 1891 clipping, Seidl Society Archive. *New York Outlook,* June 27, 1894.

41. Letter: undated clipping, Seidl Society Archive. *Musical Courier* Aug. 5, 1894.

42. David Nye, *Electrifying America* (1990), p. 50. Seidl letter in Seidl Society Archive.

43. *Brooklyn Daily Eagle,* Sept. 1, 1890.

44. Clippings, Seidl Society Archive (*Brooklyn Daily Eagle,* December 1894).

45. Clippings, Seidl Society Archive (*Brooklyn Daily Eagle,* Aug. 1894).

46. "A Card to the Public" in April 1892 program book. Seidl Society Archive.

47. Correspondence, Seidl Society Archive.

48. A lesson: handwritten speech, delivered April 21, 1894, and *Brooklyn Daily Eagle* April 22, 1894. Rocking chair: *Brooklyn Daily Eagle,* Dec. 20, 1889. Carusi: undated clippings, August 1896. Seidl Society Archive.

49. *Brooklyn Daily Eagle,* Nov. 24, 1895.

50. *Brooklyn Daily Eagle,* April 27, 1896. Correspondence, Oct.–Nov. 1895. Seidl Society Archive.

51. *Brooklyn Daily Eagle,* May 2 and May 6, 1896.

52. *Brooklyn Daily Eagle,* Sept. 14, 1889. *Musical Courier,* Oct. 28, 2896.

53. Finck (ed.), p. 42. Speech (undated) in Seidl Society Archive.

54. Horowitz, *Wagner Nights,* p. 237.

55. *New York Herald,* May 31, 1896.

56. *Brooklyn Daily Eagle,* July 28, 1895.

57. *Musical Courier,* Dec. 8, 1897. "Advanced thinker," undated clipping (March 1898), Seidl Society Archive.

58. Printed in 1893 Seidl Society program. Seidl Society Archive.

59. *Brooklyn Daily Eagle,* May 3, 1898.

60. Evans cited in Sasson, "'Dear Friend,'" p. 172.

61. Sasson, "'Dear Friend,'" p. 172.

62. Sasson, "'Dear Friend,'" pp. 174–176.

63. Sasson, "'Dear Friend,'" pp. 177–178.

64. Sasson, "'Dear Friend,'" pp. 183, 186.

65. Maretzek and Thomas quoted in Joseph Horowitz, *Classical Music in America: A History* (2005), p. 170.

66. Ezra Schabas, *Theodore Thomas: America's Conductor and Builder of Orchestras* (1989), pp. 222–228.

67. Linda Whitesitt, "Women as 'Keepers of Culture': Music Clubs, Community Concert Series, and Symphony Orchestras," in Ralph Locke and Cyrilla

Barr (eds.), *Cultivating Music in America: Women Patrons and Activists Since 1860* (1997), pp. 74–75.

68. Whitesitt, p. 76.
69. Whitesitt, p. 72.
70. Whitesitt, pp. 67, 69.
71. Erich Leinsdorf, *Cadenza: A Musical Career* (1976), p. 118.
72. Lears, p. 46.
73. Horowitz, *Wagner Nights*, pp. 218, 226–230.

CHAPTER 4

1. Jan Swafford, *Charles Ives: A Life with Music* (1996), p. 175.
2. Swafford, p. 184.
3. Swafford, p. 186.
4. Tom Owens (ed.), *Selected Correspondence of Charles Ives* (2007), pp. 36–39.
5. Owens (ed.), pp. 42, 45.
6. Swafford, p. 97.
7. Charles Ives, *Essays Before a Sonata* (1920), in *Three Classics in the Aesthetic of Music* (Dover, 1962), p. 128.
8. Ives, p. 117. Swafford, p. 190.
9. Owens (ed.), p. 47.
10. John Kirkpatrick (ed.), Charles Ives, *Memos* (1972), p. 129.
11. Swafford, p. 303.
12. Vivian Perlis (ed.), *Charles Ives Remembered: An Oral History* (1974), p. 78.
13. Ives quoted in MacDonald Smith Moore, *Yankee Blues: Musical Culture and American Identity* (1985), p. 55.
14. Swafford, p. 61.
15. Antonín Dvořák, "Music in America," *Harper's* Magazine, Feb. 1895.
16. Kirkpatrick (ed.), pp. 49, 115.
17. Kirkpatrick (ed.), p. 70.
18. Swafford, p. 394.
19. Swafford, pp. 411–412.
20. Kirkpatrick (ed.), p. 15.
21. John Kirkpatrick, "Charles Ives," in Stanley Sadie and H. Wiley Hitchcock (eds.), *The New Grove Dictionary of American Music*, vol. 2.
22. Kirkpatrick (ed.), p. 131.
23. Swafford, p. 198.
24. Perlis (ed.), p. 56.
25. Perlis (ed.), p. 53.
26. Kirkpatrick (ed.), p. 131.
27. Swafford, p. 198.
28. Anecdotes in Perlis (ed.), pp. 60, 63, 50; and Swafford, p. 200.
29. Perlis (ed.), p. 75.
30. Perlis (ed.), p. 59.
31. Ives, p. 110.

32. Ives, p. 132.
33. Ives, p. 119.
34. Ralph Waldo Emerson, *Complete Works,* vol. 12, part 1. www.rwe.org.
35. Ives, pp. 121, 114.
36. Ives, pp. 132, 127. "Unfinished" in Kirkpatrick, p. 79. "Experiment" in Owens (ed.), p. 86.
37. Ives, pp. 136–139.
38. Cited in R.S. Perry, *Charles Ives and the American Mind* (1974), p. 23.
39. Ives, pp. 153–155.
40. Daniel Gregory Mason, *Contemporary Composers* (1918), p. vii.
41. *New York Times,* March 19, 1916.
42. Perlis (ed.), p. 211.
43. Quoted in Rochelle Gurstein, *The Repeal of Reticence: A History of America's Cultural and Legal Struggles Over Free Speech, Obscenity, Sexual Liberation, and Modern Art* (1996), pp. 22–28.
44. Kirkpatrick (ed.), p. 130.
45. Moore, p. 55.
46. Ives, pp. 172, 158, 159. Perlis (ed.), p. 192.
47. Ives, p. 170.
48. Kirkpatrick (ed.), p. 207.
49. Joseph Horowitz, *Classical Music in America: A History* (2005), p. 26.
50. Kirkpatrick, p. 142.
51. Kirkpatrick, p. 184.
52. Ives, p. 165.
53. Ives, pp. 163–164.
54. CD note for DGG 429220–2.
55. Quoted in Perry, p. 107.
56. Swafford, p. 270.
57. Kirkpatrick, p. 240.
58. Swafford, p. 90.
59. Kirkpatrick, p. 129.
60. Ferruccio Busoni, *Sketch of a New Aesthetic in Music,* in *Three Classics in the Aesthetic of Music* (Dover, 1962), p. 79.
61. Kirkpatrick, p. 66.
62. Ives, pp. 17, 128, 109.
63. Gayle Sherwood Magee, *Charles Ives Reconsidered* (2008), p. 75.
64. Jackson Lears, *No Place of Grace: Antimodernism and the Transformation of American Culture 1880–1920* (1981); the Lowell poem is cited on p. 154.
65. Magee, p. 74.
66. Cited in J. Peter Burkholder, *All Made of Tunes: Charles Ives and the Uses of Musical Borrowing* (1995), p. 294.
67. Henry Krehbiel, *How to Listen to Music* (1896), p. 68.
68. Owens (ed.), pp. 145, 107. Perlis (ed.), p. 152. Kirkpatrick (ed.), p. 137.
69. Owens (ed.), p. 107.
70. Perlis (ed.), p. 136.
71. Perlis (ed.), p. 197.

72. Swafford, p. 314.
73. Swafford, p. 313.
74. Swafford, p. 211.
75. Kirkpatrick (ed.), p. 65.
76. Swafford, p. 364.
77. Kirkpatrick (ed.), p. 133.
78. Perlis (ed.), p. 104.
79. Swafford, p. 375.
80. Frank Rossiter, *Charles Ives and His America* (1975), p. 22.
81. See Michael Hicks, *Henry Cowell, Bohemian* (2002), especially pp. 162–163.
82. Owens (ed.), pp. 244–245.
83. Perlis (ed.), p. 205.
84. Perlis (ed.), pp. 42–43.
85. Owens (ed.), p. 357.
86. Swafford, p. 427.
87. Perlis (ed.), p. 98.
88. Owens (ed.), p. 369.
89. Owens (ed.), p. 290.
90. Perlis (ed.), pp. 65–66.

SUMMATION

1. For the performances of Dec. 23 and 24, 1910.
2. Henry Krehbiel, *Chapters of Opera* (1909/R1980), p. 396.
3. Joseph Horowitz, *Classical Music in America: A History* (2005), p. 82.
4. All Hale quotes from Jean Ann Boyd, "Philip Hale, American Music Critic, Boston, 1889–1933," dissertation, University of Texas at Austin (1985).
5. Loeffler quoted in Horowitz, p. 114. Hale quoted in Boyd, p. 44.
6. Boston aestheticists as ephemeral sublimation in Martin Green, *The Problem of Boston* (1966). George Santayana, "The Genteel Tradition in American Philosophy," in Santayana, *The Genteel Tradition* (1967), p. 39.
7. Justin Kaplan, *Mr. Clemens and Mark Twain* (1966), p. 358.
8. Ron Powers, *Mark Twain: A Life* (2005), p. 562.
9. Howard Mumford Jones, *The Age of Energy: Varieties of American Experience, 1865 to 1915* (1970), pp. 104–105.
10. Thomas Kessner, *Capital City: New York City and the Men Behind America's Rise to Economic Eminence, 1860–1900* (2003), p. xiii.
11. Ronald Story, *Harvard and the Boston Upper Class: The Forging of an American Aristocracy 1800–1870* (1980), pp. 9, 18, and chap. 9.
12. Story, p. xiii.
13. "One's peers" in Story, p. 164. For Higginson as a tyrannical monopolist, see Lawrence Levine, *Highbrow-Lowbrow: The Emergence of Cultural Hierarchy in America* (1988). "Cultural policeman" in Green, p. 110. "Slings and arrows" in Paul DiMaggio, "Cultural Entrepreneurship in Nineteenth Century Boston," parts one and two, in *Media, Culture and Society,* vol. 4 (1982), p. 318.

14. *Musical Courier,* Dec. 23, 1910. Kessner, pp. 238–239. "Prominent historian" is Sven Beckert, *The Monied Metropolis* (2001), p. 267.

15. Levine.

16. Horowitz, *Classical Music in America,* pp. 172–173. Mark Clague, "Chicago Counterpoint: The Auditorium Theater Building and the Civic Imagination" (dissertation, University of Chicago, 2002).

17. Paul Fussell, *The Great War and Modern Memory* (1975), p. 8.

18. Igor Stravinsky, *An Autobiography* (1936), p. 53. Schoenberg letter to Alexander von Zemlinsky, Feb. 13, 1918, cited by Henry Raynor, *A Social History of Music* (1978), p. 9.

19. Cited in Henry F. May, *The End of American Innocence* (1959), p. 346.

20. May, p. 213.

21. Horowitz, *Understanding Toscanini.*

22. Horowitz, *Classical Music in America,* pp. 416–432.

Index

About the Author

Joseph Horowitz was born in New York City in 1948. He was a music critic for *The New York Times* from 1977 to 1980. His previous books are *Conversations with Arrau* (1982, winner of an ASCAP/Deems Taylor Award), *Understanding Toscanini: How He Became an American Culture-God and Helped Create a New Audience for Old Music* (1987, a National Book Critics Circle best book of the year), *The Ivory Trade* (1990), *Wagner Nights: An American History* (1994, winner of the Irving Lowens Award of the Society of American Music), *The Post-Classical Predicament* (1995), *Dvořák in America: In Search of the New World* (for young readers, 2003), *Classical Music in America: A History* (2005, an *Economist* best book of the year), and *Artists in Exile: How Refugees from War and Revolution Transformed the American Performing Arts* (2008, an *Economist* best book of the year). From 1992 to 1997 he served as artistic advisor and then executive director of the Brooklyn Philharmonic Orchestra, resident orchestra of the Brooklyn Academy of Music, and there pioneered in juxtaposing orchestral repertoire with folk and vernacular sources, engaging gamelan orchestras, flamenco dancers and singers, and Russian and Hungarian folk artists. He has subsequently served as an artistic advisor to various American orchestras, most regularly the Pacific Symphony. He has also cofounded, with the conductor Angel Gil-Ordonez, PostClassical Ensemble, a chamber orchestra in Washington, DC. For the NEH he has directed a National Education Project and a Teacher-Training Institute, both dealing with "Dvořák and America." He has taught at CUNY, Colorado College, the Eastman School, the New England Conservatory, the Manhattan School of Music, and Mannes College. He regularly contributes articles and reviews to the *Times Literary Supplement* (UK); other publications for which he has written include *American Music, The New Grove Dictionary of Music and Musicians, The New Grove Dictionary of Opera, The Musical Quarterly, The New York Review of Books,* and *Nineteenth Century Music.* He is the author of "Classical Music" for both the *Oxford Encyclopedia of American History* and the *Encyclopedia of New York State.* His website is www.josephhorowitz.com. His blog is www.artsjournal.com/uq.

TEXT
10/13 Sabon

DISPLAY
Sabon

COMPOSITOR
BookMatters, Berkeley

INDEXER
Kevin Millham

PRINTER AND BINDER
Maple-Vail Book Manufacturing Group